Praise for
Wildflower

"Featuring an extraordinary real-life heroine, exotic settings, a love triangle, and a mysterious death, Seal's riveting portrayal of famous wildlife filmmaker Joan Root is not to be missed."

—*Good Housekeeping*

"You gotta read: Lucky us—renowned journalist Mark Seal has written *Wildflower: An Extraordinary Life and Mysterious Death in Africa.* It's the engrossing tale of environmental activist Joan Root. . . . [*Wildflower*] boils over with romance and adventure. . . . Grab this compelling story as soon as it hits store shelves." —*Los Angeles* magazine

"The best aspect of *Wildflower* is Seal's ability to pull various elements into a compelling narrative: the personal love story. The physical splendor of Africa and its endangered wildlife. And the desperate Africans living on a dollar a day, their poverty and lethal tribal conflicts legacies from European colonial policies." —*USA Today*

"Extraordinary." —*The Washington Post*

"Exhilarating." —*Vogue*

"[A] richly detailed portrait . . . Thanks to Seal's meticulous re-creation, [Joan Root's] extraordinary life lives on." —*People*

"[A] gripping read." —New York *Daily News*

"[An] amazing new book about the mysterious murder of naturalist and Oscar-nominated filmmaker Joan Root."
—*The Dallas Morning News*

"Empathetic . . . absorbing." —*BookPage*

"Seal gives us the sad details up front and then leads us, gently and sensitively, through the story of this shy yet remarkable woman. . . . This is a great story built from many interviews of friends and family and from Root's extensive diaries and letters. What an adventure! What an example! Highly recommended."
—*Library Journal* (starred review)

"[A] riveting portrait . . . Seal's gripping chronicle of naturalist Root's life of adventure and loss, beauty and brutality, is fascinating on many fronts and will remain in demand." —*Booklist* (starred review)

"[A] zesty biography of wildlife documentarian and conservationist Joan Root . . . Seal captures both the extraordinary quality of [Joan and Alan Root's] work and Joan's personality. . . . Seal expertly draws out the drama of the Roots' days afield. . . . Even more compelling is the author's portrait of the years Joan spent alone on the shore of Kenya's Lake Naivasha, her fortitude in trying to protect the ecologically fragile area from poaching and illegal fishing and the fallout of the flower industry that sprang up on its shore. . . . [*Wildflower*] transports readers into the midst of an incandescent, doomed life."
—*Kirkus Reviews*

Wildflower

RANDOM HOUSE TRADE PAPERBACKS

NEW YORK

Wildflower

AN EXTRAORDINARY LIFE
AND MYSTERIOUS DEATH IN AFRICA

Mark Seal

2010 Random House Trade Paperback Edition

Copyright © 2009 by Mark Seal

All rights reserved.

Published in the United States by Random House Trade Paperbacks,
an imprint of The Random House Publishing Group,
a division of Random House, Inc., New York.

RANDOM HOUSE TRADE PAPERBACKS and colophon
are trademarks of Random House, Inc.

Originally published in hardcover in the United States by Random House,
an imprint of The Random House Publishing Group,
a division of Random House, Inc., in 2009.

ISBN 978-0-8129-7909-1
eBook ISBN 978-1-58836-861-4

Printed in the United States of America

www.atrandom.com

1 2 3 4 5 6 7 8 9

Book design by Dana Leigh Blanchette

Title-page photograph courtesy of Alan Root

Photographs by Alan Root and Guillaume Bonn

To Laura Blocker, my wife, best friend, and fiercest editor, whose love, strength, and patience made this book possible.

And to Wayne Lawson, executive literary editor of *Vanity Fair,* who has guided me by his constant grace, generosity, and editorial genius since we first met in Dallas, Texas, in 1986.

As always, to Jan Miller Rich, who opened the door of her literary agency to me in 1989 and transported me into a new world of possibility.

AUTHOR'S NOTE

I read about the murder of a woman in Kenya from several oceans away. I had never heard her name before. But through the miracle of technology, I sent an email to her ex-husband and, within a week, he invited me to attend the woman's memorial service and write about her life. "I am sure you would get a wealth of material from the great cross section of the Kenyan community that will be there," wrote the woman's ex-husband, whose name was Alan Root. Not only did Alan introduce me to the people who could tell me about the woman who died—my interviews with them provide much of this book—but he also gave me her letters and diaries, all of which helped me re-create scenes, recall dialogue, and find truth. Of equal importance, Alan opened his heart and told me *everything,* which was surely difficult, heart-wrenching, and frequently painful for him. For his unsparing openness and unflinching candor, I give Alan Root my profound admiration and endless thanks. This book could not have been written without him.

PREFACE

She always knew he would come back to her.

He would climb into his helicopter at first light one Nairobi morning and rise above the screaming madhouse of the city, tilting west over East Africa's largest slum, and flying out into wonder: out over the Great Rift Valley, the cradle of civilization, a three-thousand-mile-long seam in the earth that stretches from Syria to Mozambique but is at its most glorious here in Kenya. As the floor of the world dropped away; opening into endless sky and a breathtaking vista, he would follow this corridor straight back to her.

There were things she longed to tell him, things only he would understand. Everything she'd been too shy and self-effacing to say before would now come pouring out, just as it had in all of the letters she had written him, letters she never sent:

> A lifetime has passed since we split, and yet some memories of things we did together seem [as if they happened] only the other day. There is so much I would like to say and share with you—now I know I am not inferior to you.

She waited for him in her blue house beside the lake, which looked so perfect and placid from the air. But this was merely another extreme in a country where great beauty coexists with unimaginable brutality, where the border between life and death is the thinnest of lines, where nothing is ever as it seems.

> Now in contact with others, I realize how knowledgeable I am about the natural world. . . . People respect me nowadays. But the only love of my life is one of the few people I cannot communicate with, even as a friend.

She could leave all that pain behind as soon as he came back into her life. Flying over the mountains and dormant volcanoes that form a natural amphitheater around the lake, he would hover over the emerald-green water, taking in its wide, verdant, wildlife-infested expanse.

> When you flew over and saw the blue house you were probably happy you didn't live here anymore, but I am really such a different person, I hardly know myself. I have written you so many letters in my head but when I try to write I go to pieces.

She imagined him buzzing the house, as playfully as he always had, then touching down on the grass landing strip and stepping out, as if returning from only a brief safari instead of half a lifetime. Then at last she would impress him with her independence and accomplishments and show him the abiding endurance of her love.

Finally, he did come back to her, flying in with the dawn on January 13, 2006. It was not, however, as she had dreamed for so long. He hadn't come to reunite with the woman who had once been his wife, partner, and best friend, the woman he'd left to live alone in Africa for sixteen years.

He had come to collect her remains.

INTRODUCTION

The report was chillingly brief.

> **Conservationist Killed**
>
> Joan Root, 69, animal lover and conservationist who collaborated with her husband, Alan, on wildlife documentaries in the 1970's, was killed on Jan. 13 in Naivasha, Kenya. Root was shot to death by assailants who invaded her farmhouse, the police said. Two men were arrested, officials said. One of the couple's films, *Mysterious Castles of Clay,* narrated by Orson Welles, showed the inner workings of a termite mound. It was nominated for an Oscar in 1978.

As a contributing editor at *Vanity Fair* magazine, I am always in search of great stories, and this one seemed to have plenty of the right ingredients: conservationist and wildlife filmmaker, nominated for an Oscar for a film narrated by the legendary Orson Welles, murdered for unknown reasons in Africa.

As soon as I began to research her, I quickly realized that Joan Root wasn't just another wildlife filmmaker. She and her husband, Alan Root, were, for a time in the 1970s and 1980s, the world's *greatest* wildlife filmmakers, mythical figures to nature lovers of all ages. You didn't watch Joan and Alan merely on television and on flickering classroom screens across Africa and Great Britain, you traveled with them, whether they were sporting with ferocious crocodiles and hippos in exotic lakes, sailing over Mount Kilimanjaro in a hot-air balloon, or being chased, mauled, bitten, gored, and stung by every conceivable creature as they drove, flew, ran, and swam across Africa, determined to capture the continent and its wonders on film before this wild world was lost forever. They were pioneers, filming animal behavior without human interference decades before films such as *Winged Migration* and *March of the Penguins* were made. Their movies were often narrated by top movie stars, including David Niven, James Mason, and Ian Holm, and in 1967 one of their films had a royal premiere in London, where the couple was presented to the queen.

They introduced the American zoologist Dian Fossey to the gorillas she would later die trying to save, took Jacqueline Kennedy up in their hot-air balloon, and covered much of Africa in their single-engine Cessna and their amphibious car. Then, for reasons the public never really knew, they suddenly vanished from the screen as mysteriously as some of the endangered species they had documented. They separated and later divorced. Alan, the more outspoken of the couple, went on to become a wildlife-filmmaking icon, winner of awards, tributes, and accolades. The blond, bronzed, beautiful Joan, who was intensely shy and always in the background—as both her husband's capable backup and the unheralded producer of their films—dropped out of filmmaking altogether, retreating to live alone on eighty-eight acres in Naivasha, Kenya, where she devoted herself to saving the ecologically imperiled lake just beyond her home. It was there, in her bedroom at one-thirty A.M. on January 13, 2006, that she was brutally murdered by assailants with an AK-47. Screaming in Swahili that they would fill her with so many holes she'd "look like a sieve," they pumped bullets through the glass and the bars of her bedroom windows until Joan—who, at sixty-nine, had become one of the most indomitable conservationists in the world—lay dead in a pool of her own blood.

Within a week of reading the paragraph in the *Times Digest,* I had gotten an assignment to write an article about Joan Root for *Vanity Fair*. I sent emails to everyone I could find who might be remotely connected with her, with special emphasis on finding Alan Root. A few days later, I received a one-line email from him: "I hear you are looking for me."

After expressing condolences over the loss of his ex-wife, I told him how much I would appreciate his help when I got to Kenya. Two days later, he responded:

> Dear Mark
>
> I am sorry, I was just not up to a late and long phone call early this week. I had buried Joan's ashes on Tuesday morning and planted a fig tree above her—(she will always be surrounded by "roots"). I'd also spent a lot of time with the police, and I was just shattered.
>
> I am glad you were able to contact Adrian [Luckhurst, Joan's business manager] and he has passed on your message. Please do not take my silence as a lack of interest. I want you to write this story and will do all I can to help. Unless it is going to delay things too much I really think it would be great if you could attend the celebration of her life that we are holding at Naivasha on March 4th. You would be welcome there and I am sure you would get a wealth of material from the great cross section of the Kenyan community that will be there . . .
>
> With best wishes
>
> Alan

Within a few days, I was on a flight bound to Nairobi, Kenya. I had never been to the city or the country. I had no idea that I was embarking on a journey that would keep me in Kenya, off and on, for over three years.

After landing in Nairobi, I drove fifty-five miles west to Joan Root's home on Lake Naivasha for her memorial service. Hundreds of the world's leading naturalists, wildlife experts, and filmmakers sat outdoors on her magnificent lawn to celebrate this extraordinary woman.

The memorial service was held beside Joan's stretch of Lake Naivasha, a wonderland of wildlife straight out of a Walt Disney film that one of Joan's friends said is "like *Doctor Dolittle* times one thousand," where 1,200 hippos swim by day and mow the grass by night amid the music of the area's 350 species of birds. Throughout the extremely emotional service, her friends and colleagues all wondered aloud about her senseless death. Who would murder this sweet and gentle woman who rarely spoke above a whisper and had spent decades passionately helping the desperately poor and needy of Kenya? Some, including the police, were convinced that her murder was the result of a simple robbery attempt. But if robbery was the motive, others asked, why was nothing stolen from her house? And why the barrage of bullets when the threat of one would have persuaded most people in crime-ridden Naivasha or nearby Nairobi (known familiarly these days as "Nairobbery") to surrender their cash?

The likely explanation, many of her friends felt, was that Joan had been the target of a contract killing—easily arranged in Kenya for about a hundred dollars a hit—because of her conservation activities around the lake. The gentle animal lover had become a rare dissenter in a bizarre, only-in-Africa scenario that had turned her beloved lake into a war zone, in a conflict created by, of all things, roses. Over the preceding two decades, peaceful, pastoral Lake Naivasha had been invaded by armies of flower growers who created some of the biggest flower farms in the world. These farms covered the lakeshore with huge plastic hothouses, inhibited the natural migration of wildlife, and attracted a desperate tide of hundreds of thousands of impoverished migrant workers, resulting in slums, squalor, crime, and, some insisted, ecological apocalypse. Crime in the area had become commonplace, murders routine, poaching of fish and wildlife epidemic. The lake, from which the flower farms sucked up water and into which they spat back pesticides, was so contaminated that its demise was predicted within five years if immediate measures were not taken. While others just talked about this situation, Joan put her words into action in a fearless and, some said, extremely dangerous way. Her vigilante campaign to preserve her land and the lake around it ended up alienating the authorities she stood against, and even the desperate African workers whose livelihood she was trying to save. All of this may well have marked her for death. Even though four suspects were taken into custody after her murder, they were eventually released. It was a strange and brutal story, ending with more questions than answers.

"Everyone here knows what I mean when I say Joan's death is only part of the dark waters slowly engulfing this country," said Joan's friend Ian Parker in his eulogy. "Collapsing law enforcement is the darkest side of corruption and lack of political principle. When the law enforcers cannot protect citizens or bring criminals to justice, and when individuals are denied the means to defend themselves—and most Kenyans are not allowed firearms—people will take the law into their own hands. This is not a threat from some cranky old *mzungu,*" he continued, employing the Swahili word for "white person." "It is a lesson history teaches us over and over again. When a defenseless public benefactress like Joan can be sought out and killed, history speaks again. Take heed! This society is in a dangerous state. Joan's death demands that now is the time for us to speak out, protest, and be counted." He noted that three of his friends, not counting Joan, had been murdered in the previous year, 2005, "an improvement of fifty percent over 2004," when five friends had been murdered and "two badly injured in attempted murders."

The eulogies were extraordinary—passionate and heartfelt. Watching Parker at the podium, I witnessed an old man become young again as he shook his fists at the heavens and seethed with anger over the brutality that had befallen his longtime friend. Parker, a consummate adventurer, conservationist, pilot, and nature photographer, was now a slightly built, white-haired man of seventy. He resembled the actor Frank Morgan, the balding, beaming carnival barker who played the Wizard in *The Wizard of Oz*.

Parker and I met in the bar tent at the memorial. As we talked, he told me nostalgically how he had met Joan on a lark when they were teenagers. By the time she was nineteen, Joan's beauty had become legendary in Nairobi. When five soldiers from the Kenya Regiment decided to ask out five of Nairobi's most beautiful girls—whether they knew them or not—Ian Parker chose Joan. He brazenly drove up to Joan's father's coffee farm unannounced. He rang the bell, told Joan of his mission, and asked her for the date. "Why, thank you," she said politely, "but no thanks." Then she disappeared without another word.

Ian Parker may have tried, but Alan Root was the only man to capture Joan's heart—though, by his own admission, he had failed her in the end. On the day after the memorial service, Alan Root wanted to tell me about Joan's life, and we agreed to meet up for an interview. He still knows how to make a dramatic entrance. He had instructed me to wait for him in the backyard of his business manager in the Nairobi suburb of Karen. I was standing there, expecting him to walk through the back door and into the garden, when the quiet was broken suddenly by the sound of a helicopter flying in from the direction of Nairobi National Park. When it came down for a landing, kicking up grass and dirt in the yard, I could see Alan at the controls in the glass bubble, looking like the dashing daredevil from his films, except that he was now sixty-eight. He had thick glasses and a gray beard, but he was still powerfully built, wearing black jeans and a casual shirt.

"I've crashed two of these," he said once I was in the helicopter beside him. We lifted off, and he tilted the helicopter toward the Ngong Hills, blue and shadowy in the distance, and flew at high speed over the game-filled plains. I could make out the zebras, Cape buffalo, and gazelles in the national park below as Alan pulled back on the throttle and we shot like a bullet through the clear African sky. I could see right away the extraordinary life force that drove him, that made him so charismatic in life and in his films.

Alan Root had lived his life dangerously, recklessly, completely: getting gored by wild animals, crashing planes, wrecking cars, leaping into raging rivers, drinking with the best of them, getting caught in love affairs. Yet of all the women he had known, it was Joan, quiet, beautiful Joan, who had the most powerful impact, especially on his early life, and he wanted to help me tell her story. He was transporting me into another world in his helicopter that day, which would turn out to be the best story I had ever encountered as a journalist. Until that moment, I had been mainly a collector of cold, hard facts. Then Alan Root flew me across Africa, and the ride of a lifetime began.

The article I wrote, which was published in the August 2006 issue of *Vanity Fair,* was just one more dispatch in the deepening mystery of a fascinating woman. Yet, like the chilling paragraph that had galvanized me in the beginning, the article seemed to make a visceral connection with readers. People would stop me on the street to discuss this indomitable individual. A dozen feature-film makers expressed interest in obtaining rights to the article. Several publishers urged me to expand it into a book.

Most magazine stories tend to come and go, but this one wouldn't die after the next issue hit the stands. It seemed to have a life of its own. Working Title Films optioned the movie rights for a feature film, with Julia Roberts's company, Red Om, set to coproduce and Julia attached to star as Joan Root, all of which was announced at the 2007 Cannes Film Festival, making international headlines. Still, I thought the story was over, at least for me. Joan Root was dead, and because she had rarely expressed her feelings, much less verbalized them, even to her closest friends, most of her personal story was presumably buried with her.

Then something incredible happened. Joan Root began speaking.

"I understand you believe that this woman didn't talk much." An email out of the blue from Alan Root. "You were right about the talking," he continued. "But I have millions of words she wrote to her mother, diaries, etc." I was instantly intrigued and thrilled at the possibility of learning more about this extraordinary person.

Another stroke of luck arrived when I tracked down Anthony Smith, the bestselling London author, explorer, BBC presenter, adventurer, and best friend of Alan and Joan Root. He had twice ridden a motorcycle the length of Africa, and became the first Brit to obtain a balloon license after World War II and cross the high Alps in a balloon. Then eighty, Anthony was living in a small and cluttered London flat, where he had invited me for what he'd advertised as "one of my famous spaghettis." I brought a bottle of California chardonnay. "Brilliant idea to bring the wine," he said when I arrived. He was extremely tall, funny, and effervescent, speaking in a clipped British accent, filled with "hmmm's" and "Oh, my's!" punctuating endlessly glorious stories of his years with Alan and Joan both before and after their divorce.

I liked him at the outset. Anthony Smith had no edit filter to his conversation. Not only did he tell me everything about the Roots honestly and completely, he also gave me a fat folder full of letters to and from Alan and Joan. "You're lucky," he said. He'd just found the letters the day before my visit, while moving out of his house in the middle of a divorce. "If you had come a week later, I would have thrown them away."

What others said about Joan while she was alive was compelling, but more astounding were her own revelations in thousands of pages of letters to her mother, husband, and friends, as well as decades of meticulously kept diaries, the last entry of which she made shortly before her death. Reading her diaries and letters, I realized that this amazing woman's story demanded to be fully told, and that she had provided posterity with much of it herself.

Running through every line Joan Root wrote, from her adventurous youth to the perilous days just before her death, were affirmations of her affection for Africa and its wildlife, and for Alan, the only man who was as wild and free as they were, the only man she ever loved.

Wildflower

Chapter One

One can only imagine what British colonialists felt when they first sailed from chilly and proper England to hot, exotic Kenya. They were rough-and-ready pioneers, coming to tame the vast and mysterious country that had been claimed for the Crown in 1895. They came in the name of civilization, building railways, erecting Nairobi and other cities, and forcing the Maasai from their ancestral grazing lands, and yet what made them famous in books and movies was hedonism: a handful of wealthy and aristocratic British colonialists raging in what became known as the "Happy Valley" lifestyle, Kenya's version of the Roaring Twenties, when khaki-clad, trigger-happy, wife-swapping British transplants scandalized the world with their antics.

There may have been only a handful of Happy Valley hedonists in Kenya, but they made one hell of a noise. Most of the colonialists were, by contrast, hardworking, diligent citizens, as made famous by the writer Karen Blixen, the Danish author who, under the pen name Isak Dinesen, wrote *Out of Africa* and other books about the years she ran a coffee plantation outside Nairobi with her cousin Baron Bror von Blixen-Finecke, whom she married in 1914. "The British people came to Kenya and brought a bit of Britain with them," remembers one of Joan Root's friends. "Raising the British flag, pulling it down at sundown, dressing up formally for dinner, gin on the porch, and then the headwaiter would come in full uniform with a gong and say, 'Dinner is ready.' Everyone would raise their glasses and exclaim, 'To the Queen!' "

That era came crashing to an end in the 1950s, when the colonial era ended with a bloodbath. In 1952, Kenya's most prominent tribe, the Kikuyu (whose population counted for 1.5 million out of Kenya's 5 million inhabitants), and members of several other tribes rose up violently against the British presence in what became known as the Mau Mau Rebellion. "A Kikuyu became a Mau Mau by taking a sacrilegious oath that separated him from his normal life and turned him into a kamikaze human missile aimed at his employer, the European immigrant farmer," wrote Patrick Hemingway in an introduction to *True at First Light,* a memoir about time in Kenya by his father, Ernest Hemingway. "The most common agricultural implement in the country was called in Swahili a panga, a heavy-bladed, single-edged sword, stamped and ground from sheet steel in the English Midlands, able to cut brush, dig holes and kill people under the right conditions. Almost every agricultural worker had one." The Kikuyu killed two thousand African dissenters and attacked the British army and the police.

"Reacting as if this were another Battle of Britain, the European community had several infantry detachments dispatched from Britain and the entire white civilian population armed themselves," wrote John Heminway in his book *No Man's Land.* "For four years no one sat down for dinner in Kenya without a revolver by his plate."

Declaring a state of emergency, the British government arrested Jomo Kenyatta, the well-educated and widely traveled Kikuyu leader who had returned to Kenya to unleash the Mau Mau insurgency among his Kikuyu tribesmen and who rightly believed the European farmers had stolen the most precious resource: their land. Hunting Kenyatta down, however, took some knowledge of the local landscape. Joan Root later told a friend that one of the leaders of the manhunt was a man named Edmund Thorpe, her own adventurous but quiet and exceedingly well-mannered father. After capturing Kenyatta, the British battalions killed more than 11,000 rebels, hanging 1,000 and sending

150,000 to prison camps, compared with only 30 Europeans killed in the "emergency" before the British quelled the revolt in 1960.

Although they repressed the uprising with brute force, the British realized that they could not sustain white rule in Kenya, and in 1960 they conceded that Kenya's leaders should be elected according to the principle of one man, one vote. Kenyatta was released from prison in 1961, and a year later, he negotiated the terms that led to Kenya's independence in 1963. Kenyatta became the leader of the new nation.

Joan Root's father, Edmund Thorpe, would write later of the futility of the bloodbath in a letter: "When the British arrived, the Kikuyu were a small tribe hiding in the Aberdare and Mount Kenya forests being decimated by the Maasai from the south and Somali from the north. To stop this, Britain put a line of farms in the no-man's-land to stop the raids. In no way were the Kikuyu great warriors and would have been obliterated if the raids had not been stopped. They were despised by all other tribes when I got to Kenya in 1928. Of course, this is no longer true because they have bred up to be the largest tribe and they are clever."

Kenyatta turned out to be a pragmatic leader: He included non-Kikuyus and even whites in his administration and turned Kenya into something of an oasis of political stability and economic power. Meanwhile, he remained true to his Mau Mau roots. "When the missionaries arrived, the Africans had the land, and the missionaries had the Bible," he once said. "They taught us how to pray with our eyes closed. When we opened them, they had the land, and we had the Bible."

Many black Kenyans believe that their country never truly reverted to African hands, and they still feel enslaved to the colonial system and British rule, which left a festering wound that has yet to heal. Such was the feeling in the country at the time of Joan's death; indeed, many believed it may have contributed to her murder. But the world she was born into in 1936, nearly twenty years before the Rebellion, was very different.

Joan Wells-Thorpe was born in Nairobi on January 18 and taken home to the mud hut where her parents were living while building a house on their coffee farm. Her father, Edmund, was the son of a British yachting family, and he had taken off from gray, cold Devon, England, in 1928, after deciding that he'd had enough of his drab job with National Westminster Bank. An adventure gene raged through the Thorpe family, and when Edmund and his brother, Richard, reached their twenties, they immediately followed their lifelong dream of setting out for the colonies. Richard went to India to raise tea. Edmund chose Kenya.

Stately, bespectacled, sweet, and soft-spoken Edmund Thorpe lived a wild life and died on March 1, 1997. Like so many British pioneers, Edmund always stressed that he had come to Kenya to work, not play. "Survived the Depression panning for gold," he wrote in an undated résumé. In 1929, a year after his arrival, he enlisted in the Kenya Defense Force. Marauding gangs of poachers had been routinely raiding the bush, killing everything in sight and hauling away game. With only a handful of other wardens and a few native Kenyan scouts, Edmund brought poaching under control. Given the countless times he had escaped violent death, Edmund liked to tell friends that he was protected by a guardian angel.

On his résumé, Edmund related a few of his adventures—how he swept the oceans for mines; worked as a part-time policeman in a savage country where bandits were murdering schoolchildren; posed as a playboy on a yacht while actually serving as a naval military spy; and finally settled down to start a family. In 1933 he married Lillian Walker, a white South African. She complemented Edmund perfectly, keeping him organized, handling the follow-through, making him a home to return to from his endless adventures.

Eventually, Edmund decided to enter the coffee business. He and a partner bought a derelict 240-acre estate in the high, lush coffee country outside Nairobi, then subdivided it into approximately twenty-acre estates. Edmund kept three of the estates for himself, for a total of sixty-five acres, along with a coffee factory beside a river, and called his farm Lyntano. He planted thirty-nine thousand coffee trees and later claimed that every growing season, he had a mile of coffee beans drying out on tables and a hundred workers harvesting them in the sun.

For him, Kenya was paradise. "I could swim in the Indian Ocean, fish in a primeval stream, or camp just below snowline," he once told an interviewer. Hippos and crocs lived in his garden, as did sunbirds, cranes, and all kinds of monkeys. It was such an evocative landscape that *Tarzan* films were shot beside the river that ran through Edmund's acreage. (In one movie, however, Tarzan wore rubber booties and had to be assisted as he swung on fern-covered wire "vines." Edmund Thorpe was, by contrast, the real adventure man.)

One idyllic afternoon when Edmund and Lillian were picnicking on Crescent Island, a verdant peninsula that juts out into Lake Naivasha and is situated an hour and a half outside Nairobi, they conceived their only child. Thus began the circle of Joan Root's life on the lake, where she was born and where she would die. From the moment of her birth, Joan's life was unlike those of other little girls. "A friend had left me Mabel, a big red monkey with very long arms," Edmund later told a newspaper reporter. "She'd steal kittens, puppies, anything young. One day someone happened to glance in Joan's room, and there was Mabel, perched in the window, holding Joan. We exchanged our baby for a banana."

They never *really* got her back. From that day forward, Joan Thorpe would remain in the arms of the wild.

In a country where little child-rearing advice was available, Edmund and Lillian turned to the published advice of authorities who advocated a regime that emphasized self-reliance, wherein you did not comfort a crying baby no matter how much it howled. Baby Joan would lie awake crying in her crib for hours on end, but nobody was allowed to intercede. She grew up wailing for attention that she never received, until she finally quit crying forever. As she grew into adolescence and then young adulthood, Joan became increasingly unwilling to show weakness or ask for help.

She grew up in the wild, where even as a small child, she accompanied her father on his safaris. By then Edmund had become a professional hunter, leading tourists into the bush. His expeditions stretched from Kenya to Uganda and Tanganyika (now divided into Tanzania, Rwanda, and Burundi). One day, with the sound of rifles ringing in his ears, he had a brainstorm: Why not trade the guns for cameras? Just like that, Africa's earliest photo safaris were born. He advertised them as Kenya Thru the Lens.

The photo safaris were audacious in size and scope: twenty days, twenty-one clients per tour, two thousand dollars per person, including airfare from New York. They were such a hit that Edmund couldn't handle the business alone. He enlisted the help of his wife, who organized the tours and supervised the details. Soon the size and scope of the expeditions grew, until at the end clients were so exhausted by the wonders they'd seen—each day packed with up-close encounters with elephants, hippos, lions, crocodiles, giraffes, and rhinos, on the peaks of Africa's jagged volcanoes and in the valleys of its sprawling, barren plains—that they practically had to be shoveled into their airplane seats and shipped back home.

As the photo-safari business continued to grow, Edmund and Lillian reached a point of exhaustion. Desperately needing more help, they eventually turned to the most reliable, detail-oriented, stoic individual they knew: their daughter. She was nineteen by then, tall, attractive, intelligent, fluent in French from the years she had spent in a Swiss boarding school, yet most at home in the African bush. However, her strict, unpampered childhood had left her painfully shy, and she was uncomfortable around people, preferring the company of animals.

After being "finished" in Switzerland, she had come back to Kenya and gone to work. Few people in the white community of Kenya continued their education in those days, because there were plenty of jobs available. For four years she worked as a secretary for Shell Oil in Nairobi. Then her father made her a proposition: Help me with the photo safaris now, when we can teach you the business, and one day the company will be yours. Joan happily went to work for her parents in the role that would come to define her: chief in charge. She did everything effortlessly—drew up the itineraries, coordinated the tourists' arrivals and departures, handled the staff, bought food and supplies and oversaw setup and preparation, managed the caravan of Land Rovers (the one she drove had a roof rack covered with straw and filled with cages of cackling chickens—fresh meat and eggs for the clients), helped erect the tents, tended the fire, cooked the food, loaded the cameras, even pointed out the animals—in short, everything except click the shutters of the clients' cameras.

> Driving east across the Serengeti, with frequent stops for game photography, we climb to accommodations in a well-appointed safari lodge on the lofty rim of vast Ngorongoro Crater, another of the principal strongholds of Africa's wildlife. A full day will be spent on the crater floor, reached by a spectacular descent over switchbacks cut into the crater walls. In addition to the predictable animal photography awaiting us at Ngorongoro, we may also encounter our first *manyattas* [community dwellings] of the nomadic Masai tribesmen.
>
> —brochure copy for Kenya Thru the Lens

The brochure put it mildly. The Ngorongoro Crater, located in the highlands of northern Tanzania, is known as Africa's Eden. Ngorongoro is believed to have the greatest concentration of wildlife on the continent—leopard, lion, cheetah, eland, black rhino, golden jackal, Thomson's gazelle, lappet-faced vulture—all within the confines of a vast collapsed volcano, a walled enclave approximately the size of Paris. At its northern edge is the Olduvai Gorge, ninety yards deep and thirty miles long, which leads to the Serengeti, the area of endless yellow plains famous for their thunderous wildlife migrations, including the annual migration of almost a million wildebeests.

"These Americans are a very pleasant bunch, and they're enjoying the trip," Joan wrote one day in 1960 as she was shepherding a photo safari in Uganda. "The roof rack on the Land Rover is a success. It was good riddance to that trailer! I'm not getting tired driving. In fact, I'm enjoying it better than when I just sit."

She was always doing the driving, leading the caravan, leading everything, until, one rainy day in Africa's Eden, she met Alan Root. Later, Alan would say that he had already spotted Joan in and around Nairobi but that he had never known how to get her attention. He finally had his chance.

Alan Root felt that he had been born anew as soon as he set foot in Kenya at age ten. From that moment on, neither he nor the African bush would ever be the same. Alan was a rare combination of wit and intelligence, a natural-born comedian, always dominating a crowd. A full-out daredevil, he feared neither man nor beast, and he took pleasure in teasing and testing both. As John Heminway would write of him, in his book *No Man's Land,* "He is the success story of the bush. Much to the pleasure and anguish of his friends, he remains the absolute eccentric, the clown, the daredevil, the mimic, the misanthrope, the life of the party, the irrepressible idealist of nature. . . . He will die for a sequence in a film, a joke, a game of tennis. In short, Alan is so consumed by living that every day requires some proof that he has cheated death."

In contrast to Joan, who still wasn't sure where she wanted to go in life, Alan had decided his own destiny not long after he landed in Kenya. He was the son of a Cockney meatpacker who had emigrated from the London area to run a slaughterhouse and meatpacking factory in Nairobi. Alan determined early on that his life would be dedicated to *living* animals. His wildlife education began with the tiniest creatures—insects, reptiles, birds.

The Roots lived on the Athi Plain, at the edge of Nairobi National Park, where, Alan's father wrote, on a clear day you look out the windows onto the snows of Mount Kenya on one side and the snows of Kilimanjaro on the other. On weekends, Alan spent every spare moment in the bush with the Kamba, the hunter tribesmen and women who worked as cooks and gardeners in his parents' house. Soon the British boy was as at home in the wild as they were. He grew smart, strong, and handsome, his hair bleached blond by the sun and his future shaped by his experiences in nature—not merely observing animals but collecting them. "Root's Reptiles" was one of his early exhibitions at the Prince of Wales School in Nairobi, where he attended classes usually with a snake in his pocket and a practical joke on his mind. Crazy, funny, wild, taunting—that was Alan Root.

Collecting animals evolved into filming them with an eight-millimeter Bolex, which he focused on snakes and rhinos. He called his product a home movie, and one night he showed it to a small audience at the Nairobi Museum. Afterward, he was introduced to an East African Airways pilot and amateur wildlife photographer who asked if Alan would like to help with a film project that the pilot wanted to do but was short on time. *Would* he! With a borrowed camera, Alan made his first real film, about a bird called the lily-trotter, which spends its life on mammoth purple-flowered lily pads on Lake Naivasha. With their striking brown, white, and yellow plumage, these small birds have extremely long toes and claws that distribute their weight over a large surface area and enable them to walk on the lilies. Alan camped for weeks in a tent beside the lake and marked his days by recording the activities of the lily-trotters. By capturing them unobtrusively in their natural habitat, without human interference, Alan discovered what would become his trademark style.

Soon the lily-trotter footage caught the attention of another pair of potential patrons, Armand Denis and his beautiful blond wife, Michaela, the reigning king and queen of wildlife filmmaking in the 1950s and early 1960s. Their BBC series of half-hour-long programs, called *On Safari,* was more about them than the animals, however—Michaela once said on camera that she would never get into a crocodile-infested river before applying her eyebrow pencil—so they relied on bush cameramen to provide their animal footage.

Originally, they hired Alan not to film animals but to look after the tame ones they took with them on their travels. Then Armand Denis mentioned he wanted footage of an egg-eating snake, and not only did Alan have an egg-eater in his collection of reptiles, he'd already filmed it eating an egg. When he saw Alan's home movie, Armand Denis said, "What the hell are you doing looking after animals? Why aren't you filming them?"

They stationed Alan as an assistant to their cameraman, Des Bartlett, in the Serengeti, where he quickly met an even bigger supporter: Dr. Bernhard Grzimek, whose 1956 film, *No Place for Wildlife,* was a manifesto against safari hunting in the Belgian Congo and was regarded as perhaps the first conservation film. Grzimek was visiting the Serengeti with his son, Michael, and they were looking for a knowledgeable cameraman for a film project. After Alan was recommended by the local game warden, the Grzimeks asked the young cameraman if he would film the migration paths within the Serengeti for them. The resulting film, *Serengeti Shall Not Die,* won the 1959 Academy Award for Best Documentary. Twenty-two-year-old Alan Root was credited as cameraman.

Then Joan Thorpe drove into his life.

On this particular day, Alan was filming, knee-deep in the Ngorongoro mud. Suddenly, the Thru the Lens convoy rolled past, heading up to the top of the Ngorongoro Crater, where the group would stay for the night. As he looked up, something incredible flashed across the viewfinder of his camera: the tall twenty-one-year-old blonde driving the Land Rover. Alan watched Joan climb out of her vehicle, dressed in khaki shorts and a short-sleeved shirt, as beautiful as anything he'd ever seen. When she signed the group in at the visitors' book, Alan made his move: "Hi, I'm Alan Root." Just then, her parents walked up and invited the young man to join the group for dinner.

Joan must have already known who Alan was, but she hadn't spoken to him before. She listened while he introduced himself to the others in the camp, telling them who he was and where he'd been. Being Alan, he threw in a joke or two. The others laughed appreciatively, but from Joan, nothing. She was too shy for small talk, especially with strangers. Over drinks and dinner, Alan was utterly charming. He seemed to know everything about the crater and every animal in it. All those around the campfire listened eagerly as he told of his adventures in the wild. From Joan, still nothing, not even a smile. An occasional "oh" was all she said, if that. When they finally sat down to dinner, Alan managed to find a seat next to her.

At one point in the evening, Edmund mentioned that he wouldn't be needing Joan to drive in the morning, as most everybody would be staying in camp. He suggested that she take the day off. Alan deftly made his move. Why don't you take the day off with *me*? he suggested. He added that he'd pick her up in the morning and they could drive into the crater together.

Alan was so nervous the next morning that he forgot he had stored a pound of butter in his glove compartment the previous night. As he and Joan drove down the winding switchbacks into the Ngorongoro Crater and the temperature soared, the melting butter began dripping onto Joan's long, shapely legs. Accustomed to the unexpected things that happen on African safaris, Joan calmly did her best to wipe off the butter. Alan couldn't help but stare down at those glistening legs as he apologized for his forgetfulness and tried to shift his focus to the passing lions and buffalo and the grazing herds of wildebeest below. Meanwhile, he kept doing what he did best: talking.

He told her how he had come to Kenya with his family and how they had then moved to Rhodesia, where his father ran another slaughterhouse. But his mother and father weren't getting along too well, so he moved with his sister and mother back to Nairobi in 1951.

Joan nodded and smiled occasionally but said nothing.

He told her about his duty in the Kenya Regiment when the anti-British revolt known as the Mau Mau uprising happened, and he put on a uniform and was sent to hunt down fugitives in the Aberdare mountain forest. He didn't catch any Mau Mau, but he did manage to raise a bongo—the only one in captivity at the time.

She looked over and nodded. Like everyone in Nairobi, she knew that Alan had raised a bongo, the most elusive animal in the East African bush. The large Kenyan species of the chestnut-colored antelope, with bright white stripes and lyre-shaped horns, was rarely seen and had seldom been captured alive until a friend of Alan's found an orphaned baby in a snare and brought it to him. It was such a precious find that Alan kept the bongo in his bedroom, and from there he traveled with it to the Cleveland Zoo, which paid him a lavish sum of eleven hundred pounds for the animal and made him a local celebrity.

Alan still lived with his mother and sister in a very rustic house. His bedroom had mud walls, a thatched roof, and a dirt floor. So his mother didn't really mind that he kept a bongo in his bedroom. And she was used to animals in the house. He even kept a baboon in there until the ape became a bit overaggressive and made a pass at his mom.

He glanced over at Joan again. She still hadn't said one damn word.

Now he was collecting all sorts of animals to sell to zoos, and filming them. That had become his real career. He told her about his friendship with Michael Grzimek, who had died recently in a plane crash. From now on, Alan said, his mission would be to capture the essence of Africa on film. Not the typical staged, saccharine version. He wanted to capture the glorious continent's animals in full roar, without any technical fakery. Whether or not Joan was impressed, she didn't say, just kept staring straight ahead.

She was, Alan would soon learn, engaged to be married to a young man in Nairobi named Ted Goss.

They spent most of the rest of the drive in silence. Alan knew "Goosey-Goss," as his friend Ian Parker said he had been called in school. How the hell had Ted Goss ever gotten Joan Thorpe? In years to come, Ted Goss would become a legendary game warden, instrumental in saving Tsavo National Park (East Africa's largest) from poachers, and known for fighting gangs who decimated herds of elephants with everything from AK-47s to rocket-launched grenades. But back then, in the early 1960s, Goss was just another big, burly white Kenyan looking for a break. And he had landed Joan Thorpe! Alan realized he would have to find a way to win her over, to break through her shyness.

—

Soon the photographic safari moved on, leaving Alan stuck once again in the mud of the Ngorongoro Crater, still filming, but now obsessing over the woman who had just driven away. The two of them would make a perfect pair, though he couldn't have known that he needed her much more than she needed him. She was organized; he flew by the seat of his pants. She handled details and logistics with ease; he was a big-picture guy. She was a skilled producer, able to do everything at once; he was a natural-born star. He would just have to find a way to get her.

Not long afterward an animal appeared, as it always would for Alan, to give him his lucky break. Looking for locations for future photo safaris, Joan and her father had driven to Wamba in the northern frontier district, one of the country's most remote and inaccessible wildlife preserves. This beautiful mountainous landscape—dissected by rivers, home to the peaceful, hospitable Samburu tribe—was perfect for camel expeditions, and Edmund and Joan knew it would make an incredible photo-safari destination.

They were scouting for potential campsites when they heard a cry coming out of a well, one of the wide and deep waterholes the Samburu tribesmen dug to catch water for their cattle and camels.

They walked over to the well and peered in, only to discover an oil-black three-week-old abandoned baby elephant stuck in the mud.

Aided by a team of Samburu tribesmen, they managed to pull it from the well, but the rescue was only a first step. In those years, no baby elephant had been successfully raised by a human. Feeding a baby elephant was next to impossible because elephant's milk contains a vastly higher percentage of fat than cow's milk, and you couldn't milk an elephant. (This was long before the great naturalist Daphne Sheldrick invented the formula that replicated an elephant mother's milk.)

Nevertheless, Joan was hell-bent on saving her find. Constant contact with its mother is essential for a baby elephant, so Joan became a surrogate mother for this one, which she named Bundu, the Bantu word for "wilderness." She lived with Bundu on a pile of hay in a storeroom outside her father's house. Every night Joan slept with the animal, feeding it with a giant baby bottle, never leaving its side.

In the white community of Nairobi, everyone knows everything about everybody. So it was natural that Alan would hear about Joan's attempt to raise a baby elephant, and just as natural that he would rush to give her a hand. If anyone could help her save Bundu, he could. Alan not only helped her feed and care for the baby elephant. Most important, he helped Joan love it. For four weeks, Joan never left the little creature's side. But just for a moment she did.

Alan was away, and Joan had an urgent errand to run. She told her father's stable keeper that she would be *right back*; under no circumstances was he to break the chain of human contact, not even for a moment. But most African men don't hug elephants, and once Joan was gone, the young man let go. When Joan returned, Bundu was dying.

"Oh," Joan must have said, "oh," over and over again, and in that single word she expressed all her anguish and grief. The day the baby elephant died, she must have said it many times in her soft, barely audible voice. Then, for the first time in a very long time, she must have cried, and Alan didn't turn away. Nature had taken the baby elephant from Joan, but it gave her Alan Root.

As for Ted Goss, he was history, if their engagement had ever really begun. According to a friend, it was a lark after one of her friends had gotten engaged on a vacation when Joan and several friends had taken a trip to the Kenyan coast, and Joan had thought she should get engaged, too. Ted Goss had simply seized the moment. The love she found with Alan was real, sparked by sudden loss and by a deep kinship between two nature lovers, neither of whom had ever known true romantic love. It was an attraction of two opposites who, together, made a whole. Everything Joan was not—outgoing, extroverted, silly, utterly incautious—Alan was in spades. She would later claim that she loved Alan from the moment she met him, and much, much more as she got to know him. She had just been far too shy and overwhelmed when they first met to show it. She loved his flamboyancy, the way he took the stage, the way he was always the center of attention—which meant that she didn't have to be. She loved propping him up, protecting him, propelling him to places he might never have gone alone. No one else understood her the way Alan did, she would later say. They didn't have to talk about their love. Like the nonverbal communication between animals, it was just there—deep, primal.

A later magazine article about Joan says of this turning point in her young life:

> How do you get on TV? One way (*not recommended*) was taken by beautiful blonde Joan Root, who could double for Ingrid Bergman. . . . Joan made it by first tugging a baby elephant out of the mud, then taking it home to her parents' coffee plantation in East Africa and, finally, marrying the neighbor who showed her how to get milk into it. . . . The neighbor was Alan Root, a transplanted Englishman and nature photographer, who provided the formula that won her (and the puny pachyderm's) heart. It was love at first gulp. "Zap!" she says.

Zap! That was all laconic Joan could think to say to an interviewer of the moment she fell in love with Alan Root.

Chapter Two

Who is this Alan Root, and what is he going to become? Edmund Thorpe had been asking himself this for weeks. Eventually, he asked Alan. At twenty-two, the young man had still only one goal: to become the greatest wildlife filmmaker in the world. He was on his way, having already been chief cameraman on a film that had won an Oscar. Now, however, he'd caught something equally elusive and far more precious than his famous bongo: Edmund's beautiful daughter, to whom he'd proposed one day while on safari merely by blurting out, "Will you marry me?"

The wedding took place in February 1961 at the Anglican All Saints Cathedral in Nairobi. Joan's dress was the color of *leleshwa,* or wild sage, and an elaborate veil billowed around her porcelain-white face. The normally unshakable Alan, in a double-breasted suit and tie with a flower in his lapel, was so nervous that his knees knocked throughout the ceremony. "They looked like twins—tall, blond, blue-eyed, and both wearing glasses," remembered Alan's only sister, Jacky, who was Joan's maid of honor.

Afterward, Joan's parents hosted the wedding reception in their living room at Lyntano, where forty or so guests celebrated the match before a roaring fire. Alan's best man and fellow cameraman, Des Bartlett, gave a toast to the happy couple.

At the end of the evening, the newlyweds were heading out into the bush to begin what Alan called a working honeymoon ("So we're either still on our honeymoon, or we never had one") in what Joan later described as "a safari that would last twenty years."

Parked outside the reception, their Land Rover and trailer were packed with everything they owned—cameras, tent, clothing, supplies, food—enough to last them for months. Instead of throwing rice, several of Alan's drunken buddies had put fresh elephant dung under the Land Rover's wheels and poured boiling water on it, so when the newlyweds drove away to the cheers of their friends and family, elephant shit sprayed in all directions. It was, everyone agreed, a real Kenya wedding.

Then they were out of the city and away from everything safe and contained, on their own and ready to capture on film an Africa they both worried was expiring before their eyes. Wild animals were the true wedding court of this bride and groom, and the animals would soon rise up in an astonishing procession that would lead Mr. and Mrs. Alan Root into a future neither one of them could have conceived of that February day.

Their first destination was Tsavo National Park, home to one-third of Kenya's elephants, to film footage for Armand and Michaela Denis's television series. Alan had telegrammed Hunters Lodge in Kibwezi, a hundred miles south of Nairobi. When they arrived, however, the lodge was full—no room for the Roots. They had to drive two hours farther to an ordinary roadside inn somewhere between Nairobi and Mombasa. It was anything but luxurious, yet Joan, who was quite at home sleeping in a tent or under the stars, couldn't have cared less with Alan at her side. In that forgettable town, in that very little room, the blissful couple spent their first night together as man and wife.

From the moment they left their impromptu honeymoon accommodations, Alan had a full-time companion, partner, and unofficial producer in his wife. Starting from day one of their life together, Joan would do for Alan what she had done so expertly for her father: help him by handling the details.

It really was a working honeymoon, centered on Alan's filming for *On Safari*. The newlyweds planned to set up camp on the Athi River, the second-longest in Kenya, which flows through Tsavo East National Park, and which, during rainy seasons, swells to a depth of thirty feet and is filled with hippos and crocodiles. It was the dry season when they arrived. They planned to sleep beside the dry riverbed and record elephants making waterholes by digging in the sand. Even before they unpacked, they hid behind a pile of rocks and filmed the elephants in the moonlight. There were also plenty of rhinos, zebras, and buffalo to film. They complemented each other perfectly—Alan filming, Joan loading the cameras, Alan out front, Joan always watching his back. After a long night, they returned to their campsite, where Alan discovered a major lapse in planning.

The tent he had brought was too big, an army tent. He wrestled with its huge wooden poles and the heavy canvas, which was designed to be raised by soldiers. As usual, Joan was unfazed. She helped him pound the tent pegs into the ground, then tied a cable to the main tent pole and attached it to the winch of the Land Rover, which did the heavy lifting.

They didn't have a cot, just a thin mattress on the ground. As it turned out, sleeping on nothing but a mattress beside an African river is an invitation for every insect or creature that creeps, crawls, or burrows. One night, a sand-colored scorpion with a black tail—one of the nastiest, most poisonous varieties—crawled out from under the mattress and stung the bride. The pain from such a sting is excruciating, but Joan uttered only a muffled "Oh." She took two aspirins and went back to sleep.

At four-thirty A.M. on the same night as the scorpion bite, there was another diversion: eight lions 150 yards or so from the tent, in the act of bringing down an impala. Their commotion awakened the newlyweds, and Alan shouted what had by then become his two-word mantra: "*Film it!*" They got into the Land Rover and recorded the kill, then followed the pride to the riverbed where the animals went to drink after their meal. Near the Roots' camp, as they were both aware, was the Tsavo River railway bridge, where, during its construction, two large male lions had killed and consumed nearly 140 workmen—the most famous man-eating lions in Africa's history. Joan slept only an hour that night, and the pain from the scorpion bite lasted four days. Still, she never complained—she was, she wrote her parents, "terribly happy."

They both were. Alan would later reminisce:

> Neither Joan nor I went in for any little romantic interludes—no fancy dinners, no special birthday or Christmas stuff (without kids that's no fun), no weekends away lolling about somewhere expensive. We had candle-lit dinners together under the stars most nights, and we watched the sun—and the moon—come up and go down over some of the most beautiful places on earth. We were together, alone, among animals, and in country that we loved. *Is that not a good description of a great honeymoon?* We shared the same powerful feelings—of joy to be out in the wilds, of excitement at discovering or filming something never seen before, of exhaustion after a long day of hard work, of the satisfaction that came from doing that work better than most in the business.
>
> When we were married, we went straight off to work in the harsh country along the Tsavo and Tiva Rivers. It was during a terrible drought, hot as hell, and we had no help to put up camp, to cook and clean, carry water, firewood, or equipment. But it was a fantastic time. We agreed that it was the best possible honeymoon, and then it just segued into more and more of the same. We began to work out how to live in our camps as simply and efficiently as possible—something we got down to a fine art—and soon we were completely self-contained, ready to go anywhere.
>
> When we did meet up with friends—usually game wardens or hunters in the bush—we'd party hard and drink and dance, but we were always glad to get away again. We didn't do holidays at all, as I said, but when we had finished a difficult sequence, or were ready to move out of an area, we would often take a couple of days off. Then we'd go exploring places we hadn't visited, just picnicking, bird-watching, looking for river crossings or future

campsites, or just walking in the bush and enjoying being together and knowing that the other was getting as much pleasure and excitement as you were.

Their lives became a dizzying succession of campsites in astonishing locations, all across East Africa and beyond. Their toilet was a trench in the ground, with a wooden board with a hole in it, elevated by coffee cans, bricks, or wood. Their shower was a perforated bucket filled with water heated over a fire, hoisted up to the limb of a tree. While Alan concentrated on the ideas, cameras, equipment, and cinematic aspects of their film safaris, Joan saw to it that the fire was always lit, coffee brewed, bread baked, food cooked, cocktails ready, cots erected, itinerary meticulously planned—every detail checked off.

They soon fell into a routine. Alan would say, "We're off to Karamoja," or wherever.

Joan would then pack up everything and they would roll on to their next destination, where she would unpack and set up camp all over again. Joan not only helped Alan but also took care of his friends. Very soon Alan's endless clique of daredevils and adventurers began erecting their tents alongside Alan and Joan's.

In these and later years, Joan sent a continuous stream of letters to her mother. She wrote in a precise hand on Alan's blue tissue stationery, which had ALAN ROOT in big block letters at the top and the black silhouette of one of Kenya's animals—monkey, giraffe, gazelle, elephant, or striped African skunk—in the top right-hand corner. Joan always began each letter with "Dear Mum" or "My darling Mum." She would write long, detailed letters of her adventures, some dispatches stretching to ten or more pages. Snippets from this correspondence convey the couple's early lifestyle:

> Alan has gone out with Ian [Parker] to shoot an elephant [for a film about the first attempt to cull wildlife on a scientific basis], so I have time to get down to letter-writing.

We spent about 6 days on the Tiva, and got many species of animals drinking during the day, but due to freak rains from a week ago, there is water on the surface, so elephants have dug holes everywhere and therefore are not concentrating near the blinds. The night we spent in the blind, we only saw about 30 elephant and 10 rhino that were frightened by a lion.

Tomorrow we are going to Tsavo-West . . . where we will be filming poachers in their hide [blind] making poison. We went into the river to look for crocs with a flashlight. Alan and Ian wanted to catch a little one, but decided against it when we counted 25 pairs of eyes glowing.

Last night, Alan and [a friend] went croc hunting with a spotlight and caught one two feet long. They brought him to the house, and we got a recording of his pitiful little cries and then let him go this morning. The river is full of crocs because of the Waliangulu [an elephant-hunting tribe] who cut up the elephants and hang the meat to dry, then throw lumps in the river when no one is looking so they have less work to do. They're lazy blighters.

Ian shot an elephant this morning so Alan is filming the cutting up and loading on the lorry. . . . We're both very fit and very sunburnt.

Out in the wild with Alan, far from the safari tourists, Joan underwent an amazing transformation. Her shyness fell away, and an adventurer emerged, though not one of Alan's ilk. She would never sneak up on a snake, pluck the hair out of an elephant's tail, or taunt a lioness—all of which Alan was apt to do, especially if there was a crowd around to watch. Instead, Joan had a profound empathy for the animals they followed and filmed.

But above all, she was the wife and partner of Alan Root. He was front and center in everything she did. Her love was there when they returned to camp each evening, when she cooked his food and made his bed. And her love was reciprocated. "Romance?" Alan mused years later. "I would often put a bunch of wildflowers on her pillow. Joan would surprise me with homemade ice cream after a hot day, or a hot whiskey and honey after hours of following gorillas in the freezing rain. We'd skinny-dip in clear springs or in rivers as brown and thick as chocolate sauce, and damn the crocodiles. Instead of entertaining chattering guests at the dinner table we'd have baobab buds in a jug so we could watch them open, or praying-mantis eggs that would hatch as we dined. We had the best job in the world, and we both loved everything about it—where it took us and what we experienced together along the way. Really, our lives were so full of adventure and discovery that they were a great romance in themselves."

The couple could not live on love alone, though, and the money they earned from the Denises was more a stipend than a salary. Then Alan remembered the bongo he had raised; it was now in the Milwaukee Zoo and needed a mate to establish a breeding herd. The zoo would pay for the mate. He and Joan headed for bongo country, high in the rugged Aberdare Mountains. Alan had devised a safe trap, a sort of tunnel that he would place on a trail. A bongo passing through it would trigger a mechanism that released doors at the trap's entrance and exit. Night after night for a month, Alan slept near the trap, which blended into the landscape, while Joan camped nearby, researching and gathering all the plants in a bongo's diet.

One day they awoke to find a fine specimen in their trap. At first they fed it through a small window in the enclosure, until it was acclimated to their sound and smell. Then Joan, as still as the antelope itself, climbed into the trap and fed the bongo by hand.

The Roots made an early film of their bongo-catching exploits called *Box Me a Bongo*. In it, Joan's youth and beauty are in full bloom. A gentle yet indomitable presence, she is as tall as a fashion model but as quiet as a fawn. Even in the rugged wilderness of the Aberdares, she didn't have a hair out of place or a wrinkle in her khakis.

This early film also marks a debut of sorts for the people who would become Alan and Joan's biggest fans and unofficial film crew: the black Kenyans, the Maasai, Kikuyu, Luo, and other tribesmen and women who would be there at every turn, in this case helping to carry the bongo crates down from the mountainsides and later rushing by the hundreds to the hot-air balloon landings, where schoolchildren laughed and sang and got tangled in the balloon fabric, and forever running after the Land Rover.

Joan and Alan had found both home and family in the wilds of "good old Africa," as Joan would put it in a letter to her mother. Home, for Joan, meant Alan, wherever he chose to be. This became even more clear on a trip back to Lyntano, her father's coffee farm. Although it was her familiar world, it was no longer home. After years of quiet acrimony—Edmund would later write that he had "never been in love ever before, *ever*"—her parents had filed for divorce, and her mother had moved back home to Durban, South Africa. Her father was packing up, leaving Joan to sell the sixty-five-acre farm.

Before the divorce, Edmund had become enamored of another woman, a beauty named Jean Bowie Nathan Shor, who was an adventure journalist. She had served as a Red Cross captain in Italy during World War II, worked for the UN in China, climbed Kilimanjaro, and written numerous articles for *National Geographic*. She became the first woman to follow Marco Polo's route across Afghanistan and China, a journey she chronicled in her book *After You, Marco Polo*. Twice divorced, she had been working as a tour leader for the U.S. offshoot of Thru the Lens in San Francisco when she was assigned to go to Africa and conduct a photo safari. Edmund furnished the supplies and manpower for her tour, and he became so fascinated with her that he signed up for her next trip, a cruise on the Mediterranean. In a letter to Jean's sister, he wrote, "I can assure you that I am not normally at all emotional—only about Jean and as far as I'm concerned she is the whole world, all of it."

Edmund was preparing to depart for that Mediterranean cruise—on which he planned to propose marriage to Jean—when Joan arrived home. She had come with Alan to pick up her car, and she found her father sheepish and evasive about his travel plans, not to mention his new infatuation. When she discovered his intentions, she was horrified. She poured out her heart in letters to her mother, who was awaiting the finalization of the divorce. Lillian Thorpe, so long a great colonial lady who did almost everything to extremes—working, drinking, smoking, laughing—was becoming more and more introverted as her joy turned to depression and discouragement and the Kenya she had loved became emblematic in her mind of all that was wrong with the world.

"No one thinks [ill] of you, Mum, who had a completely unblemished past," Joan wrote. "Don't let that old bastard upset you." She said how disgusted all her friends were by Edmund's treatment of his wife, after all Lillian had done to support him and build up his business. She vented her anger that her father was traveling with his new love "only a few weeks before the divorce case." Later, after the divorce was final and Edmund had a new partner, Joan tried to comfort her mother. She assured her that "his good name (if it still exists) will soon perish. . . . Anyway, Mum, don't get in a twist about it and forget the man (at least forget him when you have got the last cent possible out of him)." At that moment Edmund seemed to embody all the worst attributes of the human male. Alan, on the contrary, two years into their marriage, continued to embody all the best. "I have a wonderful husband who is working terribly hard to build up something," she wrote her mother.

As she and Alan drove out of Nairobi, headed for another tent beside another river, Joan's husband had some news of his own for her: He had accepted an offer to film an expedition across East Africa in a hydrogen balloon.

It was taken for granted that Joan would follow the balloon in the Land Rover, fetch the crew wherever they landed, and have the camp ready. There was one more thing, Alan added: He'd asked his bosses, Armand and Michaela Denis, for a leave of absence in order to go on the balloon safari, and they had fired him on the spot.

—

One of the men who had enlisted Alan to take the balloon trip, Anthony Smith, was a popular writer for London's *Daily Telegraph* and a longtime Africa aficionado. He had met Alan and Joan at a wildlife conference in Arusha, in what is today Tanzania, after being told "The people you need to help you are Alan and Joan Root." Smith had told Alan that he was determined to fly a hot-air balloon over the wild places of Africa, to follow the lead of Jules Verne's 1862 novel *Five Weeks in a Balloon*, in which the author detailed the idea of a flight from Zanzibar westward across Africa. *Would they be interested in filming the voyage?* Smith wanted to know.

Of course, Alan assented immediately, adding that his wife would be a necessary adjunct to any project he signed on for. It took two six-ton trucks to carry enough fuel for a flight, and it took twenty-four people three hours to inflate the balloon. Soon, however, Alan and his new friends were in the air, with Africa spread out below them like a magnificent carpet. According to one local newspaper account:

> President [Idi] Amin saw a mysterious flying object descend into Lake Victoria and then take off again, Radio Uganda reported yesterday. It quoted him as saying the object was to be taken as a "sign of good luck to Uganda," and added: "Any person who might have seen the object is advised to go for prayers in their respective places of worship."

As always, Joan handled the details and took her custodianship of the balloon project quite seriously. Anthony Smith remembered one typically problematic day: "We were having *terrible* trouble with the balloon. A storm had blown in, and the balloon was being blown across the ground, straight into the thorn trees. We hitched it to the Land Rover, but that didn't seem to help. Joan went to the tent to get something, and found ten or twelve Maasai in the tent, certainly not helping, just sheltering from the storm. Joan was *so* angry. The Maasai had piled up their spears right inside the doorway to the tent. She picked all of the spears up and just threw them out into the rainstorm. A warrior's *spears* . . . Joan kept everything going."

"She was the spear carrier," added her friend Dee Raymer, another Nairobi-based wildlife expert. "Not only the spear but the entire armory. Alan was the front man, the man with the gab and the charisma, and the incredible talent behind the lens. That doesn't make a movie. You've got pre- and post-production, processing, records of what's in the footage, the nuts and bolts of shopping for your safaris, packing the vehicle for them, having everything on hand when it's needed . . . I mean *everything,* which Alan would later discover normally takes a team of people to do. Joan did all of that single-handedly."

Yet Joan always downplayed her role, calling herself Alan's "assistant." As Alan would later explain to *People* magazine, "If she were a great career woman, she might not be interested in helping me with mine. I'm the guy who's got the ideas. But she's a great manager." To which the writer added, "The Roots are a team, and that's what makes it work so well."

> A wildlife cameraman's wife has to be willing to share many of her husband's hazards. Joan Root has had her own share of mishaps. She was bitten by a scorpion on a wedding night spent under canvas in the bush. A two-inch acacia thorn passed through the sole of her foot. Alan had to remove it with a pair of pliers. And, of course, there was the case of the hippo that bit off her face mask in Mzima Springs. She accepts these things. Less easy to accept, I feel sure, are the strains put on her nervous system by some of Alan's escapades. . . . Recently she has been learning to fly, perhaps in self-defence. Alan is a lucky man to have her. I'm sure he knows it.
>
> —Colin Willock, *The World of Survival* (1978)

After his first balloon flight, Alan knew he had found the perfect vehicle for his filmmaking future. Joan had a radically different experience of this adventure, however, since she was responsible for chasing the balloon as it made emergency landings in craggy mountains, negotiated calamitous descents amid boiling thunderheads, and thudded into villages filled with curious natives. Unplanned and crash landings became almost routine.

At the end of the three-month trip, Anthony Smith felt that he knew *everything* about the thoroughly outgoing Alan Root—and they became such good friends that Alan would later name him as one of the beneficiaries of his will. When Smith returned triumphantly to London after his balloon adventure, he regaled his mother with tales of his conquest and of Alan, the bush boy who had guided and photographed their adventure. He also mentioned Alan's wife, Joan, and told how she had tracked them everywhere.

"It seems that Joan had the more dangerous job, having to pick you up wherever you landed," said Smith's mother. "What about her?"

Smith thought for a second, recalling what Joan did when they landed and how she took care of them in camp. Outside of that, he couldn't recall anything specific about her. He couldn't come up with a solitary thing that Alan had said about his wife or what she had said about herself. She was so integral to the project, yet so self-effacing and happy to be working behind the scenes, that she blended in instead of ever standing out. After three intimate months in the Roots' company, he realized he knew absolutely nothing about Joan. "We never gave a thought to the carefree girl who casually drove through all sorts of country to pick us up from wherever we happened to land," Smith would later write in England's *Guardian*. She was too shy and modest to reveal anything about herself.

Everywhere Joan went, she involved herself in what would become her lifelong mission: the care of wounded creatures. She told her mother about one night when four tribesmen stopped by their camp, "clutching a bedraggled red-billed hornbill. It was terrified and so dirty . . . its wing feathers so scraggly, it could not fly." The bird, a species of South African hornbill, was no larger than a human hand. It has black and white feathers and a blood-red beak almost as large as its entire body.

The tribesmen wouldn't say how they had caught it, but most likely, it was the runt of a litter, and when the other chicks had flown the nest, the littlest hornbill was left behind, too weak to fly. The men wanted a shilling for it, which Joan immediately gave them. For twenty-four hours, the chick was too panic-stricken to accept food, but eventually, Joan and Alan got it to eat. Joan named the little hornbill Scruffy, and soon it became so tame that it would perch patiently in a tree outside their tent, waiting until they walked outside, whereupon it would swoop down and land at their feet, breaking into "ecstatic singing and dancing displays." In the months that followed, Joan often wrote about Scruffy in her letters to her mother. In one she said:

> He really must have a charmed life, because at our last camp, at Vipingo, he was loose in the bushy tree above our tent, and I was trying to entice him down with a *dudu* [insect, in Swahili], when to my horror I saw a green mamba only a foot away from him. He also noticed it and hopped up to it and started pecking its middle section. Mambas eat birds, so I was petrified, but Alan got a long stick and poked the mamba so that it slid off a few feet, and we managed to catch Scruffy. It was bright green and at least 6 feet, and if it had bitten Scruffy he would have died instantly, and we can't understand why it didn't.

Scruffy was further evidence for Joan that animals could be rehabilitated, and that humans can make a difference in the wild. This belief was wholeheartedly shared by a formidable individual who was intent on taking wildlife films to a new level of quality and daring, and whose sponsorship would allow Alan and Joan to move into an even larger arena of filmmaking. His name was Aubrey Leland Oakes Buxton.

Buxton was the epitome of the 1960s British nature nut. Frequently outfitted in a khaki safari suit, he had been crazy about animals since his days in the Royal Artillery during World War II, when he spent time in Africa and Burma. Back in London, wealthy from his work in the pharmaceutical industry, he drove a Bentley and married the daughter of a baronet. Later he would be involved in the founding of the World Wildlife Fund, which Prince Philip headed for twenty years. In the late 1950s, convinced that the British public's appetite for footage of animals in the wild could become as strong as his own, Buxton and several colleagues snapped up the Anglia Television franchise for the east of England, intending to introduce nature films into commercial programming.

Buxton's series wouldn't merely show wild animals in nature; it would attempt to save them. Back then few people even knew what "conservation" stood for, and that worried Aubrey Buxton to no end. He created a club with friends and associates who shared his sense of the urgent need to popularize wildlife conservation efforts by showing endangered animals and their environment on television. "The intention," Buxton said, "was to put together the best team in the world—the best photographers, the best naturalists, the best of everything—and they all had to be dedicated conservationists."

After giving this new series the name *Survival,* he went to Africa to enlist the leading wildlife filmmakers of the day. He had already signed several of the best cameramen on the continent, but Alan Root, whom he knew by reputation, remained elusive. "And I knew he could be the most brilliant and innovative cameraman in the world," Buxton would later say.

Alan and Joan were camping on the border of Uganda and the Republic of the Congo (later Zaire, now the Democratic Republic of the Congo) when Buxton found them in the midst of a torrential rainstorm. Unable to cross a submerged bridge into Uganda, they were temporarily marooned on the Congo side of the roaring Rutshuru River, in a terrifying but exhilarating landscape they shared with white-headed fish eagles and vultures.

Buxton was comfortably camped with his wife on nearby Lake Edward, into which the Rutshuru River feeds, when the game warden mentioned that the Roots were nearby. "Take me to them *immediately*!" Buxton exclaimed.

He and the game warden drove out into the raging storm. Arriving at the swollen river, Buxton stood on the Uganda bank, screaming greetings across to Alan and Joan. To better hear the curious gentleman in the safari suit, Alan waded across the flooded bridge as far as he could. Buxton introduced himself and shouted out a few words regarding his lofty ambitions for a new television series. He intended to make the greatest wildlife films in the world and he wanted the Roots on his team.

Joan let out a shout, and Alan looked down into the rapidly rising river.

"Sounds great!" Alan shouted, retreating to Joan's side. "Send us a letter!"

"Is there anything you need?" Buxton yelled back.

Alan calculated that they had enough food, but he remembered that they had run out of food for a parrot they'd brought. "Parrot food!" he said. "Bring us some birdseed!"

Buxton yelled not to worry. Sure enough, the next morning a plane flew over and dropped a big bundle of peanuts on the Roots' campsite.

"My first payment from *Survival* was peanuts," Alan would later say, laughing.

One of their first assignments for the *Survival* series was to film not wildlife but a vanishing way of life, the primitive Karamojong tribes of Uganda. "A requiem for a spectacular people," intones the voice-over of the later film *A Tear for Karamoja.* "Half a century ago, Karamoja was a country into which a white man ventured at the risk of his life." Later, this cattle-breeding tribe, whose diet consisted of cow's milk and blood, would be decimated by Ugandan prime minister Milton Obote and Ugandan dictator Idi Amin, who systematically slaughtered the Karamojong along with other native tribes. Those who remained were stripped of their weapons, as well as their most prized possession: their cattle.

Children were also highly prized by the Karamojong. "A man can have as many wives as he can afford," Joan wrote in one of her frequent letters to her mother. But the tribe's marriage ceremony was merely a prelude to childbirth. Indeed, there were eight or nine stages before a woman was fully acknowledged as the wife of a tribesman. "Not until she has a child," Joan explained. "And it is not until she has reared at least two children to walking age that she leaves her own mother and goes to live in her husband's homestead."

Where were Joan and Alan's children? the Karamojong incessantly asked as they eagerly offered to initiate the couple into their tribal practices. They actually inducted Alan in a manhood ceremony, which, Joan wrote, "consisted of the stomach contents of an ox being smeared down his face and chest, and then being lightly hit with sticks by the elders. . . . They then chanted strings of blessings for us, which went on and on. One of them was that the next time we visited them, I would have *a child!*"

Her hope and anticipation is palpable here, as if to say, *Yes, someday we will have children of our own.* Alan loved the idea as much as Joan did. He was great with children, and his desire to have his own would grow even stronger. But at this critical juncture in their lives as filmmakers, there was neither time nor space in their lives for a baby.

Africa constantly called to them, not only with its glories but also out of need.

Lake Magadi is an eighteen-mile soda lake an hour outside of Nairobi. It lies in one of the lowest and hottest spots in the Great Rift Valley, a hellish, shallow body of extremely high-alkaline water that produces several-foot-deep soda deposits—called *trona*—on the surface of the lake. These deposits burn the skin on contact, and the fumes scorch the eyes. The lake's soda sparked a local industry in the town of the same name: The Magadi Soda Company, the world's second-largest source of sodium carbonate, which is used to make soap and other industrial products. Though great for the local economy, the soda itself is awful on humans and wildlife.

One day in July 1962, the sky over Lake Magadi turned pink with flamingos. A flood in the birds' ancestral breeding ground had forced them to migrate en masse, and they ended up in the worst possible place for a flock of anything to breed. As the flamingos settled in, someone at the Magadi soda company alerted the bird expert at the Nairobi Museum, who called Joan and Alan, asking if they would be willing to guard the flock against predators.

They'd be happy to, they answered, as long as they were allowed to film it. They drove straight to the lake, where once again they pushed the limits of conventional filmmaking—not by what they did but by what they didn't do: Specifically, they didn't interfere with the animals and instead filmed them in their natural habitat doing their natural activities. Alan and Joan set up a blind in a bare patch above the water level, with flamingos all around them, and waited weeks to start filming until the flock had become accustomed to them. Eventually, the flamingos laid their eggs in nests made of soda mud, which hardened into thousands of rocky mounds. Once the eggs began to hatch and the birds began stepping into the soda lake, a terrible drama unfolded. Because of the intense heat and the stinging soda deposits, when the flamingos went in search of food to feed their chicks, they had trouble returning to their nests. For long periods, thousands of screaming birds and chicks were in the open, unprotected, inviting vultures and hyenas to move in for an easy kill.

Soon large concentrations of chicks stopped moving altogether. "I'm going to see what the trouble is," said Alan, and Joan followed him from their blind. They found a pitiable scene: thousands of dead flamingo chicks in boiling, crusted alkaline lagoons. The birds had been imprisoned by the soda in the lake and starved or drowned. It stained their feathers, burned their skin, and crystallized on their spindly legs from ankle to knee until it grew into heavy deposits. Tens of thousands of these young birds had been manacled by half-pound soda-ball shackles. Unable to move, they were doomed either to starve or to sink into the poisonous water.

Joan and Alan discovered that one tap with a knife or hammer would break a deposit, freeing the bird's leg. Working as quickly as they could, they freed a hundred birds, but thousands more were immobilized all around them. They put out an SOS, and help arrived in droves: first local volunteers, then the army and air force, then schoolteachers and their students, all braving the hundred-degree heat, the stench of dying birds, and the scalding soda.

SAVING THE FLAMINGO: MAGADI RESCUE OPERATIONS BEGIN was the headline in Nairobi's *Daily Nation* on September 23, 1962. A photograph of Joan and Alan kneeling over two tubs of shackled baby flamingos accompanied the story. In the end, they freed more than 27,000 chicks and prevented another 200,000 from entering the shallows, where the high concentration of soda would have imprisoned them. They had accomplished the largest bird-rescue operation in the history of Africa.

Once the salvaged flamingos flew safely away, however, the hungry media descended on the filmmakers. Newspapers in Africa, England, and elsewhere ran stories with Joan's picture—in some cases alone, rather than beside or behind Alan—and the world at large got its first glimpse of the tall, attractive blonde in a white sleeveless shirt, a floppy red hat, and the briefest of shorts.

Requests for Alan's film footage and Joan's still photographs of the rescue mission poured in from magazines all over the world. *Reader's Digest* cabled that it would pay Alan sixty pounds for every picture it published; plus, it would cover all his expenses. *National Geographic* commissioned on the spot an article that would be called "Flamingos Freed from Anklets of Death." *Afrikaner* magazine and *Das Tier* (the German publication edited by Dr. Bernhard Grzimek) also contacted the couple to say they would like pictures as soon as possible. The Roots were on their way to wildlife filmmaking stardom.

For now, everything was focused on the two of them and their career. That was how Joan showed her love—by working for her husband, fighting for him, suffering with him through his infinite injuries, and reveling in his many triumphs. The summit for wildlife filmmakers at this time was, of course, the BBC, where the wildlife content was being produced and hosted by David Attenborough, brother of the British actor Richard Attenborough. "Anyway, he's really keen to see Alan's poaching film with a view of putting it on BBC TV and also to get more of Alan's work because he says people are getting tired of Armand and Michaela and yet there is a vast public demand for wildlife films,"

Joan wrote her mother. "We're delighted because he is the most important person to know if Alan wants to sell anything to the BBC." With Attenborough's support, a deal was soon struck, and Alan and Joan were on their way. "You know, it never rains but it pours!" she wrote her mother at the end of 1962. "Three jobs for Alan have all cropped up at once—the BBC contract for 13 programmes in Tanganyika parks over a period of two years; Anglia now wants Alan to work for them full time, which means filming in Madagascar, possibly South America and elsewhere in the world; and now on top of those two wonderful offers, Grzimek comes out with a contract with Radio Frankfurt for seven 45-minute TV programmes a year and he wants Alan to do the photography, which also means filming anywhere in the world."

They were headed to the top of their profession. And if giving the world what they saw as the last throes of their continent meant postponing their chance to have a family, well, that was a choice they could happily make, at least for the time being.

Chapter Three

Survival next sent the Roots to the Congo, where they were the first to film the storied mountain gorillas at length. Few people had ever even seen these animals, much less tried to capture their world on film for mass audiences. Before the 1963 publication of the landmark book *The Mountain Gorilla,* in which field biologist George Schaller determined that it was actually possible to study such dangerous animals in their habitat, the giant apes had a reputation as a vicious, murderous lot. Schaller's book quotes one observer describing the gorillas' supposed bloodlust:

> When stealing through the shades of the tropical forest, [people] become sometimes aware of the proximity of one of these frightfully formidable apes by the sudden disappearance of one of their companions, who is hoisted up into the tree, uttering perhaps a short choking cry. In a few minutes, he falls to the ground a strangled corpse.

Yet Schaller maintained that the gorillas were peaceful if unprovoked. With his book in hand, Alan and Joan planned a safari to Mount Karisimbi, the highest of the eight volcanoes in the Virunga mountain range. These are part of a vast network of peaks that "rise out of the middle of Africa like the exposed vertebrae of some gigantic fossil," as the narrator says in Alan's film made twenty years after their first trip there, *Virunga: Rivers of Fire and Ice,* which includes some of their footage. "The Rwenzoris are not the highest mountains in Africa, but with twenty peaks of over forty-five hundred meters along a hundred-and-twelve-kilometer spine, they are by far the most spectacular."

Joan packed the Land Rover with enough supplies to last a month, and they set out for Rwanda. A half hour outside Nairobi, they reached a spot overlooking the seemingly infinite expanse of the Great Rift Valley. This was a place of myth and magic, "a moon landscape strewn with lava, soda lakes, and thorn and furrowed by stony rivers," wrote Judith Thurman in her book *Isak Dinesen: The Life of Karen Blixen.*

> The highlands lay at altitudes of between five and eight thousand feet, rimmed by a range of ancient mountains and extinct volcanoes, and dominated by the snowcapped peak of Mount Kenya. The air was exceptionally clean and pure, and it was said, then, to produce "euphoria" in white people, who were therefore not held strictly accountable for their behavior. B.E.A. (British East Africa) had a highly erotic atmosphere; it was a place where, within the sanction of Nature, civilized inhibitions were let go.

In the distance stood Lake Naivasha, where Joan had been conceived and where Alan had made his first real film, about the lily-trotter. "Let's stop in Naivasha and have a coffee," he said.

Like most areas in Kenya, Naivasha was a place of extremes, with burning-hot days and very cold nights; it had a lake of wondrous beauty and an exceedingly sensational past. Even its name stood for turmoil, deriving from the Maasai word *nai posha,* meaning "rough water." It was a rare and mysterious freshwater lake that had no apparent outlet, so no one knew for sure how it remained fresh. Sudden storms frequently turned the huge lake from placid to angry, and the inexplicable falling and rising of the water level caused it to fall precipitously in some years and to overflow in others. Throughout modern history, its wonders have been extolled by a number of famous visitors. Even President Theodore Roosevelt went hippo hunting there in 1909 and called it "a lovely sheet of water, surrounded by hills and mountains."

Naivasha was later famous for being the playground of the hedonistic Happy Valley set, the notorious handful who overshadowed the much larger, hardworking influx of British colonialists who came to Kenya in the 1920s to launch bold new lives in the wild. Some of the most famous Happy Valley revelers erected vast mansions around the lake. In the words of the British writer James Fox, who chronicled their high-flown antics in his bestselling book *White Mischief* (which was later made into a popular feature film):

> Friends from England brought home tales of glorious entertainment in an exhilarating landscape, surrounded by titled guests and many, many servants. In New York and London, a legend grew up of a set of socialites in the Aberdares whose existence was a permanent feast of dissipation and sensuous pleasure. Happy Valley was the byword for this way of life. Rumors circulated about endless orgies, of wife swapping, drinking, and stripping, often embellished in the heat of gossip. The Wanjohi River was said to run with cocktails, and there was that joke, quickly worn to death by its own success: "Are you married, or do you live in Kenya?"

At the time, Joan and Alan didn't care about Lake Naivasha's past. They drove into Naivasha town, a dusty little village near the lakeshore, and had coffee at the Bell Inn. During the 1920s, the well-heeled white Kenyans had gone to the inn to "take a stiff gin and tonic as they waited for a horse-drawn carriage to whisk them to a lakeside estate for a weekend of parties and shooting." By 1963 Happy Valley was a distant memory, and the Mau Mau revolt had come and gone. Since then many whites had fled the area, and the grand houses they had built by the lake were now going cheap.

As they drank their coffee, Alan picked up a newspaper, and his eyes chanced upon a real estate ad: eighty-eight acres with a house right on the lake. They decided to take a look. Just this once the wildlife would have to wait.

They drove out in their overloaded Land Rover, bumping down the rutted South Lake Road and turning in to an unlikely paradise that Ewart Grogan, the British explorer who walked the whole of Africa and wrote about it in his book *From the Cape to Cairo,* called "the most beautiful home site I have ever seen."

The road opened up to an endless green vista. Beyond that was the lake, covering an area of sixty-two square miles. In those days it was crystal-clear, filled with fish, and considered one of the world's top bird-watching spots. The property for rent in the newspaper was named Kilimandege, the hill of the birds.

Kilimandege had belonged to the McRae family, who once kept a caged cheetah in their front yard. The McRaes were dead, the cheetah was gone, and the house was empty, but the eighty-eight acres remained in all their glory. Thick with vegetation, the area had become something of a mini–game preserve, a migration path for giraffes, gazelles, waterbuck, and many other species that routinely crossed the acreage. The house was a simple structure, with a wide veranda shaded by eucalyptus and flat-topped yellow fever trees, a sort of grandstand from which to view the endless parade of animals. The doors were locked. But they looked through the windows and could see that the place was a wreck. "Dust and bat droppings and wet patches on the ceiling and so on," Alan would later remember. "Obviously in need of tender loving care."

From the veranda, Joan and Alan could see the lake, where the black eyes and twitching ears of hippos rose and fell. They spotted a family of giant white-headed fish eagles nesting above the roof. They could hear a loud commotion of twittering birds from the garden, and when they went to investigate, they found a puff adder eating a frog.

They looked at each other and knew *this was home.* "You'll go broke if you try to farm this place," the manager at the house next door told them when they went over to call the Realtor. "God, we'd never farm it," said Alan. "We just want to live here."

For a modest sum, it was theirs. They would be back soon, they promised themselves. But first they had to go and film the mountain gorillas.

They stood at the foot of the Virunga Mountains, prepared to follow the trail toward the gorillas—Alan, Joan, and Anthony Smith, accompanied by twenty-six porters, including the park ranger Senkwekwe, who had guided George Schaller (and later would guide Dian Fossey) up these treacherous heights. With Schaller's book practically memorized, the group began their trek skyward. The trail was not only steep but also slippery, packed with fallen wet bamboo. The temperature swung wildly. The higher they climbed, the rougher and rainier it got. The bamboo was soon replaced by thick mud that gave way underfoot, causing the hikers to slip downward and lose hard-won ground. There were also six-foot nettles, nasty, prickly burrs with long stinging hairs that exuded a liquid poison—which left their clothes wet and sticky and any exposed skin itching and burning.

Joan wore a leather jacket, leather gloves, and patches of heavy canvas that Alan had applied to the front of her jeans, like a cowboy's chaps, to protect her from the treacherous vegetation. These safeguards were quickly rendered useless, ripped to shreds and covered with nettle thorns.

The air grew thinner with each step. When they arrived at their base camp on the mountain, the porters unloaded the gear and immediately turned and raced back down. They apparently had no desire to stay in gorilla country any longer than necessary. The first thing the remaining trio saw was the tombstone of Carl Akeley, the father of modern taxidermy, who had come to the mountains in 1921 and died from a fever in Rwanda. Exhausted, Smith collapsed by Akeley's grave. Alan, by contrast, was exhilarated and ready to film.

They had to find the gorillas fast, before the heaviest rains came.

Their base camp between two volcanoes was the same hut where George Schaller had stayed and where Dian Fossey would later stay. Half of the roof had been destroyed in a fire, so they slept with a ceiling on one side and stars on the other. As soon as the sun set, the temperature plummeted. Then came the wind and hail. They threw on every stitch of clothing they had brought and huddled together for warmth. At last the sun rose, and with it the temperature.

11/7/63

My darling Mum,

We had to prepare for this gorilla trip in a hurry because Dr. Grzimek wanted us to come immediately and try and film the gorillas before the rains start in the Congo. . . . We have enough food to last a month and are prepared to stay here as long as is necessary. The day before yesterday we had an exhausting 5.5-hour walk. . . . Yesterday we walked for six hours trying to find gorillas, only to find a poachers' camp of at least 15 men, who had pulled out only a few hours previously because the word had got around that some Europeans were in the area (their fires were still burning), so temporarily the gorillas have been frightened (the poachers kill buffalo and do not hurt the gorillas, but they do shout at them and throw rocks). Today is Tony's last day, so they have gone out again to try and find gorillas, but I decided to stay behind because we will be here for weeks and are confident that the gorillas will come back into this area, now that the poachers have left.

On their second day, they found the gorillas. Alan, Joan, and Anthony Smith climbed higher, through the heat, wet bamboo, and nettles, until they came to what looked like giant birds' nests on the ground but were in fact the piles of motley vegetation into which the gorillas defecated. According to Schaller's book, mountain gorillas could be tracked by their feces: The fresher it is, the closer they are.

They smelled the gorillas before they heard them: an odor resembling a combination of pungent human sweat, manure, and charred wood—not unlike the stench of burning rubber. Walking on, they came upon a nest of gorilla dung so fresh it was still steaming. Alan described what happened next:

> We had to get very close for pictures, so slowly and cautiously we edged through the bush. We could hear them and we knew we were sneaking up on them, and we moved up so quietly in the dense vegetation that we realized we had got far too close.
>
> There we were, smack in the centre of about 15 gorillas.
>
> One spotted us and gave a warning scream. Others joined in and for the next few minutes they put on a show that was obviously meant to impress us—and impress us it did!
>
> The whole time we could hear them screaming and thumping their fists and knuckles on the ground and beating their chests. My commonsense told me that they were only excited at our being there and merely extremely curious.

After Smith went home, Alan and Joan were alone with the gorillas. For a month they dwelled peacefully among the reputedly vicious beasts and successfully filmed them. "They seem to be such nice, gentle animals—no other big animals would allow humans so close," Joan wrote to her mother.

Over several weeks Joan and Alan accustomed themselves to living in the burned-out hut, sweating by day and freezing by night. When they felt that they had enough footage, they climbed down Karisimbi and spent some time recuperating at a friend's house near Nairobi, after which they almost immediately headed back to the Congo to film an erupting volcano, Mount Nyiragongo. There had been a military coup in that country, and the road to Nyiragongo was blocked by soldiers.

The drunken, bullying soldiers reveled in creating a climate of palpable fear. Members of rival tribes were pulled out of their cars, tortured, and shot. Whites weren't being targeted, but Alan and Joan were constantly stopped and searched, and the soldiers did their best to humiliate and frighten them. At one roadblock, a group of particularly surly soldiers demanded their passports. Alan knew that if they surrendered the passports, they'd never get out of the country. Reaching back as if to get them, he came up with a fist and punched one of the soldiers in the belly. The couple roared off to the ominous sound of several rifles being cocked. Fortunately, the soldiers didn't have time to aim and fire.

Having passed the roadblocks, Alan and Joan climbed up to the volcano's exploded peak, which Joan described in a letter to her mother: "The crater was obscured by cloud, and we were sheltered from a hailstorm in a cave. When we emerged, we saw waterfalls of melting ice tumbling into a lava lake that opened out beneath us, the red molten mass glowing and smoking on the surface."

The ground was so hot that Joan soon felt her rubber-soled shoes melting, too. It was indicative of what had become her recurring role in the marriage. "Many in the trade considered them to have been the best wildlife filming team, with Joan often performing the more daunting role," Anthony Smith later wrote. "Who was up a thorn tree ready to warn of a wildebeest herd thundering their way? Who had her goggles pierced when a hippo grew aggressive? Whose shoes melted when the hot volcanic lava became too much for them?" As Alan said, "I don't know what I'd do without Joan. I'd probably have to marry three women at the same time."

She had been Mrs. Alan Root for just two years, and already there had been too many trips to count, always without a word of complaint. She was happier than she had ever been, hopelessly in love with both her adventurous husband and their ultra-adventurous life. Best of all, she had found a home, the house on Lake Naivasha.

Just when everything seemed to be going so well in their career and relationship, tragedy struck. Joan had a character of immeasurable strength, but soon her body broke down—not because of nettles, soldiers, or gorillas, but because of something unseen and inexplicable. Not long after their return from the gorillas in the Congo, she began getting weak, then so exhausted she couldn't lift her eyelids. Alan took her to a doctor, who wasn't sure what was wrong and put her on tranquilizers, which made the symptoms even worse. A second doctor recognized the symptoms as myasthenia.

Myasthenia, like so much in Africa, was a mystery; no one knew what caused it or how to treat it. A neuromuscular disease, it weakens the signals between the brain and various muscles. Additionally, it can alter the production of estrogen and lead to premature menopause. As it turned out, Joan suffered from full-blown myasthenia.

December 31, 1963

Dear Mum,

In my last letter I probably mentioned that I had been in the hospital and rather weak. . . . I probably caught a virus in the Congo, which is working itself off. The symptoms were the same as something very rare called myasthenia, which would have lasted for many months, probably years, and nothing's much known about it.

Alan was devastated. One night shortly after the diagnosis of Joan's illness, he went to his mother's house to tell her and his sister, Jacky.

"You don't know how sick she is!" Alan exploded. If they hadn't caught the disease as quickly as they had, it could have led to permanent paralysis.

Not concerned for herself, Joan was focused on how hard it was for Alan to carry on without her. She was determined to get well quickly and, as usual, show him her strength. After months of reporting to doctors on a regular basis, she decided that she'd had enough. Alan *needed* her. She would will herself well.

A scant eight months after they had returned from the erupting volcano, they were hiking in the Aberdare Mountains. Still weak and shaking, Joan paused before a two-foot-wide trickle of a stream, unable to walk or even wade across it. She didn't think anyone was watching her, but Alan was. "I was some distance away, and I was in tears as I watched that athletic woman, who could run and climb and swim as well as any man, and she was trembling with fear of failure of a two-foot jump.

"Then with a banshee yell, she threw herself forward. She only just did make it—stumbled, almost fell, then steadied herself. Then she slowly turned around, with a huge grin, and yelled back at me, 'This is a tributary of the Tana!'"—referring to one of Kenya's mightiest rivers, a quarter mile wide. "'Tell those ruddy quacks I don't need them anymore! I just jumped the Tana!'"

> I know you'll be happy to hear that Joan has mended and is in her usual good shape. She still has to take the odd pill, but is strong and well again. She proved it the other day by going up Mount Kenya with me on a trip to film a very rare sunbird that lives up near the snowline.
>
> —Alan Root to Anthony Smith, April 4, 1964

Whoop! Whoop! That's the sound a chimpanzee makes to call its mate in the wild, and Joan and Alan adopted it as a kind of code, meaning: *I'm here, dear. Where are you?* They sometimes had trouble communicating with words, but their *whoops* became a private language. They spoke it not only in the bush but also in the home where they had settled on Lake Naivasha.

The Roots' property lay off South Lake Road. A long drive led through flat-topped acacia trees and thornbushes, and then past the camp where Alan and Joan's staff—cook, driver, groundsmen, and various film-crew assistants—would reside. At the end of the drive was the house, whose verdant acreage sloped down toward the emerald-green lake.

Here, in this modest house on the pristine but turbulent lake, Joan Root finally felt at home. "Unless you built a house halfway up a mountain with all of East Africa at your feet, there would be few more beautiful settings," Colin Willock would later write in a 1978 book about the *Survival* television series. "The freshwater lake lays down its papyrus-fringed carpet of purple lotus lillies within fifty yards of the verandah. Bushbuck and dikdik, little bigger than a hare, nibble the flowers."

The lake would soon become host to a growing community of

naturalists. Across the lake from the Roots, the elephant expert Iain Douglas-Hamilton and his wife, Oria, would create a lodge for visitors. George and Joy Adamson—who in 1956 had taken in three orphaned lion cubs after George and his partner had been forced to kill the parents—came to live down the road from Alan and Joan. Joy took a particular liking to the smallest cub, which she named Elsa and, with much effort, successfully trained to live on her own in the wild. The experience was the basis for her bestselling book, *Born Free,* and the Oscar-winning film of the same name.

They could not have picked a better place from which to base their adventures—a spot so wild and fabulous it could have been a Hollywood set. If the Rift Valley is the cradle of civilization, Lake Naivasha is its Garden of Paradise. There is green everywhere, from the papyrus— that lines the lake with its tall green stalks and pom-pom heads, to the water itself, with floating islands of shrubs and flowers drifting by. Along the shore are the remaining houses of the Happy Valley era, the miles-long expanses between them home to masses of exotic animals, from gazelles to crested cranes, giraffes to pythons. At night an army of hippopotamuses rises from the lake to feed on grass and other vegetation, literally mowing the lawn every evening and returning to the water before sunrise. Their nightly path takes them through a field of papyrus and lotus lilies, up a hill of eucalyptus and fever trees, to a simple bungalow with a corrugated roof and a wide veranda that serves as front door, observation deck, and feeding ground. There Joan always kept a box of mealworms so that guests could offer one up to the local birds, which would happily come eat it out of their hands.

By the mid-1960s the lake house had become their headquarters, where they came for research, post-production, and rest between safaris. It was as much a home for animals as it was for people: There were creatures everywhere but few creature comforts. The living room was lined with shelves of books about wildlife and Africa. Joan had a production office filled with files, film, pictures, and production notebooks, and

Alan had a studio where he edited their films and stored their equipment. There were three small bedrooms, for them and their guests, and a big kitchen—separated from the main house—where Joan routinely cooked for anywhere from two to twenty visitors.

The Lake Naivasha property was also home to some of the animal stars of the Roots' films. Joan was in charge of maintaining this ever-growing menagerie, which included Chekky the porcupine, who would shake her quills in greeting; Minnie, the striped aardwolf, a small hyenalike animal whose diet consisted of termites; Sally the orphaned hippo; and Million, the mischievous aardvark. Joan did not consider the animals pets but, rather, visitors recuperating until they could make their way once again in the wild.

For Alan, Naivasha was the laboratory where the ideas for his films were born. Whether it was a hippo in the garden or a mongoose family under a tree, he wanted to film everything. At cocktail hour, Alan, Joan, and their friends would gather for drinks and appetizers on the veranda, and tiny red-billed oxpeckers would swoop down, perch on the humans' chins, and peck at the food between their teeth. Alan and Joan filmed that, too.

Charming as such scenes were, Africa existed in its full ferocity here, too. Frequently prowling beneath the Roots' dinner table was Joan's caracal, a large wildcat with razor-sharp teeth and claws. If guests leaned down to pet the cat, nine times out of ten it would roll over and let them. But the tenth time it might very well scream and lunge like a living bale of barbed wire.

"On one occasion, what I thought was a waterbed, on the far side of the living room, got up, walked out the door, across the grass, and into the lake—a pet hippo named Sally," wrote George Plimpton in an August 1999 *New Yorker* profile about Alan. Hippos kill more people in Kenya than any other herbivore in Africa, but Joan always fed Sally by hand.

"We are presently staying at Alan's house in Naivasha and are having great fun," one guest wrote friends back home. "I have so far been bitten by mosquitoes, leeches, a mongoose, a bush baby, a lizard, a small green snake, and a pet cormorant. Apart from swimming in a crocodile-infested pool, and holding a python's tail, my adventures include nearly leaving my right eye and ear hanging in a thorn tree as I rode on the roof of the Land Rover. This, I feel, is not a bad record for one month's stay, and I will undoubtedly have many stories to tell when I get back to the 'Mother Land.'"

As for the staff, they were perfectly capable when sober, but Joan and Alan had to hide their liquor from their longtime senior staff member, a short, cheerful Kikuyu named Kiari. Joan's diaries and letters are filled with stories of drunken escapades that take place "when Kiari slips off the rails." (Alan wasn't much better when he was sloshed. "Alan damaged his knee badly by fooling around on a motorbike under the influence of a Punch!" Joan wrote her mother after one holiday, adding that he had also engaged in "karate chopping the blazing Christmas pudding and setting fire to everyone's paper hats.") Kiari had worked for Joan's parents on their coffee farm, and his children also lived and worked for Alan and Joan at Naivasha. His son Babu tended the aardvark and filled in the countless holes it dug; Kiari's daughter, Wambui, helped with the cooking and cleaning; his son-in-law, Ngure, looked after the vehicles.

"Memsaab," as Joan's employees called her, was regaled with wild tales of fierce fights, robberies, and mayhem. In one letter, Joan tells of their safari driver, Gichuhi, throttling Kiari over ten Kenyan shillings (under ten U.S. cents back then) and then stabbing Kiari's wife in the face with a penknife when she tried to release Gichuhi's stranglehold on her husband. "The kids then grabbed pieces of firewood and beat Gichuhi until they broke his arm," Joan wrote. "Naturally, there was no alternative but to sack him." She said Gichuhi had also been moonlighting during their absences, using the Land Rover to take "goats up to Kinangop at night and bring back vegetables, and innumerable [other] little rackets." Joan also suspected some of the employees of stealing their film equipment to sell on the black market.

These were petty crimes; but perpetrators from the outside were much worse. Thieves stole truckloads of copper wire from telephone poles on Joan and Alan's property, disrupting phone service for months on end. When the phones worked, there were sometimes threatening calls at midnight or later, especially when Joan was staying in the house alone. Someone she had never met was arrested on ten counts of forging her name.

And yet somehow, everything worked. Some nights Alan and Joan would stretch a sheet between two fever trees and show their films to the staff, who would stare wide-eyed at the incredible action, just as millions of adults and children in living rooms and schoolrooms across England and Africa were doing. The animals they saw on screen, however, were quite different from those that roamed about the Roots' home by the lake. The animals in their films were deep in the bush and not always friendly to the filmmakers. "A lot of the time, Joan was sort of an intensive-care nurse," Alan said. "She was here to nurse me when I crashed planes and motorbikes, when I fell out of trees in New Guinea, out of boats on the Amazon. She was there with the Glenfiddich and the bandages when I was bitten by a whole menagerie of animals."

Joan took similar care of numerous others, including Dian Fossey, who flew to Nairobi in 1963, intent on studying gorillas that the Roots had already begun filming. Not only had Fossey relied on Alan and Joan's knowledge of the gorillas when she first came to Africa; they personally led her through the trails of Virguna, an expedition she described in her memoir *Gorillas in the Mist:*

> On my first visit to Kabara in 1963 I was fortunate in meeting Joan and Alan Root, photographers from Kenya who were camped in the meadow while working on a photographic documentary of the mountain gorillas. Both Joan and Alan kindly overlooked the intrusion of a somewhat hobbly and inquisitive American tourist into their secluded mountain workshop and allowed me to accompany them on some of their extraordinary contacts with the relatively uninhibited gorillas. . . .
>
> I shall never forget my first encounter with the gorillas. . . . Joan and Alan Root, some ten yards ahead on the forest trail, mo-

tioned me to remain still. The three of us froze until the echoes of the screams and chest beats faded.

Four years later, when Fossey returned to begin her infamous campaign to save the endangered gorillas of Virunga, she had a lucky break when she ran into Joan at Heathrow airport, an encounter that Joan described in a letter to her mother.

Amboseli, 2/12/67

Dear Mum,

As you know I flew from London a few days before Alan, and at London airport waiting to get on the plane I met a girl Dian Fossey who was going to Nairobi on the same plane. We had met her in 1963 when she came up to see the gorillas when we were filming them. She is an American girl and in the States she had met Dr. Leakey, and he had arranged to finance her going back to the Congo to study the gorillas. She was overjoyed to see me at London because we are her only friends here. We were most concerned about her traveling to the Congo on her own and getting up into the volcanoes, knowing no Swahili. Anyway, to make a long story short, I helped her buy all her supplies and equipment, and Alan traveled with her to the Congo, got her through the Congolese customs all right, introduced her to the bigwigs of the Albert Park, found porters, climbed up the volcanoes to the gorillas, installed her in the hut, gave her a few quick lessons on how to avoid the elephants, and how to find the gorillas, and gave all the scouts stern lectures to look after her. . . . It is a bit worrying leaving an inexperienced girl, isolated up there, but without our help I don't know how she would have managed. The Congolese park scouts are very nice types, and she has the scout who stayed with us when we were there. She is hoping to study the gorillas, as closely as Jane Goodall has studied the chimpanzees in Tanganyika.

On December 26, 1985, over twenty years later, Fossey would be murdered in her hut in Virunga, her head split open with a panga brandished by, as most believed, either a poacher, or a Rwandan incensed over her standing in the way of financial exploitation of the park for tourism and the animals she loved. By then the dark waters that would engulf Kenya were swiftly rising. The Roots' neighbor, *Born Free* author Joy Adamson—a woman so famous for peace—would be speared through the heart in January 1980 by a laborer who later confessed to killing her but insisted that he had done so only after Joy had shot him after he complained about not being paid for fourteen days of work. In 1989 Joy's husband, the lion-maned George Adamson, would be ambushed, probably by poachers, and gunned down in a hail of bullets outside his caged lion preserve. For now, however, the most dangerous things Joan and Alan had to contend with were wild animals.

"My *bibi,*" Alan would call Joan, using the Swahili word for "wife." Joan didn't have a pet name for her husband. It was always just Alan, which, with alarming frequency, became "*Oh, Alan!*" She expected him to do the unexpected—whether pulling the tail of a bull elephant or taunting a poisonous snake—and she was ready to handle whatever outcome these antics wrought.

Since he had launched his wildlife career with his snake farm, Alan's skin had turned into an archipelago of scar tissue, prompting George Plimpton to title his *New Yorker* piece "The Man Who Was Eaten Alive." There was a daredevil encounter behind each wound—especially the one where his index finger used to be.

About seven years into their marriage, Alan and Joan had flown with an American movie producer to visit Joy Adamson in her camp at Meru National Park. While the producer and Adamson were discussing her possible involvement in a movie about animals, Alan went for a walk. When he returned, he was carrying a four-and-a-half-foot-long, very fat, extremely poisonous puff adder.

Puff adders cause more human deaths than any other snake in Africa, but Alan was typically unafraid. He was showing the movie producer how the snake's fangs work—"lifting them out of their recesses with a knife edge," he later told George Plimpton—when Adamson brought out her camera. "I put the snake down to let it sidle off into the bush," Alan said. "Just then Joy announced that she didn't have any film in her camera. So I went after the puff adder and tried to catch it. It was waiting for me, and it struck, getting me on the knuckle. Excruciating pain—right from the start."

Alan's last snakebite, courtesy of a burrowing viper, had been quickly cured with a shot of anti-venom, but anti-venom can cause the body to go into shock if used a second time, so Alan chose to forgo it. Joan commandeered a plane at a nearby lodge, and on the flight to Nairobi, Alan began vomiting and fainting. "I decided I'd better have the anti-venom," he said. Joan gave him a shot of three cc's, but by the time the plane landed, Alan couldn't walk. At the airport, Joan hailed a taxi to the hospital, where emergency-room attendants rushed Alan inside on a stretcher. By then he was in a severe state of anaphylactic shock, which the doctor on duty assumed was caused by the snakebite. Not knowing it was actually a reaction to the anti-venom, the doctor gave Alan a second shot. That one nearly killed him.

Puff-adder venom kills by breaking down the body's blood vessels. Soon a blood blister the size of a baseball rose on Alan's hand, and his whole arm and half of his chest turned black. Gangrene was setting in.

We'll have to amputate his arm, the doctor told Joan.

Joan said no, insisting that Alan would get better.

Sure enough, after a few days, he did. But he was still in critical condition.

We'll have to amputate at the elbow, the doctor said.

Again, Joan said no.

Alan's condition improved, but not sufficiently.

We'll have to amputate at the wrist, insisted the doctor.

Again Joan said no.

In the end, Alan lost the index finger of his right hand, where the puff adder had bitten him. He later told an interviewer he put the severed finger in a jar and took it to the National Museum in Nairobi, "the first installment of bits bitten off, the rest to follow in various jars," he said, although the finger and its jar of formaldehyde eventually found their way back to Alan and Joan's home on the lake.

Whoop! Whoop!

As happy as they were together at Naivasha, increasingly, only the animals would whoop back to Joan. Alan, the darling of the wildlife-film world, began to spend more and more of his time far away, editing his films or meeting with his producers in London. His handsome profile gazed from a photograph of Alan and his fellow *Survival* film-makers on a wall in Anglia Television's office on Park Lane across from Hyde Park, in regal quarters that once served as Lord Mountbatten's London communications center during World War II. To his employers and admirers, Alan was Africa personified—daring, dangerous, charismatic. He was in his prime, at the height of his powers as a film-maker and of his prowess as a man. "He loved it when Anglia TV would send eight secretaries to meet him at Heathrow airport and take him to a show that night," said Anthony Smith. "He was the star!

"There was always a girl at the party," Smith continued. "And there was an elephant, and Alan went up and pulled some hair out of the elephant's tail, to make the girl an elephant hair bracelet."

Didn't the elephant charge?

Of course it did, Anthony said, but Alan knew which way to run—or at least where to stand—when pulling the tail hair out of a big bull elephant. The elephant was on the other side of a pile of rocks, and Alan knew elephants can't run across rocks.

For his part, Alan would later insist that the elephant-hair bracelet was for Joan, although he would also admit, "I mean, there were a couple of—I don't know what you would call them—not affairs, anyway," but short dalliances, nothing serious, nothing permanent. And what did Joan think of Alan's proclivities as the alpha male? "Joan was fine with it," Anthony Smith said of Alan's early dalliances. "It's *Alan.* Joan knew there were infidelities. But Joan's mistake was not being part of London, part of New York. Joan always had to get back to the animals."

For Joan, whose picture was not on Anglia's office wall, who rarely came up to London even when Alan was there for months at a time, the most important thing was their work. Who else could acclimate the caracal and wean away its fear of human beings by letting it sleep in her bed, so that when Alan said, "Action!" in the Serengeti, the wildcat "leapt skyward, struck a bird out of the air with its paw, and became a star in slow motion," as their friend Delta Willis later wrote. "Joan was out of the frame, but back in the groove." Joan had faith that Alan would always come back—and for a long time, she was right—so she gave him his freedom. In the meantime, confident in her marriage, she was content to stay in Naivasha, caring for their animals, keeping up the home and office, planning the next film. They were on their way to fame and wealth, and it was up to Joan to ensure that everything would be ready for the next adventure.

Very quickly, the *Survival* wildlife television series gained enormous popularity. Shown in nearly a hundred countries, it would be in regular production from 1961 to 1971, longer than any other wildlife series in British television history. According to *The World of Survival,* Colin Willock's book about the series, it did "more than any other medium to interest the public in wildlife and to popularize the cause of conservation."

One thing was certain: There would be no *Survival* without Alan Root. But what only a few people knew was that there could be no Alan Root without Joan.

Chapter Four

In 1964 Aubrey Buxton, the Roots' boss at Anglia Television, had sailed to the Galápagos Islands with Prince Philip on the royal yacht *Britannia.* These islands off the coast of Ecuador, which had inspired Charles Darwin's landmark book *The Origin of Species,* were rife with an amazing diversity of wildlife—the ground thick with marine iguanas, the ocean teeming with sea lions and giant tortoises, the sky filled with Darwin's finches, vermilion flycatchers, and frigate birds—all so unafraid of humans that they flocked, swam, and leaped toward the yacht. The natural setting for this animal life was a majestic backdrop of rugged, lava-strewn crater lakes, patches of woodland, grassy glades, and tide pools covered in pink waterweed.

The untouched beauty came at a price: The Galápagos stood totally unprotected, almost an invitation for pillaging and poaching. This unique group of islands was populated almost exclusively by birds, reptiles, and sea creatures. Other than bats and sea lions, mice were the only mammals that had ever successfully made it through the treacherous waters to the Galápagos, located six hundred miles from the nearest landmass—except for human beings. Pirates and hunters had also recently introduced a few domestic animals to the islands—donkeys, goats, pigs, dogs, cats—a potential catastrophe for the ecosystem and its indigenous wildlife.

We've got to save it, thought Buxton.

On his trip back from the Galápagos, Buxton outlined a plan for a wildlife film, as he did on his way home from many of his adventures. In Buxton's vision, "with plenty of time on hand, [a cameraman] vanishes for weeks or months, ultimately to reappear with thousands of feet of superior film." He needed a top cameraman, and two years after his first voyage to the Galápagos he dispatched his star, Alan Root. Just getting to the Galápagos would be quite an undertaking, Buxton realized, at a time when there were no established sea or air routes to the islands. "Film all the wildlife you can!" he implored in his telegram to the Roots. "Film everything that bears on Charles Darwin's observations!" Joan and Alan had just returned from leading an exhausting Thru the Lens safari when they received this directive from Buxton, who asked them to meet him in London a week and a half after receiving his cable.

Joan packed for a land-and-sea safari, and they flew from Nairobi to consult with Buxton. Four days later, they flew to Lima, Peru, and from there they sailed the six hundred miles to the Galápagos on the *Beagle II*, a leaky trawler named after Darwin's original ship; this *Beagle* was owned by the Darwin Research Institute and manned by a crew of scientists and naturalists.

For two months they filmed the entire animal community, not only the obvious sea lions and marine iguanas but everything from blue-footed boobies diving in formation to albatrosses beak-fencing in courtship to a now-classic scene of a woodpecker finch picking cactus thorns to use as a tool to dig insects out of wood. "It was quite exciting being the only people on an island," Joan wrote. They filmed large herds of wild donkeys, descendants of imported pack animals, which walked right up to Joan and Alan, probably expecting they were also donkeys. "They seemed so bewildered when they saw we weren't—they just stood and stared."

To Joan's astonishment, even the sea lions, which have been known to charge intruders with their giant incisors, were perfectly calm as she played with their babies right in front of them. "It is the strangest thing that when we are under the water and a mere 10 feet off-shore and playing with the youngsters, they ignore us, apart from swimming up to us occasionally."

By the time they were done, they had shot twenty-three thousand feet of film for a program that typically required six thousand feet at most. Joan shipped it all off to London with their copious production notes. When the brass at *Survival* watched the footage, they knew they had something extraordinary. The story it told went to the heart of what *Survival* was all about: not just watching wildlife but urging audiences to protect it.

It was a terribly important story, and Alan felt that as the one who had created the footage, he was the best person to shape its final telling. He had been feeling this way for a while now, but when he approached his bosses at *Survival* and asked for creative control of the project, they said no. "You're an excellent cameraman, Alan," one told him. "Stick with what you do best, and leave the rest to us." He grudgingly acquiesced, but he decided it was for the last time. *The Enchanted Isles,* as the documentary was called, was a triumph. Everyone loved it—except Alan. He was sick of producers taking his footage and "jazzing it up." He felt passionately that it wasn't necessary. So once the film was finished and Alan's contract with *Survival* was up, he had some news for the producers: He was leaving Anglia and moving to the BBC, where he had been introduced through David Attenborough and where he would be allowed to make films his way. Anglia's executives begged Alan to renew his contract, offering twice the two thousand pounds per film the BBC had promised. But Alan had had enough. He was determined to show them that he was more than a cameraman—he was a *filmmaker*.

As this drama was unfolding behind the scenes, the film itself was becoming a major success. *The Enchanted Isles* was the first British wildlife film to be shown on American television, with special save-the-Galápagos-now commentary by Prince Philip. A royal premiere was scheduled, and the filmmakers were to be presented to the queen. It was rather an awkward time to be quitting Anglia.

"There's no doubt that [Anglia's] commercial television is where the money is," Joan wrote her mother. "It's not that Alan will sell to the highest bidder. He just wants to make decent films that satisfy him, and he doesn't know if Anglia will do this. However, it seems that Anglia will go to almost any lengths to keep him, and so I don't know what he will do. Really a lot of thought should go into this problem, but time is just running out on us."

In the fall of 1967, a cable arrived in Naivasha from Buxton regarding the royal premiere: "We have always been very frank, and I find myself in a dilemma about your visit. In the past, we would have simply asked you to come and it would have been an Anglia job. Now I am not sure what to say. The program has involved enormous costs, the Royal Event is going to cost a hideous sum, and I am not sure how to justify the cost of the two flights from Nairobi for somebody who no longer works for us. I am sure you understand." If they could pay their own way to London, he continued, he would pick up all expenses during their visit. They didn't think they could afford it, yet they knew they had to be there.

"My knees knock together at the thought," Joan said of attending a royal premiere in London with the queen. "It will help get our names out in England when our films start appearing on the BBC," said Alan. She must have liked the sound of that.

It cost 194 pounds round-trip—around $2,500 today, adjusted for inflation—and that was for an excursion fare that required a nineteen-day stay. "We really ought to be there. Because it *is* our film," Alan said.

They took the post-midnight flight from Nairobi, which was delayed until four A.M. It was midafternoon by the time they arrived in London. They got off the plane and rushed to the baggage claim, worried not for their suitcases but for the coral fish they had shipped from Mombasa to give to the BBC's David Attenborough. Some were swimming around in their sealed polyethylene bag of seawater pumped with oxygen, but the rest were belly-up on top.

Since the Roots' normal uniform of khaki would not do for a royal premiere, they had to shop for clothes—not to buy, just to rent. They were directed to Moss Brothers, where Alan chose a dinner jacket and slacks and Joan picked out an elegant, shiny, high-necked blue evening dress. She also spied a small mink cape that she thought would keep her warm. (The anti-fur movement had not yet taken off, even among conservationists.) She phoned Buxton's wife, Maria, and asked, "Might the mink be a bit pretentious?"

"Every woman will be dripping furs, dear," Maria told Joan. "*Definitely* get it."

On the morning of the premiere, *The Enchanted Isles* was shown to the press. Afterward Joan and Alan took questions. One question that came up that night and then often at subsequent screenings of the Roots' films was "Are you trying to save wildlife or merely film it?"

Alan would always say his approach was to show nature in its unadulterated glory, not to preach about it, joke about it, or use film as an attempt to preserve it. If he had his way, he said, his films wouldn't even mention the fact that the animals were endangered. "My job is to show what was there, and not to spoil it by having a presenter for the last five minutes," he later said. "If we had one film about North America before the white man came . . . would you want to hear an Indian chief or a white man talking, or would you just want to have an hour to see what it was like?" He added, "I don't think our environment has a hope in hell. I don't think mankind is smart enough to do anything about it. And Africa is going faster than anything."

After dinner with the Anglia staff at the Festival Hall, the Roots were ferried by Rolls-Royce to the National Film Theatre. As celebrities arrived on the red carpet and cameras clicked away, the Roots stood there in their rented clothing, recognizing nobody. Joan was out of her element.

While everyone settled into their seats in the theater, Joan and Alan and Aubrey Buxton took their places in a receiving line. Finally, the lobby filled with the blinding lights of a hundred photographers, beyond which they could see a diamond tiara—the queen.

"She started shaking hands with the first person in line," Joan wrote her mother. "She went along very fast, not speaking to anyone. Apparently, the people she is to talk with are put at the end of the line, and that is where *we* were."

The crowd of photographers around the queen was so dense that Joan could hardly see her. Then, all of a sudden, Elizabeth II was standing right in front of them. Joan curtsied as Buxton said, "Your Royal Highness, I would like to present Joan and Alan Root."

The queen held out her gloved hand, shaking first with Joan, then with Alan.

Next came official greetings with Prince Philip and the teenage Prince Charles. Then the royal party waited in the lobby for a few minutes, studying the photographs of Joan, Alan, and the wildlife of the Galápagos, while the filmmakers went into the auditorium. The royals followed, the lights went down, and the screening began.

The audience was captivated by underwater scenes of Joan swimming with herds of sea lions, the mating ceremony of four-hundred-pound tortoises, marine iguanas feeding on the ocean floor, and other wildlife scenes never seen.

When the credits rolled, there was wild applause and a standing ovation. Afterward, Alan and Joan were taken by Buxton and his wife to the Savoy Hotel for "a select party" that Buxton was hosting for them. The only "Anglia people" invited were Alan and Joan—otherwise, it was all VIPs and royals, "with only champagne to drink," as Joan said in her letter to her mother.

> I don't know the names of any of the titled big-wigs we met there, I never catch names when I am introduced to people. Prince Charles was monopolized by the young Buxton daughters. (Aubrey has 8 or 9 children, from 22 to about 3. Mrs. Buxton is very attractive and looks no older than her daughters and they are all good at horse riding and win lots of prizes.) Alan was most unimpressed with Charles, he certainly looks a drip, but then he's only 19 and will probably improve. Prince Philip was rather egotistical, and told us he-man stories of what he had done in the Galápagos,

and how he had struggled daringly 200 yards over some lava to see some hawks. He was only there 5 days, and slept each night on the royal yacht Britannia, so it was rather ridiculous expecting us to be impressed after what we had done there. We pretended to be impressed, of course. While he was talking to us, he suddenly faded away, and within seconds we saw him dancing with some gorgeous slim blonde, which amused us. He had had enough champagne to not want to talk about the Galápagos when there were more interesting things to do.

The next morning they took a train to the headquarters of the BBC Natural History Studios in Bristol to discuss the full-length wildlife films that Alan would create and Joan would unofficially produce for the network. On their last day in London, the Roots said goodbye to Aubrey Buxton, goodbye to *Survival,* and goodbye to pomp and civilization, as they prepared, in Alan's words, to "start off with a bang" for the BBC.

Alan and Joan hoped to capture the world of wildlife at a level that had never been done—by letting the animals act naturally—and thus tell a story that producers wouldn't tamper with and audiences would adore.

The problem was money. Two thousand pounds a program was not even sustenance pay for an Alan Root film, which generally took a year or two to complete. So they again turned to the animal that had made Alan's name—the bongo. The Roots financed much of their work for the BBC by capturing bongos; the bounty had gone up considerably since Alan sold his first one. Most zoos were now willing to pay for one of the creatures. It wasn't just the money: By sending bongos to zoos around the world, Alan later explained, they would establish a "breeding pool of bongos in zoos so the wild bongo population would never again be jeopardized." Thus, the species would be both recognized and preserved. Soon they had a score of bongos awaiting shipment in large pens on the Naivasha property. From a letter Joan wrote to her mother in 1969, it is clear how the business had grown:

> Alan left on Tuesday morning . . . and the baby [bongo] was born during that night, with no trouble at all. The bongo boy came running over in the early morning to say the baby had arrived, and there it was still a bit wet and wobbly and having its first drink. This morning the baby was still fine and full of beans. I came up to Nairobi to arrange a plane to go down and collect Alan from safari, as he wants to film it at this stage. . . .
>
> The mother of the baby is the fourth bongo that we caught at the beginning of May. Straight away Alan thought and hoped she was already pregnant, because of her shape. We were concerned about whether she would look after it alright, considering only being in captivity for 4 months and it being her first-born as well. . . . We have been really feeding her up for the past few months and giving her three big bowls of milk every day, and so she is very healthy, and remarkably quiet. She is far quieter than the big and little one that you knew. (By the way we received a cable last week to say that those two have arrived in New York and are fit and well. Now they do a month's quarantine there before going to the Milwaukee Zoo.) . . .
>
> The bongo pens have now been all rebuilt [and] we have put a fence of strong wire to keep the hyenas out. . . .

In addition to the bongo business, the Roots also freelanced: ramping up the photo-safari business Joan had been given by her father; filming for Dr. Grzimek for his various television programs, and for George Schaller for *National Geographic*. In one project for Grzimek, Alan filmed the reactions of rhinos and hippos to balloons shaped like themselves. In a piece for Schaller, he filmed hunters darting lions. Always, however, their BBC debut was at the forefront of their minds and an audacious plan for Alan to become the first person to fly over Kilimanjaro in a balloon at the back.

The first subject they settled on was Mzima Springs, an oasis in Tsavo West National Park that disgorges fifty million gallons of water a day, filtered through nearby hills as it runs down a lava ridge into a series of clear pools. Mzima was an animal sanctuary untouched by modern man, and the water, as clear as the brilliant blue sky above, was filled with crocodiles and giant rock pythons as thick as a grown man's thigh. But Mzima's most dangerous—and naturally photogenic—resident was the hippopotamus.

Hippos kill more people in Africa than any other herbivore; crocodiles lead the carnivore list. The year Joan and Alan went to film at Mzima, a crocodile had killed a young boy, and another croc had bitten off a man's leg. Neither of these victims had even been swimming in the spring, which is what Alan was planning to do. He would wade in wearing a mask and snorkel, filming everything.

Incredibly, once he was in the water, the hippos were practically playful, bumping into Alan without incident. The filming went smoothly—fish eating hippo dung, birds spearing fish, crocs attacking everything.

The finished documentary, *Mzima: Portrait of a Spring,* served its purpose. Not only was it seen widely by an international audience, it soon played repeatedly in a hippo exhibit at the Natural History Museum in London. Alan Root had indeed started with a bang. Both producers and viewers were staggered.

This first effort for the BBC left Alan and Joan exhausted. But there was no time to rest, they felt, not with a continent dying around them. Their next project, *Baobab: Portrait of a Tree,* would examine nature on a much smaller scale, but it would be much more labor-intensive. Again, it would treat a subject that not even the most seasoned naturalists had thought they would ever see on film: a red-billed African hornbill raising its young inside a two-thousand-year-old baobab tree. The traditional approach would be to film the hornbill outside the tree: A female ready to lay her eggs flies into a tree hole. Her mate seals it off with mud and droppings, and the mother bird emerges weeks later with her young.

Alan and Joan planned to film the hornbill's life from the bird's point of view. So they cut a hole in a tree, covered it with a pane of glass, and erected a tent around the trunk. Eventually, a hornbill nested inside, and for nine weeks Alan lived in the tent, filming the bird's every move through the hole. At regular intervals, Joan would slip Alan food and provisions through a flap in the tent.

Baobab: Portrait of a Tree was another groundbreaking effort, showing professionals and laypeople things they never knew existed, and making the brass at Anglia realize what a mistake they'd made in allowing Alan Root to leave. "We said *au revoir* with regret but in the certain knowledge that you should never stop real talent from seeking to do its own thing," Colin Willock, Anglia's head writer, later wrote in a memoir about *Survival*. "What's more, we were fairly sure that, sooner or later, he'd be back."

So when the telegram came to Alan from *Survival* with just three words—"Lassie, come home"—Alan returned to the fold with a much better deal and with a guarantee of complete creative control. "I will be credited as cameraman/director/producer," Alan wrote Anthony Smith. "I intend on doing the Serengeti migration, the Seasons film, a portrait of a termite hill, a flick about us . . ."

One of their first projects upon returning to *Survival* was the Serengeti migration, in which he would uniquely capture the most dramatic phenomenon in Africa: the annual migration of more than a million wildebeests across the Serengeti. The couple had witnessed it in different ways many times before. Joan had described the migration in a letter to her mother:

8/24/71

We had plenty to film while we were marooned on the wrong side of the river, as thousands of wildebeeste were anxious to cross

> the flooding river to move to other grazing grounds up north. We were on the scene when a column was plunging in to cross. Very soon, the steep banks on the other side were so torn away by their hooves, that they could not get up the other side nor back the side they had come. Fortunately our very presence made the column turn back, or many hundreds more would have plunged in. It was tragic to see them being swept away and we estimated that about 500 were drowned in two days. There are now 600,000 wildebeestes on the Serengeti and every year there are dramatic occurrences such as this.

Joan and Alan had also flown over this massive migration in their single-engine Cessna, *Oscar Charlie,* with the camera fixed on the wing, filming the plains below, black with the thundering herds. Later, they'd fly over the migration in their hot-air balloon. The flight was, as Joan later wrote, "probably the best we ever had. The bulls were fighting and rounding up females, and the floating balloon caused bulls to run from under us, and into neighbouring bulls' territories with much head tossing and horn clashing. We landed fifty yards from a lioness that watched over the long grass. I never get blasé about the migration—hundreds of thousands of wildebeest horizon to horizon." For any other filmmaker, the airborne perspectives would have been the best and probably only way to film the migration. But they weren't good enough for Alan Root. He wanted more than just a bird's-eye view.

"Okay, Alan, get ready. They're coming!" Joan shouted over a walkie-talkie months later as she stood under the canopy of a fever tree and watched the black cloud of wildebeests heading their way. Inventive as ever, Alan came running out of the bush with a camera hidden in a giant tortoise shell and placed it directly in the herd's path—and then ran out of the way. Watching the documentary, the viewer can almost feel the power of the hundreds of thousands of hooves passing above and around the camera. It was an incredible cinematic event, one of Alan and Joan's finest films.

But all was not well.

Joan was in Durban, South Africa, at the time, on one of her regular visits with her mother. She was also seeing South African medical experts about the lingering effects of the myasthenia. Most of the symptoms—mild paralysis, drooping eyelids, double vision—had disappeared, but one remained: cessation of menstruation. Having put off childbearing to further her and Alan's filmmaking career, Joan was now eager to become pregnant. But the prognosis was not good.

She wanted children and knew that Alan did as well. On top of her own desire and worry, she couldn't bear the thought of letting him down. She visited numerous doctors and read countless medical books. Friends consulted experts worldwide on her behalf. "She is a healthy person now aged 36 with no children," one wrote to a fertility doctor in London. "In 1964, she suffered from myasthenia, and a year or so later ceased menstruating. She assumed it to be some temporary effect of the disease, but she has not menstruated since. . . . Bearing in mind her age and this extra drawback, do you think that her chances of becoming fertile and having a child are better than, say, 10%? I know the couple well but do not wish to complicate their lives by giving them false hopes. They have been married for twelve years and have only begun to wish for a child recently."

Joan returned to Naivasha from South Africa with a firm diagnosis: She would never bear children. "She saw several specialists in South Africa and she had her menopause several years ago apparently," Alan wrote to Anthony Smith. "She hasn't menstruated since we were in the Galápagos and has had all the hot flash business, which local quacks said was a temperature control fault from her myasthenia—but by then it was probably too late anyway, now it certainly is." *Oh, Alan,* she must have thought. But then what else could she say? She simply returned, told Alan the prognosis, and went back to work.

"I got the feeling that she felt inadequate in some way and therefore just didn't want to discuss it," Alan remembered. "And so 'It doesn't matter. We have a wonderful life. I have got all of these animals that I love, and that's it.' I always wanted children, but decided we couldn't. [Neither] of us felt strongly about it enough to adopt, which was difficult in those days anyway in a country like this. I mean, it is a nightmare, but basically it wasn't something we pursued anyway. We were having a great time and felt very fulfilled with what we were doing and that was it."

"She was a Kenya girl," Joan's friend Oria Douglas-Hamilton, the wife of Joan and Alan's friend Iain, said. "They're expected to be smart and beautiful, good wives, lovers—everything. And if you give a lot of your time to helping your husband, you'll put off having children. There came a time when she couldn't have them, and she transferred that love instead onto animals."

Despite his apparent acceptance of the situation, as the news sank in about their future without children, Alan felt increasingly torn. "I really am a mess these days," Alan confided in a letter to Anthony Smith about another woman who had entered his life. "And it's all because I have not yet been able to resolve my domestic situation, I guess. X [the other woman] continues to be an enormous force in my life." He was torn not only between two women but also between his two strongest desires: being a great filmmaker and being a father.

"The whole bloody mess is my own making," he wrote. "Since meeting her, I seem to be producing a whole different set of hormones. I'm just crazy about kids and go around like a bloody hen, fluffing out my feathers whenever I see one. I bought a Land Rover the other day—I've got more money than sense these days—and I can't imagine anyone other than Joan driving it. Yet, when I went to collect it, there was one outside with a family getting into it. The sight of a 3-year-old trying to climb up into it, scrabbling and laughing, just made me burst into tears, and I couldn't imagine anyone but X helping him up."

For Joan's part, though, she was as stoic and optimistic as ever about their future. During their two-and-a-half-year expedition to film the wildebeests, Joan seemed for the first time to have felt a power of her own. As she said in a letter to her mother, "I'm finding my feet rather well, and let's face it, it was time I ceased being a sheepdog behind Alan."

—

For all the complications in the marriage, they were still an indomitable team, and at some level each of them knew it. Though they were riding through rough waters in their personal relationship, their filmmaking work provided the glue that held them together. A longtime dream kept popping into Alan's head—the image he had seen as a boy from his bedroom window: Kilimanjaro, the highest peak in Africa. It called to him and Joan like a dare, and they began planning an audacious mission: for Alan to become the first person to fly a hot-air balloon over Kilimanjaro. However, while preparing for the historic flight, they also ran the photo-safari company they had formed with their friend Richard Leakey. Leakey was the son of the renowned archaeologists Mary and Louis Leakey, whose fossil discoveries in Tanzania's Olduvai Gorge proved that man was far older than previously supposed.

From his and Joan's earlier balloon flight, Alan knew a balloon was the best way to film wildlife from above. Airplanes go too fast to allow you to get anything in focus; helicopters are so noisy they scare away all the wildlife. But a balloon could glide quietly at an altitude that would allow the filmmaker to be right on top of the animals.

Alan had gone to a balloon show in the resort town of Henley-on-Thames, England, and after being lifted above Peppard Common for five minutes one misty day, he bought a balloon on the spot. When it arrived at Naivasha, he and Joan fired it up and rose over the lake, which became their testing ground or, more accurately, their crashing ground.

"With ballooning, you never have the faintest idea where or how your flight is going to end," Alan said in voiceover in *Safari by Balloon,* the film about his and Joan's balloon exploits. "We took off from exactly the same place each morning. But one day we'd land way out in the sticks and have to wait hours to be recovered. The next day we might land in the middle of an African village"—the film cuts to a scene of kids running in a calamitous procession around the balloon—"and have hundreds of willing but completely disorganized hands to help us back up."

Alan had the balloon license, he explained, but it was Joan who should have had one. "I'm the photographer in the family, and whenever I wanted to film something I had to hand over control [of the balloon] to Joan," he said. "In other words, I ended up trying to give her flying lessons while looking through the viewfinder. And we'd also get in situations where, because I was filming, I assumed Joan must be piloting. And we'd get into situations like this."

The balloon skitters along the ground in the Maasai Mara.

"I thought you were flying this thing!" Alan said in voiceover, as if speaking to Joan.

"No, you didn't tell me to," he said, mimicking Joan's high-pitched voice.

"Can't you see I'm filming?"

"I'm sorry, I didn't notice. I'm taking stills," he said as Joan.

"Okay, well, look, get down in the basket. These are thorny bushes. Hang on. Here we go. . . ."

And . . . CRASH! Straight into the trees, surrounded by elephants and zebras.

"Joan soon got the feel of it, and we started to get results," Alan said in the film.

When Alan heard rumors that someone else was planning to accomplish his longtime dream of flying over Kilimanjaro in a hot-air balloon, he decided he *had* to do it first. The plan was to make the flight alone, for weight purposes—"The less the load the better," he would later say. "But I'd always considered taking Joan and knew she would want to go, and actually having her there to take stills while I was filming would be helpful."

Up until the last minute on the day of the liftoff, Joan was to be part of the ground crew, with their friend Ian Parker flying above the summit in the "shepherd aircraft," from which he would film the balloon's ascent over the mighty mountain. But the morning of the flight turned out to be calm, which meant that the balloon could handle more weight. So at the last minute Alan said, "Jump in!" And Joan leapt into the basket.

At seven-thirty A.M. on March 9, 1974, Alan and Joan, with four hours of gas, were ready for their historic mission. Alan fired the burner, and with a giant *whoosh,* they lifted off. "We climbed for several minutes through cloud . . . and came out into the sunshine and an unbelievable view," Alan later wrote in a letter to Anthony Smith. "The peaks were clear and great necklaces of cloud made them even more spectacular than usual."

"Up we went, through the cloud, to have the most magnificent view," Joan wrote. "We ascended steeply beside Mawenzi until we were above it, and then we were carried by a wind going exactly the way we wanted. . . . It was a glorious day up there."

They clipped on their oxygen masks at eighteen thousand feet and rose over the frosted spires of Mawenzi, where enormous wind gusts almost pulled them down. Alan fed the burner, and they popped up to twenty-four thousand feet, passing high above Kibo, the snowy mile-and-a-half-wide crater that marks Kilimanjaro's summit. "It was just *unbelievable,* the beauty of the scene, from that vantage point," Alan wrote. "Even though it was 20 below zero, we were neither at all cold." They had not only become the first to fly over Kilimanjaro in a hot-air balloon, they had also captured footage from the summit.

Now they just had to get down. Right after they cleared the summit, Alan looked over at Joan and realized that something was wrong. Attempting to change the film in her stills camera, she was shaking, fumbling, and making a mess of a very simple task.

"You don't need to be so frightened!" Alan said.

"I'm not frightened. I just feel . . . funny," said Joan.

When she dropped the film on the floor of the basket and couldn't even bend over to pick it up, Alan's concern turned to alarm. He checked her oxygen hose and saw that it had come loose from the cylinder. For some minutes, Joan had been breathing nothing but the thin air at twenty-four thousand feet, and the symptoms of severe oxygen deprivation—inattentiveness, lack of judgment, loss of coordination—had set in. Alan reconnected her, and she took several long and deep breaths. Then she removed her mask so that Alan could hear her clearly.

She wagged her finger and scolded him for suggesting that she had ever been afraid. "Remember, I just felt funny," she said.

They made their way down to the Shira Plateau, at twelve thousand feet, where Alan had planned to land. Their four hours of gas were almost over. But he was unable to descend fast enough and therefore had to fly fifteen additional miles over deep gorges, high cliffs, and forests. Alan increased the flame, and they shot from eleven thousand feet back up to eighteen thousand in one vertiginous rush. Finally, they were out over the vast plains of Tanzania, preparing to touch down at the edge of a forest.

Then Alan made a serious mistake. "I started to relax," he recalled.

On their last cylinder of gas, with the high winds threatening to blow them over the forest edge, Alan knew they had to land immediately. He dropped the two-hundred-foot trail rope, which helps keep the basket stable in its descent. The rope knotted on the way down. Exhausted, Alan hauled it up, untangled it, and dropped it again. This time the coils began whipping off the floor faster and faster—so fast that Alan didn't notice the rope had passed around him. When it snapped tight, he was flung halfway out of the basket. "I hung there over the edge, watching my glasses turn over and over as they fell," he recalled. "Alan!" Joan cried, grabbing him by the waist and hauling him back into the basket.

As they came in for a crash landing in the village of Sanya Juu, near the town of Moshi, the locals reported the unusual sight to the authorities. "Unfortunately, while we were floating slowly towards them, the police at Sanya Juu decided they were being *attacked*," Joan wrote her mother. "They phoned Moshi for instructions. They were told to capture us on landing."

"I borrowed Joan's glasses and came in to land with an enormous *thud*," Alan wrote a friend. It was his worst landing to date—in a plowed field, forty yards from someone's house and two hundred yards from West Kilimanjaro Road. The basket rolled onto its side, and the two balloonists and all their equipment fell out. Immediately, a screaming crowd came running up. They had never heard of a hot-air balloon, much less seen one land. Alan was blowing dust off the instruments when he recognized a noise that, he wrote, "sent the hair tingling along my spine." It was the cold, metallic sound of at least one submachine gun being cocked. A dozen policemen and soldiers surrounded them. The officers would later say that they had suspected the balloonists of being "astronaut spies."

"You are under arrest," one of them said.

Staring into the barrel of the gun, Alan had only one thing on his mind: his film. Just then the Roots' ground crew arrived on the scene. "Look, we crashed and my wife is sick," Alan said to one of the officers. "Can she go sit in our car while we talk?"

"All right," the officer said.

Alan gave Joan a look, and she knew exactly what it meant. They hadn't spent all those silent years together in the bush for nothing. She grabbed his camera and went into the car, where she slipped out the exposed footage and hid it. Then she reloaded the camera with fresh film. Soon after, everyone was hauled off to the village police station, where, Joan wrote, "we spent 11 hours trying to explain our motives for wanting to float over the mountain in a balloon!" They were eventually taken to Moshi, and the head officer there knew what a hot-air balloon was and what a flight plan was. The officer said that they could go, but first he would have to confiscate the film in their camera.

"I threw a fit," Alan wrote, "but to no avail. They said they would process the film, and return it to me, if it contained no prohibited material. . . . We didn't start laughing until we were well out of Moshi." Once again she had saved him—and their most ambitious project to date.

In 1974, Jacqueline Kennedy Onassis came to Kenya for a safari and, having heard of Alan and Joan through friends, asked them to take her into the bush. She arrived at Naivasha with her two children, Caroline, then sixteen, and John, then thirteen, and some of their friends. To avoid publicity, Jackie wanted to stay at Joan and Alan's house. However, feeling it was somehow not right to lodge a former first lady in a house shared by wildcats and a hippo, the Roots put her up at the home of a neighbor.

At night Jackie and her children watched Alan and Joan's films and fed the animals. After a few days of safaris on land, Alan decided to take them up in his balloon. The first flight—with Alan and five kids in the basket—went well. The next morning he took Jackie and a safari guide named Jock Anderson on what was to be a perfectly idyllic flight across Lake Naivasha and over its promontory, Crescent Island, rising up to a high altitude so she could take in the full scope of the glorious lake and its surrounding volcanoes. As usual, Joan followed in the Land Rover to pick them up. "I was watching from the main road and was annoyed when a reporter and a photographer from *Newsweek* magazine recognized me and asked if they could follow me to take pictures of [Jackie]," Joan wrote her mother.

As Alan was coming in for a landing on the Naivasha airstrip, he flew over a grass fire. When the smoke blew into the balloon, it reduced the balloon's lift, and they began plummeting toward Naivasha's shantytown, called Karagita. Alan and Jackie were headed straight for the telephone wires. "I knew what was going to happen as I left the car and ran through the maize and was beneath them when the basket hit the lines," Joan wrote. It didn't just hit—it *crashed* into the telephone lines, bending the poles in the balloon and breaking the filaments that attached the balloon to the basket.

The basket was upside down, tangled in telephone lines. Alan shouted to Jackie and Jock to get on the bottom of the basket and hold on to the ropes. "I could only watch as the basket fell the final 10 feet onto its side, and the trio climbed out," Joan wrote. Alan was unhurt, Jock was winded, and Jackie suffered only a bruised foot. "She was very calm, even though shaken, and had enjoyed the flight despite the ending," Joan wrote to her mother.

What Alan said to the former first lady upon crash landing is now lost to time; he wasn't above teasing even his most famous guests. Returning from a trip, Alan liked to fly home in *Oscar Charlie* through Hell's Gate, the mini–Grand Canyon near Naivasha. Few people were crazy enough to attempt it; the canyon was so narrow that the wings of even a small plane almost scraped its craggy walls. But Alan loved it here, especially when he had passengers and could tell them how no one else dared to fly through Hell's Gate except his friend Iain Douglas-Hamilton. When one passenger asked what would happen if Douglas-Hamilton decided to fly through at the moment they were flying through the tiny canyon, Alan answered, "It's very simple." Alan explained, according to the *New Yorker* profile: If the two planes were approaching each other head-on, Iain was supposed to go up, and Alan was supposed to go down—or was it up? As Alan feigned forgetfulness, he scared the passenger so much that he "sat stiffly, staring straight ahead," for the remainder of the flight.

Alan wasn't bluffing about these flights. "One Sunday afternoon at Naivasha he casually suggested a recreational flight to see flamingos on Lake Magadi," remembered Alan and Joan's *Survival* colleague Mike Hay.

> We took off and all seemed set for a pleasant afternoon of sight-seeing, but we were soon at zero feet with thorn branches tapping the under-carriage. As we crossed the northern cliff to the entrance of Hell's Gate Gorge we dropped like a stone with the contour. Then, looking up, I could see the cliffs of the first left hand bend in the gorge beginning to tower above us and a crunch seemed unavoidable. I was close to incontinence as Alan made an incredibly tight turn with the wheels all but brushing the rock as we dived yet again deep into the gorge. As if those weren't enough thrills for the day, the radio crackled that the "Red Baron" was on our tail and another Cessna zoomed over us and into the abyss. Lots of pretend machinegun effects accompanied this maneuver and the Red Baron turned out to be Iain Douglas-Hamilton. The two aces proceeded with a twisting dog-fight all the way through Hell's Gate and it emerged that the duel was very much prearranged. At one point I looked over my shoulder at Joan in the rear seat. Cool as a cucumber and, if I recall rightly, calmly knitting away at a sweater. She smiled, I think with sympathy for my terror.

This probably typified their relationship. Joan never seemed put out in any way with Alan's delight in pushing the envelope and this gave him his head, when in any other marriage the female partner would invariably have insisted that such "irresponsible" behavior was curtailed. Joan was not doing so as indulgence, she knew he just *had* to do these things.

Indeed he had to do them, because he knew that the world he loved was vanishing before his eyes. As an early newspaper interview with Alan noted: "He also shares with his fellow filmmakers the belief that short of a miracle, wildlife and the world's wild places are doomed. 'I'm very cynical about it,' he says. 'I've lived in Africa all my adult life and watched it just draining away. It's like living with someone who is dying of cancer.'" That last sentence would turn out to be prophetic, but he couldn't have known that.

Each time Alan climbed out of *Oscar Charlie* on the landing strip in Naivasha, Joan would be ready—with food, supplies, bedding, clearances, permits, visas—for any conceivable trip they might make for *Survival.*

Their balloon flights soon paid an additional dividend. On June 3, 1976, they turned their balloon expertise into a side business, launching the first flight of Balloon Safaris, Ltd., specializing in the first tourist balloon flights over great stretches of game in Kenya and Tanzania. Again, Joan helped with the arrangements as well as handling the financial books. But their films always came first.

The Kilimanjaro shots were sure to be a hit, yet Alan felt he needed more to complete the film. He wanted "linking shots," additional high-adventure footage to use as segues between scenes. So they went back to Mzima Springs, hoping to get some exciting footage of the two of them swimming with hippos.

Once again the hippos were quite cooperative—except for one second-ranking bull. Lower-ranking bulls are never as easygoing as those at the top. The hippo moved away quickly after spotting Joan and Alan, stirring up so much mud and muck that they could barely see each other, much less the bull, who had stopped to appraise them from a distance. When the three-thousand-pound beast saw the bubbles rising from their scuba gear, he charged—mouth open, teeth gnashing, his whole body thrashing from side to side in the muddy water.

Joan was first in line. The bull slammed into the right side of her scuba tank, then dipped its enormous snout beneath her and, as easily as if flicking a bird off his nose, threw her up out of the water. Splashing back down, she felt water leaking into her mouthpiece and surfaced to clear it. It had happened so fast that she didn't realize until later that one of the hippo's canines had pierced her face mask, just below her right eye. A fraction of an inch higher could have meant the loss of her eye, or face, or skull.

Next the bull turned on Alan, and this time he charged even harder. The first blow rolled Alan onto his back. The bull charged again, and the next thing Alan knew, "He had my right leg in his mouth, and I really did *know* it."

Blood billowed in all directions. The hippo was bobbing its enormous head up and down, shaking Alan "like a rat," he remembered. "I was vividly aware of every detail of what was happening. . . . He got my leg into his mouth so that the left canine was slicing through the calf. While my foot and ankle were between his molars, I could feel the whiskers of his chin on the back of my thighs." Moments later, the hippo discarded him and swam away. Alan remained underwater until he figured the coast was clear. When he finally surfaced, Joan was standing twenty feet away.

"Christ! I've been bitten!" Alan shouted. Joan screamed and started to come toward him.

"No!" Alan shouted. "Get out of the water!"

He swam through his own blood, remembering the ten-foot croc that over the past week had been getting bolder in stalking them. Joan and Alan were driven to a nearby lodge, where they secured a ride in a Land Rover to the town of Kilaguni, where they caught a plane back to

Nairobi. In under three hours, he was in familiar surroundings: the casualty ward at Nairobi Hospital. Within twenty-four hours he had developed gangrene from a sizable hole in his calf, which he would alternately describe as "hamburger-sized" and "big enough to push a Coke bottle through."

In a letter, Alan told friends of his recovery: "I had some spectacular fevers—boy! I've had the sheets changed before, when I was sweating, but never the mattress! And in between the sweats, I needed an electric blanket to keep warm. After three days, 17 pints of saline, 8 pints of blood, many millions of units of intravenous penicillin. . . . I was declared OK."

Two weeks later, he began a series of painful skin grafts, with skin taken from "my right buttock," he wrote a friend. "This nicely balances the leopard bite on the other side, but unfortunately it will only be a small scar, hardly worth showing."

When it was all over, he was left with a mammoth mottled scar on his calf where the hippo had bitten him. It was a big, ugly one—definitely worth showing.

Bedridden at Naivasha for three months, Alan once again had time to plan their next project. It would be a U-turn from so many of their signature epics featuring big skies, big herds, big mountains, and big danger. For this one the Roots would go small—microscopic, in fact. They decided to spend a year documenting termites in one of the tall, spindly, fifteen-foot clay mounds that the insects erect in total darkness to hatch their young.

Termite country lay just west of Lake Baringo, in northern Kenya, where at the start of each rainy season the insects swarm out from minuscule slits in their mounds and fly off to start new colonies. To find the best, most photogenic termite mound, Alan sat on the Land Rover's hood, aiming the camera every which way as he directed Joan to drive to the next potential site. They settled on one site and observed the mounds night after night, camping near the Pokot tribe, whose members eat termites and wash them down with cow's blood. Marvels of mud architecture, the mounds rose high overhead, and inside each one thrived a tiny universe created by means of an intricate social order. Alan and Joan waited weeks for the climactic hatching. When it came, they were ready for action. Most of the mounds in the area hatched simultaneously, but ironically, not the one they'd surrounded with their lights and cameras. Watching the mass of activity occurring all around them, Joan stood there with her handheld flashlight looking around for something, anything, for Alan to film, while a giant swarm of termites covered her hair, ears, and mouth.

The following night a thunderstorm doused their lighting equipment, shattering the bulbs they used to illuminate and protect the heat-sensitive termites. On their third try, they captured a hatching mound from start to finish—only ten minutes, all told. The film would describe the winged termites as "princes and princesses who, like Cinderella, have one magical night before returning to darkness and drudgery." To capture the inside of the mound, Joan and Alan moved portions of it into a farmhouse, where they filmed the intricate inner workings, including the queen, who lays thirty thousand eggs per day. "Four inches long, and as thick as a man's thumb, this grotesque creature looms over the workers that attend her. Beside their queen, the workers look like a ground crew handling a half-inflated airship." Using surgical-grade lights to illuminate the honeycomb-like dwellings, they filmed everything, from the mound's mushroom gardens to the ventilation system to the tiny termites feeding their stilltinier infants. "People don't realize the hours it took to get every sequence," Joan wrote.

Anglia executives were wild about the film, which they entitled *Mysterious Castles of Clay.* Everyone was thrilled when the Hollywood icon Orson Welles signed on to narrate the American version of the film. It won a Peabody Award and earned an Oscar nomination for Best Feature Documentary of 1978.

Alan and Joan's friend the author John Heminway wrote admiringly:

> *Castles of Clay* is artistically as majestic as *The Year of the Wildebeest*; in addition it is suffused with mystery—worlds shrouded from man's view, lives within lives. One usually acerbic critic from the *Manchester Guardian* went beyond the usual praise: "My interest in the termite is finite. Nevertheless I believe *Castles of Clay* . . . is the finest natural history film ever seen. And, because even that seems qualified praise, I will put it among the finest films I have ever seen full stop."
>
> Here is the quintessential Root film: beneath an apparently inanimate object is concealed a command headquarters for a highly sophisticated form of life. One is tempted to conclude that beside termites, humans are as dull as river mud. . . .

Patience. That was their secret. "Sometimes, you go day after day and not get anything on film," Alan once told a magazine writer. "It's like gambling." The filmmaker and his one-woman crew were content to wait for the animals to perform, however long that might take, roaring across Africa in their Land Rover, listening to Neil Diamond tapes and reading Harold Robbins mysteries, as the natural world sprang to life all around them. They had spent two years filming the seasonal changes of the baobab tree for *Baobab: Portrait of a Tree*. For two years they had waited for the hornbill to return to the nest in the tree. For thirty nights, they had waited for the termites to hatch.

"The Roots may be the last of their breed," their friend Delta Willis wrote. "The rapid encroachment of civilization on the African wilderness means that 'it will be much more difficult for the next generation to live a life like this,' Alan says. That's one reason he and Joan plan to spend much of the decade, the 'most productive years of our lives' . . . filming the teeming wildlife that may soon disappear."

By then both Alan and Joan were as fascinating—and beloved—to audiences as the animals they filmed, and their employers knew it. Alan and Joan had been so often asked "How the hell did you get" this or that astonishing shot that Alan decided to answer the question with a "compilation film" of their greatest hits, rounded out with footage of their extraordinary life at home on Lake Naivasha. The film would air in the U.K. with the title *Two in the Bush,* and later in the U.S. as *Lights! Action! Africa!*

As always, Alan wanted to push the envelope, especially on a film about them. That was why, in 1980, they found themselves back on Lake Baringo, hunting down and gathering up the creature that would help them deliver the new film's pièce de résistance: a spitting cobra. They were after not just *any* spitting cobra but, specifically, a black-necked spitting cobra. And not just any black-necked spitting cobra would do—not for an Alan and Joan Root film. It had to be a big, angry beast of a snake, able to shoot a stream of venom with the force of a garden hose.

Assisted by some European and African snake catchers, Joan and Alan collected six "good spitters," according to Joan. Alan came up with the perfect idea for the shot—getting the cobra to spit *at Joan.* Naturally, Joan was game for it, even knowing that cobras aim for the eyes when they spit, and that their venom causes blindness if it is not immediately removed. She bought a pair of glasses with nonreflective lenses, the better for the cobra to see her eyes—two big bull's-eyes set in her beautiful face.

Of the six cobras, they settled on "a huge one who had many scales over its eyes," Joan wrote. Alan held its neck and peeled off its blinders, and when it charged the light boxes and attempted to bite the camera equipment, they knew they'd found the perfect snake for a landmark film.

Alan stepped behind the camera, Joan walked into the frame, and . . . *Action!* Feeling safe behind her glasses, Joan began to dance, bobbing back and forth, getting the cobra to bob right along with her. Since the light had to be just right to illuminate the stream in full force, they worked within a four-foot radius of the snake, with Alan and an assistant cameraman on one side and Joan on the other. Infuriated by the humans surrounding it, its hood in grand display, the cobra reared to its full three-foot height, opened its maw wide, and unleashed the money shot.

It was glorious. The spit looked like a stream of pure gold against the sunlit African savanna. As planned, the venom went straight to the eyeglasses. Not unpredictably, some also went into Joan's eyes.

She calmly backed up a few steps, pulled out a handkerchief, wiped off the glasses, and dried her eyes. Then she asked Alan if reshoots were required.

They were. Again and again they did the shot, and each time the cobra's venom found its target. Again and again Joan calmly stepped back to wipe the glasses and her increasingly burning eyes. "Alan says I look like a geisha, white face with red puffy eyes, and it shows on film," Joan wrote proudly to her mother. Luckily, she avoided any lasting damage to her eyes.

The Roots were now famous in Africa and Great Britain. In 1981 they expanded their reach into America. With *Lights! Action! Africa!* scheduled to be shown on CBS, sponsored by Kraft Foods, the couple were flown from Nairobi to New York for a national publicity tour. "We spoke to umpteen reporters doing stories about us for magazines and newspapers," Joan wrote her mother. "We had lunches in the most famous restaurants in the city. I soon got used to it and did my share of talking, but Alan was really good at answering the questions in such a way as to give them a good story for their readers and also understand that we are not taking uncalculated risks and take our filmmaking seriously. Of course, they all wanted to know about the hippo attack and the spitting cobra sequence."

They appeared live on *Today*, and in their hotel suite, they answered questions for, Joan wrote, "30 or so camera crews and interviewers for their affiliate TV stations from all over the country." After six days of interviews in Manhattan, they flew to Chicago and then to Los Angeles, where they were booked on Johnny Carson's *Tonight Show.* The appearance was canceled, however, when Carson's NBC producers realized they would be promoting a CBS film.

It didn't matter. As Joan told her mother, "Our film was shown on July 1 on CBS . . . and it got the highest share of the audience ratings, even though we were at the same time as *Charlie's Angels* [a very popular serial] on another channel." Rave reviews poured in from across America. People were writing fan letters. Kraft Foods wanted a sequel. But *Two in the Bush* was a "one-off exercise for us," Joan wrote. Their mission was to glorify not themselves but Africa. So they headed back to film more of it.

The following excerpts from the script of *Two in the Bush* may illustrate why it became the Roots' best-known film.

EXT. RAINSTORM IN THE WILDS OF KENYA

ALAN ROOT, *readying his motion picture camera*

ANNOUNCER (voice-over): We've all heard about the patience you need to be a wildlife camera team.

A red teacup sits atop jagged rocks, filling quickly with large raindrops next to Alan's camera.

ANNOUNCER: But what is life really like?

Joan's slender white hand moves into view, taking the red cup and exchanging it for a fresh one, with a plate on top of it to protect it from the rain.

ANNOUNCER: Alan Root, who ought to know, says that life is very varied for him and his wife, Joan. (Beat.) Just like anyone else, you try to keep fit.

Alan running alongside elephants.

ANNOUNCER: You try to keep clean.

Alan bathing in a river next to an African ox.

ANNOUNCER: And you try to keep regular.

Joan springs out of an outhouse, tossing a roll of toilet paper at a lioness; it bolts away.

ANNOUNCER: Alan Root and his wife, Joan, are reckoned to be the best wildlife filmmakers in the business. Just watch them.

Filmed by an assistant cameraman, Alan runs out in the middle of a field carrying a giant tortoise shell with a camera inside of it. Wildebeests soon trickle by. Joan is standing on a high limb atop a large yellow fever tree.

JOAN: Okay, Alan, get ready. They're coming. Ready!? GO!

Alan presses a button and recording starts; we see the shot from within the shell.

ANNOUNCER: If that looked easy, it's because you were not shown the many attempts that were unsuccessful, spread over weeks—but it was simple, compared to many things the Roots have managed to get on film. (Beat.) So what is life like for this unusual two in the bush? . . . For many years, they were simply photographers, sending off shots for others to make into films. Then, in 1967, they made a film for *Survival* about the Galápagos Islands, which had a royal premiere, won awards, and enabled the Roots to become independent. Now, they could do what they wanted—which meant they would make their own mistakes along with the successes.

EXT. RIVER, DAY

Alan bobs up from beneath the surface with papyrus taped to his head and to his similarly camouflaged boatlike blind, floating in the middle of Mzima Springs.

ANNOUNCER: Alan is a stimulus addict; he relishes this sort of situation, where danger and fear are finely balanced. A project is not interesting unless the odds are against him. Joan's philosophy is simpler: If Alan is going to do these things, it's less worrying and much more fun to do them with him.

[The film proceeds to show birds swarming over the Naivasha house; an antelope eating vegetables as Joan chops them on her kitchen counter for dinner; Joan reading in bed beside a genet cat; a cheetah leaping onto the hood of their Land Rover; and scenes of Alan and Joan soaring over Africa in their airplane and hot-air balloon.]

EXT. AFRICAN LANDSCAPE, DAY

Alan and Joan, running at full speed through the bush.

ANNOUNCER: But above all, they have a deep understanding and love for the creatures they film, and for Africa. They will need all those qualities in the future. And their kind of Africa is fast disappearing. Their films, and others like them, have done much to show the world what a tragic loss that would be. Alan and Joan will go on filming, and will continue to share their wonderment and understanding. And who better to record, for all time, what used to be in Africa.

They were a team, and what they did together in the bush spoke to the depth of their devotion. Despite Alan's extramarital dalliances, his deepest connection had always been, and would seemingly always be, to Joan. What they had together went deeper than love; it was music. Two people moving in tandem in absolute silence, committed to a single goal: the animals they had come to film.

"They could go for days without saying a word to each other, because they knew each other so intimately," said John Heminway, who traveled with them frequently. He remembered driving through the bush with them one day in search of cheetahs, when all of a sudden one appeared. "Most people would say, 'There it is!'" Heminway remembered. "But Joan, who had these extraordinary eyes, would do the slightest hand movement, and Alan would *understand.* The car would stop and there would be a flash of cheetah spots. It was just the way they operated, with the cozy language of what I thought was love."

It was the same when they returned to their studio and sanctuary in Naivasha: two individuals in silent harmony, working toward the same goals. If only they could have remained in the bush or at home in Naivasha. But wildlife filmmaking involves editing, post-production, promotion . . . and ego. Alan Root had "an extraordinary ego," recalled John Heminway, compared with Joan's nonexistent one. "She was one of these extraordinary people who did not want attention. Her pleasures were simply being out there and relating to wildlife. If a lame mongoose came to her house being carried by Prince Philip, she would do a cursory genuflection and take the mongoose, and the conversation would be between Joan and the mongoose. She was at her best when she was with an animal, either interpreting or anticipating its behavior."

Alan, conversely, was at his best not only with animals but also with people, as most stars are. Heminway recalled some of his practical jokes. "Here, John, hold out your hand," Alan told John once, and when Heminway did so, Alan slipped a sizable brown scorpion into it and walked away laughing. "Joan would just giggle." Heminway remembers Alan also loved playing chicken in his airplane, once forcing Heminway to take his own plane so low that he almost clipped the heads of a group of baboons crabbing on the banks just south of the Tana River delta.

A frequent passenger in Alan and Joan's plane, Heminway recalled his friend's anything-goes spirit: "If he saw two doum palms, he'd say, 'I wonder if we can get between those two,' and I'd say, 'Alan, it's not going to work!' And he'd say, 'Damn,' and he'd lower his right wing, raise the left one, and do reverse pedals. It's called crabbing—one wing lower than the other—and he'd fly through them, just missing the branches of the trees."

Heminway recalled another flight (this time without Joan), when Alan spotted a gorgeous woman beside the pool of a guest lodge in the Serengeti, he swooped so low in order to check her out that he almost crashed into the water. Alan's need for stimulation—new, exciting experiences—would always extend to all facets of his life, not just adrenaline-fueled danger. He needed, it seemed, new audiences, to make him feel alive.

In the late seventies, a friend gave Joan a diary in which she began to make entries in her neat, flowing script. She wrote of George Adamson, the aging, long-haired husband of *Born Free* author Joy Adamson, whom she and Alan regularly visited in his camp; there, after drinks and dinner, protected by only a chain-link fence, George would call lions with a red megaphone and then step out of his enclosure to feed them camel meat. Joan wrote of how, during one visit, Adamson's brother, Terence, was mauled, and how, after she and Alan brought Terence back from the Nairobi hospital all stitched up, the same lion began stalking *her*. "Still with blood on his chin, very keen." But she wasn't afraid. She wrote of their perfect little house where the lawn grew so green "it hurts the eyes," a house that was perpetually full of friends and colleagues, and of a life full of so much love and so many animals that she sometimes sounded as if she were going to burst from joy. Running through every other line was Alan: strong, smart, handsome, funny, talented, lovable Alan.

It was true that, occasionally, he had wandered. But as prophesied by the Karamojong tribe so many years ago, he always returned to her. Always, that is, until one summer day in 1982. Joan and Alan were hosting a wedding for their close friend Ian Parker's daughter at their home on Lake Naivasha when, suddenly, a woman appeared from whom Alan would find it difficult—then impossible—to extricate himself.

Chapter Five

"It was a typical Kenyan wedding," said Ian Parker of his daughter's nuptials, which were celebrated at the Roots' home on July 21, 1982. "Typical" meant a stream of planes flying in from Nairobi, guests sleeping in tents in Alan and Joan's vast backyard, and all manner of fun. As the sun began to sink over the Aberdares, Alan was standing on the roof of a canvas bar tent with a hulking young man named Jamie Roberts, stinking drunk and playfully challenging the young man to wrestle him, while a crowd of wedding guests cheered him on.

"Isn't he fantastic!" gushed one woman watching the spectacle. "And so great with children!" The onlooker's name was Jennie Hammond, and she was everything Joan Root was not. A nurse, potter, and psychological counselor, she was extremely outgoing and self-confident. A devoted mother, she had two adorable, sociable children—a girl and a boy. Yet the most striking thing about Jennie was her sexuality, Joan's business manager, the dark-haired, extremely polite, and erudite Adrian Luckhurst later remembered. "Men particularly found her *most* attractive," added one of Jennie's close friends. A brunette in her late thirties, married to a civil engineer in Nairobi, Jennie was, on that night, a dangerous combination of beauty and boredom.

Unlike Joan, Jennie was not one to stay in the background. She knew what she wanted and would do whatever it took to get it. Jennie and her husband, Bob, had known the Roots for years, but it wasn't until she saw Alan on that bar tent, horsing around with young Jamie Roberts—Alan looking and acting like a young man himself—that she decided she had to have him. And not just for a mere affair.

While everyone was watching Alan's antics, Joan was doing her usual work behind the scenes, attending to the details of the wedding. So she missed it when the tent gave way and Alan crashed through the canvas, landing on top of an icebox full of beer. Alan was a bloody mess. A doctor rushed over to stitch him up, and after the suturing, Alan was apparently still feeling limber. "I just remember being pretty drunk and making a pass at Jennie, which was reciprocated," he claimed. But some people who knew Jennie Hammond are convinced that it was the other way around. "He was *captured,*" said Ian Parker. "She turned up and said, 'Right.' She made the move, and from there I don't think Root knew what was happening."

No one—not Alan, not Jennie, not Joan, and certainly not Jennie's steady, stable, straitlaced husband, Bob, who was as different from wild-man Alan as Jennie was from Joan—wanted to discuss where things went that night between Jennie and Alan. But they certainly went somewhere. Not long afterward, Bob Hammond returned to the Nairobi home he shared with Jennie and their kids to find a note from his wife on the mantelpiece. He recalled that the note said something like "Your dinner is in the oven." The implication was: *But your wife and children are gone.*

Meanwhile, Jennie arrived on the doorstep of the house Joan and Alan had rented in Nairobi. She reputedly had two suitcases with her, as well as her two children, and she announced that she was moving in and Joan was moving out. "I don't know if she actually came with the suitcases," said the Roots' close friend Vickie Luckhurst. "But she came with a lot of emotional baggage and emotional blackmail."

Alan didn't let Jennie move in, and Joan tried to convince herself that it was a temporary fling. Alan did, however, help find Jennie a house—equipped with a studio for her pottery work—in the quiet Ulu settlement, twenty-five miles from Nairobi. And soon enough, he began paying visits to Ulu with increasing regularity.

For more than three years he went back and forth. It looked as if Joan might lose him for good. But then on July 16, 1986, Joan received word that Mount Nyamulagira, Africa's most active volcano, had erupted. Alan had been dying to film it since its last eruption. He was away editing film, and Joan contacted him immediately.

FROM: Joan Root, Nairobi—7/23/86
TO: Please give this telex to Alan Root when he visits today.

Some news to cause a quandary. Nyamulagira has been erupting since 17th, and lava flowing towards Lake Kivu. Exploding area 6 hrs. walk . . . very excited . . . Film?

That was enough—no pressure, no request for him to rush home. She knew that the mere facts would be catnip sufficient to lure her roving husband back to her.

FROM: Alan Root, U.K.—7/23/86
TO: Nairobi

Message just received. Am on island. . . . Cannot get off until this evening. Will phone you tomorrow morning from London. If volcano still active will return immediately. Can you apply for visas and aircraft permits from Zaire and Kenya.
Love Alan.

And then they were off together for thirteen days, starting with a six-hour hike up the mountain through dense forest, with eight porters carrying equipment on their heads. Joan saw to all the details, allowing Alan to work with optimal comfort and efficiency. It was just like old times. Her rubber shoes even melted on the hot lava again. It was all she wanted, to be with Alan amid the wonders of Africa again. At night they watched a fireworks display of golden embers falling around their tent—some actually burned holes in it, but it was glorious nonetheless. Each evening they would fly over the eruption, as the volcano shot lava so close to the plane that they could feel the intense heat. No one will ever beat this, Joan thought triumphantly, as she later told a friend. No one else could ever be all this—or do all this—for Alan. No woman could make him happier, more fulfilled, or more famous than she could, and, surely, he had to know it.

They returned to Nairobi with their volcano footage and began living together as before, and it seemed for a while as if Alan had decided to return to Joan permanently. But less than a month after the volcano, Jennie Hammond returned to Nairobi from a routine doctor's visit in London. She asked Alan to pick her up at the airport, and there, he immediately saw that she was in pain. "What's wrong?" he asked.

"I had to have this test," Jennie replied, explaining that the doctors had drilled a hole into her hip bone in order to take a bone-marrow sample.

"Oh, Christ, dear, what does that mean?" Alan asked.

"It means I've got leukemia," she said.

That did it. With these words, Jennie stole Alan from Joan for good. He felt "trapped," he said, and thought, I can't just walk away and leave her to die. He read a doctor's report, which said she probably had two years left to live. He would see her through this, he assured her; he would stay with her until the bitter end. And Joan? Joan would understand, he felt sure. Sensible, reliable Joan would realize that Alan could never abandon a dying woman, even if it meant abandoning his wife. From Joan's diary:

> *8/21/86: Alan came into the office from Ulu. Told me about Jennie's illness. Oh, dear. Later talked about the future—it looks unhappy on all fronts.*

The "bush telegraph," the term for the gossip network that permeates white Kenya, was soon buzzing with talk of the tortured love triangle of Alan, Jennie, and Joan. Rumor had it that Joan and Alan had made a deal: He would stay with Jennie until she died, but then he would return to Joan. According to an old friend, "She was willing to make that deal in hopes of not losing him forever. Joan was so straight; if she made a deal, it was a deal."

Reluctantly, Joan accepted this pact. If she said no, Alan would likely be gone forever; if she agreed, there was a chance that he would come back to her.

However, she could not have foreseen Jennie's increasing possessiveness of Alan and her attempted expulsion of Joan from his life. Joan's diary soon became a chronicle of heartbreak and suffering. August 29, 1986: "Got a letter from [doctor] regarding Jennie's illness. Alan very upset. We had a talk before Alan set out for Ulu for the night. They are going to a wedding tomorrow." "They" meaning Alan and Jennie. September 4, 1986: "Alan in at 1 P.M. Very low. Jennie's going bananas regarding him going to the U.S. and leaving her." The U.S. trip was one Alan was scheduled to take with Joan, to a film festival in Aspen, Colorado, where *Lights! Action! Africa!* (aka *Two in the Bush*) was to be featured. September 5, 1986: "Tea at Karen. Alan gave me addresses, etc. for the U.S., then left to take his 'family' to Chinese meal."

Over Jennie's protests, Joan and Alan flew together to Aspen and attended a screening of their film in the historic Wheeler Opera House. Just before it began—before the screen exploded with diving airplanes and hot-air balloons, with rampaging hippos, spitting cobras, and sprinting cheetahs, with scenes of the life they had shared before Jennie thundered onto the scene—there was a power failure, and all the lights went out. Joan recounted their conversation in her diary.

"Joan?" Alan said in the darkness.

"Yes, Alan?"

"You've got to fade out for the kids' sake."

"I'm angry," she said.

"I know. We have to separate to give Jennie peace of mind."

They continued the conversation the next day while walking along a river.

"Oh, Alan."

"I have to devote a lot of my future time to her."

"And our plans for Zaire?" Joan asked, referring to the films they had planned to make there—one about the volcano, another about the gorillas, and two others.

"We'll have to shelve them for now."

Alan and Joan were back together, but only on-screen. In life, they began to drift even further apart.

"They're searching for suitable bone marrow among donors," Joan wrote in her diary on November 20, 1986. "Even if found, [there is a] 20% chance of dying from operation then only a 70% chance of it working. So chances are she will die in three years. Which will be grim for Alan." Two years had turned into three, but Joan didn't seem to be shaken by the extension.

> *3/8/87: Alan told me about Jennie's visit to [doctor] yesterday. [Doctor] said she was* cured *so they rushed her to Nairobi Hospital for tests and found she was not. . . . Then phone call said she had an accident. Alan* rushed *to the hospital and found a lorry had crashed into her pickup and her head had broken glass behind it and she had stitches.*

Jennie healed fast. She would prove to be as tough as—maybe even tougher than—anything Alan and Joan had ever encountered in the bush.

> *6/13/87: Off to Naivasha.* Dammit. *Jennie is fit nowadays. Drove to Naivasha feeling very lonely.*

Joan's anger proceeded to turn into sadness, and the sadness into despair.

> Dear Alan,
>
> How ever can I communicate with you, without it constantly being taken up the wrong way? . . . I guess a lot of it is caused by the tension bottled up inside you.
>
> A part of me says it would be better for myself if I was totally

free of the distress you cause, but I also know the fulfillment I feel when we are together, and enjoying what we are doing, and I don't want to throw away the chance to have that pleasure ever again. But this does not mean I am clinging—you *are* free to do what you have to do. . . .

Actually I think I have given you your freedom in the past few years, freedom in your personal life, but there has been a lot of confusion this year.

All my love,

Joan

Jennie increasingly took charge of Alan's life. "We had thought I could still be involved in the Zaire film, until he realized it upset her too much," Joan wrote about the work Alan was planning to do for *Survival* and *National Geographic.* When Warner Bros. hired Alan to film gorilla-charging sequences for *Gorillas in the Mist,* starring Sigourney Weaver as Dian Fossey, Jennie insisted that she, not Joan, accompany him. "It hurts me that I cannot be involved in the Dian Fossey work, as Dian was a friend of the both of us," Joan wrote to a friend on July 12, 1987.

On location in Zaire, Jennie was incapable of filling Joan's shoes. She stayed in the guest quarters of a tea plantation while Alan went out to film a notoriously ill-tempered silverback named Mushamuka, who had killed a poacher after another poacher had killed his father. Possibly mistaking the camera on Alan's shoulder for a weapon, the giant ape came charging at him like a "fucking great Doberman, low to the ground, looking straight at me," as Alan told George Plimpton for *The New Yorker*. "I started filming. He went out of focus almost immediately, and the next thing I knew he was on me. He grabbed me . . . by the waist with those huge hands—I'm sort of ticklish anyway—but the bite was actually in my thigh."

Joan was sure she would have seen such a thing coming—since her vantage point would have been not from a guest house but from right behind Alan. "I also feel I may have noticed Mushamuka was getting agitated because Alan was distracted by having the big camera on his shoulder," she wrote.

By then Joan was the acknowledged expert on coaxing wild animals to perform naturally on film. When the cast and crew of *Out of Africa* came to film around Naivasha, the filmmakers enlisted Joan to provide one of her duikers—the Sudanese antelope—for a scene with Meryl Streep. "We spent the afternoon fixing the set, which meant making a faint car track through the trees, and setting up lights on top of a big lorry because it was going to be a night scene," Joan wrote. "Then at dusk Jack [Couffer, the cinematographer] shot a scene with an old Hupmobile (the car the Blixens drive in the film) driving through a waterbuck herd. . . . Then they all came round to my place with the old car, and Jack shot the scene of the light shining in my duiker's eyes, then the car driving by. Sounds simple but Jack doubted it would work, but my duiker was so good he was able to get the shot three times."

Surely Alan knew how much he needed her.

On July 10, 1987, flying over the plains of the Serengeti where they had once chronicled the thundering migration of the wildebeest, Joan and Alan talked. Not of film or wildlife or their shared passion for Africa but of pain, separation, and Jennie. Alan said it was "killing Jennie" for him to remain married to Joan. He didn't *want* a divorce, but he saw no other way out. Relying on their deal, Joan agreed to a separation; once Jennie was dead, she figured, any divorce would be moot, and Alan would come back to her. However, she soon regretted the decision. Her diary reveals how the situation deteriorated:

> *July 11–12, 1987: Alan and I both understand why the time has come to see a lawyer. I'm feeling cool and relieved to be taking some action at last.*
>
> *July 15, 1987: Divorce is not in my best interests.*
>
> *August 29, 1987: Alan behaved as if I will just fall in line as a support system again.*

October 11, 1987: Met Jennie face-to-face in Karen and said hello, but she didn't answer.

October 12, 1987: I tried to be friendly but she was cold and goading, about me doing work, and I should just leave it to Alan.

After fifteen half-hour segments of *Survival*, twenty-three one-hour films for the BBC and Anglia, and countless other projects, the Roots' professional partnership was over. Making films together in the future was out of the question—Jennie wouldn't allow it. Her possessiveness became so extreme that Joan wrote a friend, "Cannot be at the Serengeti at the same time as Alan," as if their shared presence on a 5,700-square-mile plain would cause Jennie to explode.

Still, when Alan was away with Jennie or gorillas or filming in Zaire, Joan continued to work for him, handling the accounting of the Balloon Safari business they had started together. "The dreaded accounts," Alan called them. She also filed his taxes, handled office politics (pilots quitting), typed his letters and correspondence, and even found him new office space with "a telephone girl and a man to run around town."

"I'm sure this letter bores you rigid, after all of your excitements with gorillas, but I wanted you to be able to carry on with what I have set in motion," she wrote to Alan on July 30, 1987. She would happily have kept working for her husband, and in that way she could be there for him when Jennie died and he came back to her. But Jennie didn't die. In fact, Jennie just kept getting stronger. Probably understanding what was at stake, Jennie didn't want Joan anywhere in Alan's life, even as a bookkeeper and organizer. For that matter, Jennie didn't want Alan connected to Joan through what they loved most: their films.

And while Joan championed Alan's work, one friend said, Jennie did the reverse: "She stopped him from making his films. She didn't want him leaving her. She was ill."

Alan obviously retained the utmost respect for Joan and even felt protective of her and her reputation, as the following cable shows:

7/4/88
ATTN: All involved with *Most Dangerous Game* (a television project in development)
FROM: Alan Root

Have just seen the script. I find it personally offensive and insulting to Joan that she is treated as a non-person in this film, and that I am to be shown "solo." Our current status has no relevance. Most of the sequences you are using were made with her help. Some were possible only with her help. What I do with the crew here will reflect my personal views as cameraman (albeit through a distorting lens). But I insist that Joan be seen not as an incidental gopher who got into the picture but as what she is—a highly skilled and gutsy lady. Unless I receive assurance that this is so, you can count me out.

While continuing to do Alan's administrative work, Joan stayed in his late mother's house in Karen when she came up from Naivasha. Soon mayhem descended. Thieves repeatedly broke into the cars, the storage areas, and the house itself. One night Joan woke up at four A.M. to find "a torch [flashlight] being shone in my face" by an intruder. She didn't allow him to make the first move. She grabbed a blanket from the bed and charged the man just as the agitated silverback had charged Alan. "I think this unnerved him, because he put the torch out," she wrote. But when she reached him with the outstretched blanket, the intruder swung around with "a tire lever or the blunt side of a panga. . . . A huge lump soon came up on my arm, but better than collecting it on the head." He then fled out the back door to join a gang who "ran off with my cameras, etc."

Joan realized that a woman living alone in Africa required more than a blanket for protection. "I have applied to get my own firearm, but it is proving to be a long, drawn-out process. I have since had two minor robberies at Naivasha."

Threats to her safety, though, were secondary to her tortured relationship with Alan, as the following exchange of letters shows.

> My darling Alan,
>
> My mind is a jumble of conflicting thoughts, and I cannot match your clarity with words. I do feel angry, frustrated and trapped by events. But I want to overcome these negative feelings and carry on under whatever difficulties to contribute to the projects we care about, and to help you cope in whatever way I can. It is the only way open to me to maintain contact with you and show you my love.

However, she informed him, she knew that the "devotion" she had lavished on him in all their years together had backfired and "laid me open to exploitation, which has caused my resentment and yours."

> Joan, my love,
>
> I really have no right to expect you to continue to take any interest in me. But as you know, I do so depend on you. . . . I don't want you to feel exploited by this situation. I don't know how long this is going to last, or how it will end. I can only pray that somehow, somewhere near the end of it, we, all of us, will have learned what love really is.
>
> I feel so lost and rootless. I wander from beautiful place to beautiful place, Naivasha, oh, God, the peace there. Serengeti, so much to do. Ulu, such sadness. Will that pottery wheel ever spin again? And I end up sitting alone, like my father, in the Karen house, surrounded by the ghosts of all that has happened over more than thirty years. My heart has no home anymore. It hurts even high in the sky, or in the wild places that I love so much.
>
> I have no options. I have to help Jennie, the kids, and myself to face the fact of death. To get something positive from it. I don't know. It's hard to see what good can come out of such horror.

July 30, 1987

Alan, my love

Good news is Balloon Safaris made a good profit last year. Income from balloon flights was almost double the previous year. You'll find all the radios and charging units at Karen, and also the wheat grinder. . . .

Well, soldier on, my dear Alan. I don't know why I still love you.

Joan,

I am very confused and filled with pain about what we are about to do. We had something unique and very special and I am broken-hearted that I screwed it up. I find it very hard going through life without you, and I do miss you at the times that are important and that we used to share . . . the eclipse of the moon . . . seeing some special animal or bird. I want you to know that no one will ever fill that gap in my life. It will always be empty space.

On September 5, 1990, four years after Jennie's diagnosis, Joan told Alan calmly that she would bring his financial books up to date and leave them for him to review, but he would have to take responsibility for his accounts and affairs from then on. The next day Joan stopped by the Balloon Safaris offices to see Alan one last time. Then she did what Alan and Jennie had been pushing her to do for years. After she and Alan amicably agreed on a settlement, she went to the law courts in Nairobi and took her place on a bench, along with scores of Africans waiting for their cases to be heard.

Her lawyer had arranged for the divorce to be handled during a court recess. It was fortunate that the presiding judge recognized her from her films. "You're a famous lady!" he said in a booming voice.

Joan blushed. Moments later, it was over. "Granted divorce on [grounds of] desertion," she wrote in her diary on September 6, 1990. "Three years since Alan has stayed at Naivasha."

> *Thursday, September 6, 1990, DIVORCE DAY. Felt very miserable afterwards. Went to bank to deposit money in Alan's account and* Survival *account. Had lunch alone at African Heritage Centre. . . . Very depressed.*

She became even more depressed whenever she studied herself in the mirror. Where was the beautiful young woman with the porcelain skin and perfect blond hair? The years of physically demanding work and constant exposure to the equatorial sun had taken a devastating toll. "I can picture her in my mind's eye, looking bleak and bleached, as dried out as driftwood on a solitary beach," one friend wrote of Joan at age fifty. Her skin had become lined and weathered, and her thinning hair was tinged with streaks of gray.

On January 9, 1991, about four months after his divorce from Joan, Alan married Jennie "in the Nairobi licensing office and went off that evening to separate honeymoons in the UK and Zaire," Alan wrote Anthony Smith, meaning he was going to Zaire to film and Jennie was going to London for medical check-ups. The week before the wedding, Alan had told Joan the news, leaving her feeling "upset and fragile." It was five years since Jennie's diagnosis, and the woman who hadn't been expected to live two years showed no sign of slowing down.

If Alan had fallen for almost any other woman, Joan might have stood a chance of winning him back, even after the divorce. But she couldn't win against Jennie, who wasn't content merely to have captured Alan; she was also determined to drive Joan from his life completely. Jennie expressed her thoughts in two extraordinary and undated letters to Joan: "I'm selfish and arrogant," she wrote in one. "I just wanted you to know that I'm not really nice." In the other, she explained: "Alan is incapable of decision or solution, and his insecurity does not allow him to express himself to either of us, for fear of our departure or loss. Somewhere along his life, he will possibly have to make an adult decision. But he's not very adult emotionally."

In the divorce settlement, Joan received half of the money she and Alan had in the bank; the property on Lake Naivasha; and their airplane, *Oscar Charlie*. Despite her earlier promise not to, Joan continued to handle Alan's accounts, and it was agreed once again that when she went to Nairobi for that purpose, she could stay at the house in Karen. This arrangement annoyed the new Mrs. Alan Root to no end. One night when Alan was away, Joan invited four friends, including Alan's sister Jacky, to dinner. On hearing of it, Jennie "flew into a rage," Joan wrote, and attacked one of the couples who had accepted Joan's invitation, "saying they had humiliated her and were disloyal and must never see me. And then she drove to Karen to sort me out."

"Stop shitting on my space, Joan!" Jennie shouted, demanding that Joan get the hell out of her and Alan's house, their business, and their life. She stormed around the house and screamed.

When Jennie's voice gave out, she grabbed plates, glasses, whatever she could lay her hands on, and smashed them against the walls. Joan packed up her belongings. "This is the last night I will ever spend at Karen," she wrote in her diary. She then returned alone to the only real home she had ever known, the place where she and Alan had spent twenty-eight blissfully adventurous years: Naivasha.

Chapter Six

Safely back home, Joan drew into herself, keeping her hurt and her pain deep inside where she had always kept it. If she cried, she did not discuss it, at least not in the beginning, although everyone else discussed it. The Nairobi-Naivasha bush telegraph was overloaded with talk of the tragedy of Joan Root, the Kenya girl who was now unimaginably alone.

She had arrived at a major turning point. She was devastated after losing Alan. She had lost not only her husband but also her career as a filmmaker, her role as a producer, her life as a wife. As for continuing on without Alan, one of her friends insisted that "He was without a doubt the love of her life. There was no one like him, ever, for her. . . . She was very shaken and upset by the divorce, and she needed time to lick her wounds."

Since they had married so young, Alan was intertwined with Joan at every level. "They were such a close team that, when that ended, she lost everything. She was very much at sea," said a friend.

According to Adrian Luckhurst, Joan's business manager, "As far as Joan was concerned, a breakup of their relationship—professional, private, everything—was something that she would never contemplate. Oh, it just killed her. It really did. To go from an incredibly dynamic life, and a tremendously fulfilling life, to suddenly having nothing? How do you cope with that?"

Another Nairobi friend, Jean Hartley, was impressed by Joan's strength. "I could see that she had been emotionally flattened by this divorce, and the guts that she showed by pulling herself up by her shoestrings and getting on with her life again was quite unbelievable. She just slowly, slowly, one day at a time, picked her life up and put it together again. With guts, determination, and a few friends, she built a life after Alan and became Joan in her own right—not Alan and Joan. She was tough. She wasn't soft in the middle."

Only when she was alone did Joan reveal her feelings. She poured out her heart in her diary and letters, as well as a personal notebook, writing about how she was striving to replace the hurt with hope and healing.

> *Look for the message in the negative. What is there to learn in this situation? When you have done all you can do about a negative situation, it is time to release it. There are plenty of wonderful people—wanting to give and receive love. Love exists in our minds. We limit ourselves only because of our shields of fear, our shields against love.*

After a period of deep mourning and grief, Joan began to undergo a transformation. This shy, quiet woman, emotionally mowed down in her prime, would eventually close the book on her first life and start another, emerging from the devastation and heartbreak more resolute than before. She would turn her focus once again to the animals and the natural world that had always sustained her. Now her main purpose wasn't her husband; her goal went beyond documenting the animals and landscapes of Africa on film. Her new mission would be to save them.

The animal that helped launch Joan in her new life was the same one that had brought her and Alan together so many years earlier: the elephant.

Iain Douglas-Hamilton had begun to suspect that an elephant massacre of massive proportions was happening across Africa, but almost no one believed him. Douglas-Hamilton knew that Joan, an acute observer and a painstaking researcher of everything in the natural world, could be most useful in confirming his instincts. "Joan was such a part of the local wildlife scene—she sucked information through every pore," he explained. "She was someone who loved nature, and when nature would be attacked, Joan would be there to save it."

She agreed to help him on at least two counts, the first in 1988 in Joan's beloved Tsavo National Park, once one of Africa's elephant strongholds. In the 1960s, Tsavo's elephant population had grown so great that many naturalists argued the herds should be culled. A massive drought in the 1970s took care of the overpopulation, when ten thousand elephants starved to death. On the heels of drought came an intense period of poaching, during which elephants were slaughtered by the thousands before Kenya finally awoke to the disaster. By that point, 75 percent of Tsavo's elephants had been brought down.

It turned out that Somalis with guns had been killing Tsavo's elephants, some claimed with the tacit consent of rogue members of the Kenya Wildlife Conservation Department, who stood to profit on the ivory. Joan and Iain were soon to be part of a comprehensive counting effort that would reveal this sordid story to the world. It was a multiplane counting effort, with Joan spending hours on end in a hot, cramped airplane counting both live elephants and corpses. "The results were as depressing as anticipated," she wrote in a letter. "Elephants within the Tsavo Park were 4,327, down from 22,174 in 1973 [countrywide, Kenya's elephant population had gone from 85,000 in 1979 to 22,000 in 1989]. We also counted all skeletons seen, and many of these were along the roads where the wardens and rangers were poaching from park's vehicles. . . ."

What *could* be done? The first step was to make the situation known. Richard Leakey took care of that. Joan and Alan's old friend and former partner in their photo-safari business, Leakey was now head of the Kenya Wildlife Conservation Department. Distraught over the devastation in Tsavo, he devised a public-relations triumph: the burning of a twelve-ton, twenty-foot pyre of tusks seized from poachers in Tsavo and elsewhere across Kenya. He also cleaned up corruption in the Kenya Wildlife Services, issued weapons to park rangers, worked to ban the trade of ivory, and lobbied for elephants to be on the endangered species list. He even enacted a shoot-to-kill policy to curtail poachers, who, in the case of Tsavo, were mostly Somali bandits.

But it was the bonfire that caught the attention of people around the globe. After Kenyan president Daniel arap Moi lit the pyre of tusks, Iain, Joan, and a group of dignitaries and conservationists gathered around to watch it burn.

Later, Douglas-Hamilton and Joan were involved in another count, covering the vast wilderness in the Central African Republic once known as the El Dorado for elephants. They would fly over the savannas and open forests in a small Cessna 185 and count the animals below.

Off they flew, Douglas-Hamilton piloting, Joan sitting in the right-hand passenger seat, peering down through a "counting rod" —a steel rod strapped to the airplane strut that affords the counter one specific frame to study at a time. Flying at four hundred feet, Joan stared at the ground, intent on counting every single elephant, but she saw very few. These vast areas, once home to enormous herds, were now mostly barren. "One, two, three," she began, her steady eye on the land as the cramped plane bucketed around, rocked by turbulence. "Days and days, hours and hours, of sitting in a torture chamber of a small cabin of an airplane, being bounced around, never letting her concentration flag for one second, while her eyes scanned the landscape looking for live elephants, carcasses, skeletons," remembered Douglas-Hamilton. "The qualities that Joan had were quite rare: an acute sense of observation, an ability to pick things up, first to spot, then to count, and to do it hour after hour, and at the end of the day to redo the whole damn thing on paper."

They covered much of Central Africa, from time to time picking up other experts, but Douglas-Hamilton relied on Joan and was constantly amazed at her knowledge of wildlife, especially in areas that were foreign to her. One night in camp, after listening to unfamiliar birds make what she took to be an alarm call, she said, "There must be a snake up that tree." The men looked up, and sure enough, a huge black mamba was wrapped around a limb above them.

What Joan's keen instincts told her about the elephants—a concern very much supported by the numbers—was that something was quite wrong. Joan had seen devastation before. She had agonized over her beloved Tsavo National Park, where she and Alan had filmed so frequently, when it became an elephant graveyard, with great numbers dying of starvation in 1971, followed by so much poaching that the place was littered with elephant corpses and bleached white bones. But she had never seen anything like this. In Central Africa, dead elephants outnumbered live ones to such a degree that any final count would represent an 80 to 90 percent reduction.

Who was killing off the elephants in such numbers? Flying over a fresh massacre of the huge bodies, Iain and Joan touched down to discover that the elephants had been not shot but *speared.* Why? The answer was always ivory. Teams of horsemen were riding hundreds of miles, from Sudan all the way to Central Africa, for ivory. While one horseman distracted the elephant from the front, another would attack it from the rear, driving a long slaughtering spear into the beast's haunches, then working the blade back and forth until the elephant fell. If that didn't work, they would shoot the animal with a Kalashnikov. In the end, Joan counted 4,300 live elephants and 7,900 dead ones—some corpses fresh, others years old—in an area that had once boasted an elephant population of 12,000.

The new count "was going to blow the lid off this Central African situation," Douglas-Hamilton remembered. Joan's photographs of the carnage soon became famous in a report, and later were published in newspapers around the world, and she and Douglas-Hamilton and their team prepared detailed presentation books that were shown to General André Kolingba, fourth president of the Central African Republic, complete with a detailed manifesto of what had to be done immediately to save the remaining elephants. Shocked and appalled, General Kolingba put an end to "*Le Collecte,*" the much abused system that allowed people to collect ivory from dead elephants. Such a system encouraged ivory traders to kill more elephants, from which they could then "legally" collect the ivory. The general also endorsed a trade ban on ivory, and the European Union designated millions of dollars to help stop the carnage in the Central African Republic. From this time forward, Joan would be involved in practically every count of elephants and rhinos in Kenya and surrounding countries. Her efforts in the Central African Republic and Tsavo had once again proved her growing conviction that people *could* make a difference, that wildlife *could* be saved, and that Kenya was *not* doomed.

"Look for ways to turn loss into information," Joan wrote in her notebook.

> *Join the mob or go for what you want. Give yourself plenty of quiet time alone in order to get in touch with who you are. . . . Focus power of thought. Remind yourself that the world is yours for the asking. The non-risker does not grow, you just get older. When you have decided which ideas, beliefs, relationships and situations no longer work for you, it is time to release them. Let go of negative thoughts—view them as a flight of birds crossing your path. See them fly into view and continue on their way.*

She was struggling valiantly to reestablish herself, her goals, and her beliefs in a world without Alan—struggling to be recognized on her own merits. The elephant counts were her first victories.

After the elephants, there were naturally other steps toward what would become the ultimate mission in Joan's post-Alan life. And "mission" is the right word: Joan Root always needed a mission. For her, a cause—whether it was supporting a husband, counting elephants, or rehabilitating a wounded animal—was as vital as oxygen. Without a cause, Joan Root did not feel alive. Her style of activism, however, was all her own. "She was not one to stand up in public and shout," said her Naivasha friend Sarah Higgins. "She just quietly did what she felt she had to do to try and make the world a better place."

"She was such a good person," said her friend David Coulson. "Incredibly good and very fragile. She was brave. But she was fragile. She needed another mission. I like to think we gave her back some of her self-confidence."

Coulson, the world's preeminent expert on ancient rock art, had invited Joan to accompany him on a trip to the Sahara to photograph and document ancient paintings and stone wall engravings, many of them thousands of years old. "The rock art depicted a very affluent land to the present day aridity. Their far-favorite art subjects were giraffe, elephants, ostrich, cows, hunting scenes with spears and dogs," Joan wrote to a friend.

The love of land and animals: Not much had changed in a thousand years. At night, Joan slept alone in a tent atop a cot on the sand. "In the Sahara evenings round the campfire under those incredible starry skies when you felt almost overwhelmed by the scale of the universe, Joan would regale us with stories of the adventures she had when she was with Alan," Coulson said.

These were *Two in the Bush* stories. But in the morning she was ready for work; in work, she would find revival. "She came to me, and she said, 'I want to have a role,'" Coulson remembered. "Her role was my assistant. She would follow me like a shadow. And she was absolutely meticulous, so thorough and conscientious."

He watched Joan climb up fifty-foot cliffs to find a rock-art painting, or get down on her hands and knees when, while crossing an ancient river valley, she found a "flightless grasshopper" and she just *had* to study it up close. On another occasion, Coulson remembered marveling at her toughness when, after a trip in a biting wind on the back of a donkey, she arrived at the summit where there were paintings created before the great pyramids of Egypt. "And we were standing in front of this magnificent panel, and I was photographing away, and suddenly, we heard Joan crying. And we said, 'Joan, what's wrong?'

"'Well, nothing, really,' she replied. 'It's just that my hands are so cold that I can't write down what David is saying.'"

He paused. "Later that evening, when I checked the notes, they were impeccable."

By then she could look back on her life as a wife and constant supporter to her husband with some perspective, David Coulson said, knowing what she'd done right and what she'd done wrong. "She said, 'The mistake I made with Alan is that I used to put his slippers out for him at night. I was too nice, too dutiful.'

"I think she felt she should have been a bit tougher and more her own person," he said.

From then on, that was exactly what she would be—but not for Joan, never only for Joan.

With the historic elephant counts and other adventures, Joan had embarked on her new life as a naturalist. Now she would do everything she hadn't had time to do when she was producing wildlife films with Alan. She would join and attend the meetings and events of every possible local cause and club, including local school and hospital boards and conservation groups such as the Lake Naivasha Riparian Association, for which she served as both secretary and treasurer; the Nakuru Wildlife Conservancy, for which she was a director and treasurer; and the Succulenta Society, the Nairobi-based circle that studied and safeguarded succulent plants like aloe and cactus. Joan frequently hosted Succulenta Society meetings in her home, and the society's members marveled over how the sunbirds flocked to her aloe plants and the magnificent *Anselia africana* orchids that grew on her acacia trees.

"I didn't have a lot of time for her when I first met her," said Dee Raymer, the Succulenta Society's former chairman. "I thought she was terribly stuck up and aloof. I mentioned that to a mutual friend who said, '*Don't make that mistake!* She's incredibly shy.' "

When she opened up, Dee Raymer continued, Joan was the best, most loyal, and most fascinating friend. "It was wonderful being on a field trip with her! She could tell you everything about everything. She was like a sponge for knowledge, and after Alan walked out on her, I saw her making a very methodical reassessment of herself and her life. She very much set out to become Joan Root, the individual, instead of

Joan Thorpe and Alan Root on their wedding day. Instead of throwing rice, several of Alan's drunken buddies had put fresh elephant dung under the Land Rover's wheels and poured boiling water on it, so when the newlyweds drove away, to the cheers of their friends and family, elephant shit sprayed in all directions. It was, everyone agreed, a real Kenya wedding. *(Courtesy of Alan Root)*

From the veranda of their house on Lake Naivasha, Joan and Alan could see the lake, where the black eyes and twitching ears of hippos rose and fell. They spotted a family of giant white-headed fish eagles nesting on the roof. Off in the garden, they could hear a loud commotion of twittering birds, and when they went to investigate, they found a puff adder eating a frog. *(Guillaume Bonn)*

Hippos kill more people in Kenya than any other herbivore in Africa, but Joan always fed Sally, the hippo that came to live on their land, by hand. Here she photographs hippos in the mud. *(Courtesy of Alan Root)*

Out in the wild with Alan, Joan underwent an amazing transformation. Her shyness fell away and an adventurer emerged, though not one of Alan's ilk. She would never sneak up on a snake, pluck the hair out of an elephant's tail, or taunt a lioness—all of which Alan loved to do. *(Courtesy of Alan Root)*

One day they awoke to find a fine specimen in their trap. They fed it through a small window in the enclosure at first, until it was acclimated to their human sound and smell. Then Joan, as still as the antelope itself, climbed into the trap and fed the bongo by hand. *(Courtesy of Alan Root)*

In Alan and Joan's film about their bongo-catching exploits, Joan's youth and beauty are in full bloom. She is as tall and blond as a fashion model but as quiet as a fawn, gentle yet strong, a silent, indomitable presence. *(Courtesy of Alan Root)*

Joan Root had the good fortune to have spent her life in the most beautiful place on earth. *(Courtesy of Alan Root)*

Joan and Alan put out an SOS and soon help arrived in droves, all braving the hundred-degree heat, the stench of dying birds, and the scalding soda. In the end, they freed twenty-seven thousand chicks and prevented another two hundred thousand from entering the shallows, where the high concentration of soda would have imprisoned them. *(Courtesy of Alan Root)*

While the Roots were filming the primitive Karamojong tribe of Uganda, the members of the tribe inducted Alan in a manhood ceremony, which, Joan wrote, "consisted of the stomach contents of an ox being smeared down his face and chest, and then being lightly hit with sticks by the elders. . . . They then chanted strings of blessings for us, which went on and on. One of them was that the next time we visited them, I would have *a child!*" *(Courtesy of Alan Root)*

Everything Joan was not—outgoing, extroverted, silly, utterly incautious—Alan was, in spades. She would later claim that she loved Alan from the moment she met him, and much, much more as she got to know him. She loved his flamboyancy, the way he took the stage, the way he was always the center of attention—which meant that she didn't have to be. *(Courtesy of Alan Root)*

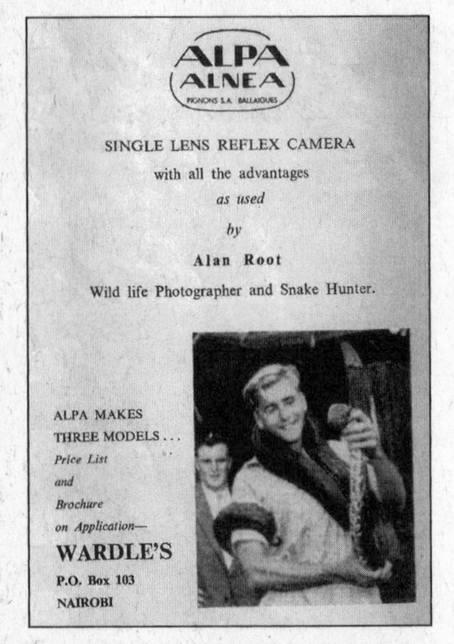

"He is the success story of the bush," author John Heminway wrote of Alan Root. "Much to the pleasure and anguish of his friends, he remains the absolute eccentric, the clown, the daredevil, the mimic, the misanthrope, the life of the party, the irrepressible idealist of nature. . . . He will die for a sequence in a film, a joke, a game of tennis. In short, Alan is so consumed by living that every day requires some proof that he has cheated death." *(Courtesy of Jean Hartley)*

Constant contact with its mother is essential for a baby elephant, so Joan became a surrogate mother for this one, which she named Bundu, the Bantu word for "wilderness." *(Courtesy of Alan Root)*

This trail was not only steep—going quickly from five thousand to fourteen thousand feet—but also slippery, because it was packed with fallen, wet bamboo. The temperature swung wildly. The higher Joan and Alan climbed, the rougher and rainier it got. *(Courtesy of Alan Root)*

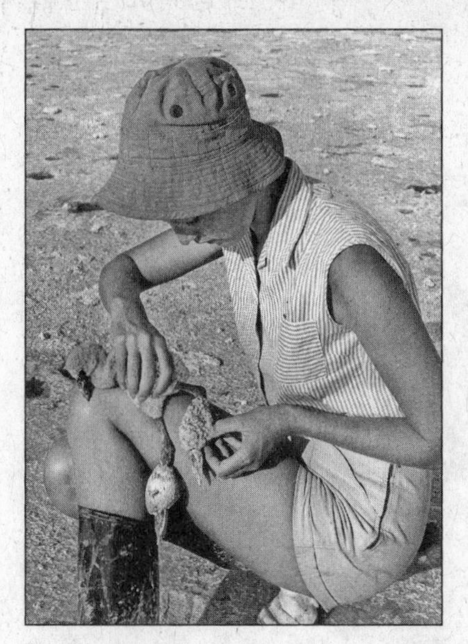

Newspapers in Africa, England, Holland, and elsewhere ran stories with Joan's picture—for the first time alone, rather than beside or behind Alan—and the world at large got its first glimpse of the tall, attractive blonde in a white sleeveless shirt, a floppy red hat, and the briefest of shorts. *(Courtesy of Alan Root)*

Joan's father, Edmund Thorpe, liked to tell friends that he was protected by a guardian angel, given the countless times he had escaped violent death. *(Courtesy of Alan Root)*

"Many in the trade considered them to have been the best wildlife filming team, with Joan often performing the more daunting role," Anthony Smith later wrote. "Who was up a thorn tree ready to warn of a wildebeest herd thundering their way? Who had her goggles pierced when a hippo grew aggressive? Whose shoes melted when the hot volcanic lava became too much for them?" As Alan himself said, "I don't know what I'd do without Joan. I'd probably have to marry three women at the same time." *(Courtesy of Alan Root)*

Audiences were captivated by underwater scenes of Joan swimming with herds of sea lions, the mating ceremony of four-hundred-pound tortoises, marine iguanas feeding on the ocean floor, and other wildlife images never seen before. *(Courtesy of Alan Root)*

"I've crashed two of these," Alan Root said when I was in a helicopter beside him. We lifted off, and he tilted the helicopter toward the Ngong Hills, blue and shadowy in the distance, and flew at high speed over the game-filled plains. I could make out the zebras, Cape buffalo, and gazelle in the national park below as Alan pulled back on the throttle and we shot like a bullet through the clear African sky. *(Guillaume Bonn)*

Frequently prowling beneath the Roots' dinner table was Joan's caracal, a large wildcat with razor-sharp teeth and claws. If guests leaned down to pet it, nine times out of ten it would roll over and let them. But the tenth time it might very well scream and lunge like a living bale of barbed wire. *(Mary Ellen Mark)*

She marveled over the natural world. She had such respect for its seasons and cycles, its ability to rejuvenate, reproduce, and sustain itself. She kept meticulous and intricately detailed logbooks, noting the times her recuperating or visiting animals were fed as well as their activities on the road to survival. *(Courtesy of Alan Root)*

"Not far from where we're gathered now, Joan Root was murdered in cold blood," a priest said at the opening of the service to celebrate her life on March 4, 2006. "It's hard to get our heads around it," he continued, trying to grasp why her life was "brutally and shamefully cut short. Although bullets could cut her down, no brutal killer could kill what she did and what she stood for." *(Guillaume Bonn)*

half a couple. . . . She had many interests. I doubt if I knew half of her friends."

No longer would she be a shrinking violet on the social level. Some thought it was out of character for Joan to join the ultra-private and storied Muthaiga Club, that bastion of white Kenyan society since the 1920s. But as a step forward in her new life, she asked Adrian Luckhurst to nominate her for membership, and of course, no one dared blackball Joan Root, even though one negative vote is all it takes. She began lunching and dining there, and on her trips to Nairobi when she didn't stay in the homes of her friends, she would spend nights in one of the Muthaiga Club's bedrooms.

Then she did something many thought was even more out of character: She went to London for a face-lift. She returned to Nairobi looking and feeling good.

During all the years she'd spent in Alan's shadow, she never thought about recognition. Now she began to question all of that. "She suffered from a lack of recognition," a friend said. "She felt she had faded into insignificance. I knew she was slightly miffed that Alan still got invited to things [in the wildlife film world] and she didn't."

"Well, by your own volition you did nothing to promote yourself," the friend said.

"Because he's the showman and I'm not," Joan quietly replied.

After the divorce, she was still following Alan behind the scenes. She wrote out the script for Alan's introduction by the British wildlife television star David Attenborough when he was given the Lifetime Achievement Award by Wildscreen, the preeminent wildlife filmmaking organization, after Alan sent her a videotape of the ceremony.

"6 minute tribute by David Attenborough," Joan wrote. "Ending. . . . So he almost single-handedly in my view made wildlife films grow up, and become the kind of professional, demanding occupation that it is today, and for that we have to thank him. But I know that we actually not only thank him, but admire him as one of the greatest wildlife filmmakers in the world today . . . Alan Root."

"Alan for four minutes," Joan wrote. "I have been lucky enough to have the love of a couple of incredible women—my first wife, Joan, who helped me to build my career in the early days. . . . And my wonderful Jennie, who helped me to see that a career is probably the least important thing in one's life. Thank you, Joan. Thank you, Jennie, and thank you, all my friends here who have walked alongside me on the big Safari."

"Thank you, Joan." She must have loved hearing those words. But she wasn't present that night or any night when Alan took the bows for a lifetime of wildlife filmmaking.

At least Naivasha needed her, counting on her talent, determination, and grace. "Stayed home all day—always plenty to do. I never catch up," she wrote in October 1994. She noted nights when huge bull hippos fed outside her bedroom window and pearl-spotted owlets were catching and hiding mice and twenty-four waterbuck were prancing across her garden.

How she loved this lake, its stillness, its peace. "Quiet day on my own," she wrote that October 1994. "Letter writing. Planting aloes and snipping plants. Raining gently at night. Grass green. Garden and lake looking lovely."

She marveled over the natural world, had such respect for its seasons and cycles, its ability to rejuvenate, reproduce, and sustain itself. She kept meticulous and intricately detailed logbooks, noting the times her recuperating or visiting animals were fed, as well as their activities on the road to survival. (A pair of cranes she named Adam and Eve, to cite just one example, had practically daily progress reports.) She noted when plants on her property came into bloom, when they went to seed, and when various animal species bred—not to interfere but to be prepared in case her help was needed. She knew that animals time their birth cycles to the rainy seasons—and in case of drought, so common in Naivasha, she might have to be there with a helping hand, a pan of water, a warm shelter, or even a nest, which she built in so many trees around her property for the birds that might become unable to build their own. This woman who could never have children of her own was serving as midwife to infinite numbers of creatures.

"Some people just see a few animals in a bit of bush," Joan would later tell a writer who had persuaded her after much initial resistance to be interviewed for a Nairobi tourist magazine about people who had made a difference in Kenya. It would be the only post-Alan interview Joan Root would ever be asked to give. "But I've developed this place into a sort of miniature Maasai, preserving the environment through animals that would be together in the wild." "She contained herself so much, but behind that was such a huge commitment to everything that belongs to the natural world, almost to the extent that you feel that she's completely part of the natural world," added a noted filmmaker. "She was so protective about the fragile structure of the land, especially the lake," said a close friend. "Her land was completely her reason to live."

Nevertheless, Joan was still scarred, a single woman burrowed deep inside herself, unable to express exactly how she felt. Despite her community service, she spent much of her time in silence, her suffering an unspoken but fully apparent burden. If she spoke at all, she spoke of wildlife. It was as if, in her wounded state, she felt an even greater connection to the animals who needed her. She took in tortoises with broken shells, defenseless owlets, crippled bushbucks, lame Thomson's gazelles. Woe to the predators who dared encroach upon the animals populating Joan's land—especially pythons, which, she wrote, slithered under the aviary "where I keep ground squirrels" and "home in on our place because of the nice smells of antelopes." She wrote that she'd caught eleven pythons in two years, the largest over twelve feet long. "I am very adept at catching them now, and Kiari is very proud and brave and he holds the sack for me to put it in."

A neighbor, Lady Sarah Edwards, told a favorite story about the time Joan attended a memorial service for a friend atop a craggy cliff, carrying a large bundle that contained a python she had caught on her property—the snakes that stalked her antelope—and planned to release that day. However, Joan deemed the cliff too precarious and steep for the snake and decided against releasing it. Instead, she went off to tea with the python in a sack under her arm.

Sometimes she stopped in to see Sarah Higgins, an outspoken joiner of local causes who shared her love of wild animals. A cheerful and engaging conversationalist, Sarah hosted something of a salon on the large terrace that overlooked her acreage. Whenever guests arrived, a teapot would always appear, covered with a perfect quilted tea cozy, along with an array of delicious biscuits. Joan would often come for neighborly visits, sipping tea and making small talk about the astonishing array of wildlife and birdlife that crossed their backyards. She would speak in measured words of the animals she was rehabilitating. But if someone Joan didn't know walked onto the Higginses' terrace, she was gone, like a startled bird.

She did express some of her acute sadness to her closest friends, leaving them impressed with both her strength and the extraordinary depth of her heartbreak. Shortly after her split with Alan, she went on a safari to Samburu country with Delta Willis, her old friend from *Survival.* She confided to Delta about the storm Alan brewed in her emotions: One day he would give her a valentine, she said, the next day a cold shoulder, so she never knew where she stood. It was a Joan Delta had never seen. From their long friendship, Delta knew how fearless Joan could be, and Delta had often been impressed with Joan's intelligence—at one memorable dinner party, Joan was seated next to Stephen Jay Gould, the Harvard professor, paleontologist, evolutionary biologist, and arguably one of the most influential and widely read science writers of his generation. "By the end of the dinner, he was asking Joan questions," Delta remembered. But in all these years of friendship, Delta had never seen Joan as emotionally flattened or confused as she was after Alan left.

Throughout these years Joan wrote in her diary of those dearest to her, including her mother, whom she visited at least once a year in her home in Durban, South Africa, until her death in her eighties in 1989. Joan also wrote of her father, with whom she was once again close, who had left Kenya to sail around the world with his second wife, then moved to America, first to Santa Fe—where he worked as a Realtor—then to

Amarillo, Texas, to retire. Always, Joan wrote of Alan, still so lovingly and desperately, noting where he was and what he was doing in his personal and professional life.

Despite her constant thoughts about him, she did try hard to purge him from her heart and to get back her adventurous spirit. Sometime during this period, she invited a South African jeweler named Otto Poulsen, whom she'd gotten to know from the many years of visiting her mother in Durban, to come and see her at Naivasha. He was charmed by the eccentricities of her unusual life among the animals. He noticed that a gate beside the landing strip had been pushed over by some powerful force—Joan explained that Sally, the orphaned hippo, had loved to rest her head on it until it buckled under the weight.

After lunch, they took a drive in Joan's SUV Pajero. "Just sit back and enjoy the ride, and I'll tell you everything about the places we're driving through," she told Poulsen. For the day, she felt like her old self again, reliving times on her father's and later Alan's safaris. When the Pajero broke down in the middle of nowhere, Joan, as self-reliant and in control as ever, told Poulsen to take her binoculars and go birdwatching while she repaired the engine, which took her half an hour. Then she drove him into the Aberdare Mountains to a famous lodge called Treetops, located at the mountains' base, where guests can look down on the ancient elephant migration route. (The lodge had been built in the 1930s in a large tree—hence its name.)

Joan was a friend of the park warden of the Aberdares National Park, whose house was adjacent to the hotel, and they stayed with him. Treetops Lodge had astonished a long line of distinguished guests, from Robert F. Kennedy to Elizabeth of England, who had checked in the night her own father died in 1952, when she became queen of England. "Here, Queen Elizabeth II went up a tree a princess and came down a queen," one newspaper reported.

As the sun set, Joan and her friend stood on one of Treetops' four viewing decks, watching elephants drink from the waterhole. "It was like sitting in a theater, looking out on a stage," Otto Poulsen remembered, adding that the stage kept getting more interesting as the elephants were joined by rhinos, antelopes, and zebras. He and Joan then returned to the warden's house for dinner. "Amazing hospitality, beautiful food, fine wine, accompanied by the chorus of the surrounding forest," Poulsen said. "The game warden had duty that night at Treetops, and he left us with sweets and another bottle of wine. Whether he was in on the plot, I don't know. But we became intimate that night."

Joan proved to herself that she was capable of sharing passion with a man who was not Alan. It was a declaration of new energy and power, and when she rose the next morning, she felt reborn. "My dearest Otto," she later wrote. "I have told you everything because I hoped you would like to hear how I am faring since I got back. As you can tell, I am still obsessed with Alan because I love him and we have done so much together and I love that way of life, but you are very special to me and I will treasure our friendship. I remember so often the warmth and ecstasy of being with you."

She confided to Poulsen that Alan was "unhappy and confused," not sure he had done the right thing in leaving her, "and is desperate to get some good filming done, but he still loves [Jennie and the children] and lives with them when he is in Nairobi, but he also loves me and our way of life, so he is in a real fix. I can understand his predicament—more so since I met you and know I could love you.

"I am feeling very strong, thanks to you, and looking forward to starting work again," she wrote in closing. The relationship was casual and went no further. Although Joan and her lover remained good friends, she would focus her passion from this point forward not on a man but on the land she loved.

For Joan, everything that mattered most to her was centered on the lake. Each landowner owned a stake in it and was responsible for protecting it under the auspices of the Lake Naivasha Riparian Owners Association, founded in 1929. Joan and Alan had been members of the association since the 1960s, but they had rarely gone to meetings, since they were always away in the bush. When Joan returned on her own, she attended regularly, though she never spoke up or offered to serve on committees.

Her attitude changed when someone tried to lay claim to her land—not all eighty-eight acres but one of the most important sections. "My riparian," she called it, her land on the shoreline, which grew or shrank according to the level of the lake. Joan's property had twelve acres of riparian land, and one of her neighbors wanted it so badly that he was willing to seize it, though most of the neighbors felt he never would have tried to do so if Alan Root had been living on the property.

Land is paramount in Kenya. Just as poor Africans in Naivasha lust for a "plot," a prized sliver of shantytown property in Karagita, white Kenyans also fight for land. Land grabs are central to the white settler's story in Kenya, ever since the British colonialists ran the Maasai and other tribespeople off their land and claimed it as their own. In 1991 a Kenyan Cowboy—the term given to any one of a group of brash, freewheeling white Kenyan landowners in the Great Rift Valley—tried to do the same thing to Joan.

First the neighbor disputed the lines that set the boundary between his land and Joan's. Then he made public his contention that the true boundary went to the center of the lake, which meant that their territorial layout should be completely altered, and six of Joan's twelve acres of lakeshore property should go to him. Next, after driving sixty of his heifers onto Joan's riparian land, he sat back and waited, betting that Joan's famously shy and gentle nature would keep her from any direct confrontation and the six acres would become his by default.

He was wrong. Although Joan stayed calm, she went to war for her riparian land—quietly, politely, even cordially, but fully determined to be victorious. First she enlisted support. Since this was Kenya in 1991, she needed a man, and of course, it couldn't be Alan, who had plenty of his own problems. She turned to Bill Hutton, a Nairobi business adviser she and Alan had consulted during their divorce. Hutton, a Scot, worked as a fraud investigator, and he had fallen victim to a similar scam when another Kenyan Cowboy had tried to steal *his* riparian land on Lake Naivasha. According to Hutton, this particular Cowboy grossly underestimated Joan Root.

While Hutton applied pressure, firing off confrontational letters to the individual in question as well as to the Riparian Association, Joan gathered evidence. She walked her land with Kiari, her old family retainer. "It's all here, Memsaab," Kiari told her. He pointed out the boundary lines that had been in place since the Roots first arrived in 1963, which matched Joan's understanding of the boundaries. The two of them then found an even older African who remembered all the details: "The pumps, the power line, and the water ditch all follow the previous track," Joan wrote in her diary. She gathered signed statements from both men, made maps, photographed the boundary lines, and took this evidence to her powerful neighbor Tubby Block, chairman of Block Hotels in Kenya, who signed a statement saying Joan's riparian boundary was right where it should be.

She and Bill Hutton then confronted the Kenyan Cowboy at his farm. Hutton had a tape recorder running as he fired off allegations, and Joan, although "feeling very tense," stood her ground. "Bill put facts to him, quite heated at times," she wrote. The Cowboy angrily insisted that they were wrong and he was right, and he was insulted that Bill Hutton had the audacity to tape their conversation. In the end, despite his protests, Joan had eleven witnesses and their signed statements, plus boundary photographs, satellite photos, and more. She and Bill Hutton took the case before the Lake Naivasha Riparian Association's president, Lord Andrew Enniskillen. (Lord Enniskillen lived across the lake on the famous 1,600-acre estate that had formerly belonged to Kiki Preston, the infamous Whitney heiress from New York who, after she moved to Kenya, became a drug addict, albeit an exceedingly proper one—people called her "the girl with the silver syringe.")

At the meeting, Joan and Bill pushed a bet of their own, arguing by means of a complex theory that the Kenyan Cowboy was actually entitled to fifteen acres *less* riparian land than he currently had, and those acres should go to Joan. The counterattack worked. The Kenyan Cowboy backed down and even tried to be friendly. "He passed and waved and came through to see me, and we made our peace," Joan wrote in her diary of the day when her boundary was restored to its previous location and her riparian land was secure.

This was a big step toward finding her own strength without Alan. Joan had proved to herself and others that she could fight and she could win. However, her next battle would be far tougher than fighting with a single landowner. It would involve a new hybrid—the equivalent of an army of Kenyan Cowboys crossed with a multitude of international businessmen, all equipped with the blessings of the Kenyan government, backed by billions of dollars, and fueled by hundreds of thousands of laborers—that would wash up on her riparian acres and create her biggest challenge yet.

Chapter Seven

Like Joan, Lake Naivasha had always seemed quietly, stubbornly invincible. No matter what you did to it—or threw in it—it would not just survive but actually thrive, emerging tougher, stronger, wilder, more resolute to face the next challenge.

The lake on whose shores Joan's parents had conceived her—so big you could barely see across it, and a constant in Alan and Joan's films—had, over the past eighty years, been host to a series of invaders both human and wild. For thousands of years, Africans had lived in apparent harmony beside the lake. In the 1920s outsiders arrived and, not content to leave the lake alone, began importing organisms. First came British settlers and wealthy Americans, including President Theodore Roosevelt, who introduced the large-mouthed bass for sport fishing. Arrivals from around the world—from American adventurers such as Ernest Hemingway to the rich British colonialists—flocked to the area for fishing, hunting, and fun.

The bass consumed the lake's indigenous small-toothed carp, and the settlers introduced tilapia, which brought commercial fishing to Lake Naivasha, according to a 1982 *New York Times* story. When fishermen complained that the lake's dense underwater weeds caught their outboard engines, red Louisiana crayfish were thrown into the mix to eat the weeds and clear the lake for water traffic. The crayfish flourished, and another fishing industry was born. Soon fifteen tons of Naivasha crayfish were exported yearly to countries as far away as Sweden, and the lake was so rife with crayfish that its floor was a carpet of crustaceans. The lake could clearly grow anything! Even the small coypu, a nutria bred for its fur. A number of the three-foot rodents escaped from a fur farm and traveled downriver to Lake Naivasha, and they, too, flourished, devouring the lake's flowering lily pads in greater and greater quantities. When the lily pads began to disappear, so did Alan Root's beloved lily-trotter, the star of his first film, as well as what a leading marine biologist called "a horde of other water fowl and aquatic fauna."

Hoping to get rid of the coypu, some of the people around the lake decided to introduce pythons. At this stage, the landowners finally rebelled, according to the *Times* story, "saying the pythons would eat their children along with the rats. They took sticks and clubs and beat the pythons to death." After that, the coypu "mysteriously went on a suicide spree, destroying their own embryonic young. As a result the lily pads are returning. Nobody knows why."

Then came the salvinia, a weed used in home aquariums, which had been dumped into the lake by a landowner along with an aquarium full of fish. Like everything else, the salvinia grew prodigiously, to such a degree that by the mid-1960s a man could almost walk across Lake Naivasha on the thick weeds. Next came pesticides, but nothing seemed to faze the lake. In 1990, however, when Joan Root returned to her home, she found a new invader, tougher than all of the previous ones combined: the hothouse flower and the economic and ecological problems it carried in its wake.

Naivasha's flower industry was founded, essentially, at the Djinn Palace, the most famous house on the lake, an exotic stark-white Moorish fantasy of domes, turrets, and cupolas, the polar opposite of Joan Root's simple cottage. Known not only for its splendor but also for its turbulent history, it had been purchased by its current owners, June and

Hans Zwager, in 1967. It had been built in 1927 by Hollywood actor Cyril Ramsay-Hill. During the Happy Valley–era debauchery, the house's original owner and designer lost everything to the greatest Lothario Kenya has ever known: Lord Erroll, real name Josslyn Hay, the handsome rogue with an aristocratic lineage seemingly intent on bedding every woman (especially every rich and married one) who crossed his path. A man of physical perfection and virile potency, he was a conscienceless cad who stole first Ramsay-Hill's wife and then his beloved Djinn Palace. "You've got the bitch, now buy her the kennel," Ramsay-Hill cabled Lord Erroll after he had run off with his wife. Erroll was perpetually broke, but Ramsay-Hill's wife got the palace in her divorce settlement, and it went to Lord Erroll after she died from chronic heroin and alcohol abuse. In 1941 Lord Erroll was brutally murdered, believed to have been shot by the husband of Diana Broughton, with whom Erroll was engaged in a very public affair.

"The butler would come in with a card, I heard, and on it was the name of the lady with whom the gentleman—or lady—would spend the night," said the palace's current owner, June Zwager, a vivacious redhead, recounting rumors of the spouse-swapping ritual for which the house was famous in the 1920s. "I think they were quite naughty. Took years for us to live down the reputation. People called it a Playboy Club because it has no outside keys," she continued, meaning keys for the bedroom doors. "You must lock them from the *inside*. That was the way he built it. There was a lot of cocaine."

The story of how the Zwagers transformed this former den of iniquity into the home of the owners of Africa's top flower farm is quite remarkable. Born and raised in the remote jungle areas of India, June had come to Kenya when she was fourteen after her father, an officer in the Royal Artillery, was posted there.

In 1953 she met Hans, who had come to Nairobi to work for a Dutch bank. June's beauty and spirit stopped him in his tracks. "A bombshell with her hair on fire," Hans later wrote. "A redhead that ignited me, and no fire-engine in Christendom could have put out the blaze."

They married six weeks after they met. Hans quit the bank and became a manufacturer's representative. "He imported all sorts of things—you name it," June said. The list included toothbrushes, grease guns, patent medicines, and wall plugs. Very soon, he launched his own importing company, which he called Kleenway. One day Hans arrived at his office to find a man waiting to see him about a certain sprayer Hans imported. The man said he needed forty of them *immediately,* which led Hans to wonder, What is he filling these sprayers with? The answer was chemicals. Coffee was the chief crop of Kenya back then, and a coffee-berry disease was decimating the plantations. Soon Hans had exclusive rights to the chemical that could fight the disease: a fungicide called ortho difolatan, later identified as a carcinogen that caused "acute aquatic toxicity," according to the Pesticide Action Network.

Coffee estates covered large areas of Kenya, and thanks to Hans Zwager's ortho difolatan, the coffee-berry disease was soon nearly eradicated. Hans and June expanded their chemical line to include other high-efficiency substances—some of which would later be listed as potentially hazardous to humans in varying degrees by the National Institute for Occupational Safety and Health in the United States. Eventually, Hans and June represented Chevron, DuPont, and Bayer.

"By the mid-1960s, Kleenway Chemicals, Ltd., had also acquired coffee farms and was in the big league of Kenya businesses," wrote Charles Hayes in *Oserian,* a book about the Djinn Palace. The Zwagers became Nairobi's couple of the moment: Hans the chemical titan, June the consummate hostess. In 1967 a friend suggested that Hans and June join a group of businessmen interested in turning the legendary Djinn Palace into a casino. "We had a canal cruiser," June remembered, "so we came through the high grass, docked at some funny old jetty, and came up here." She looked out over the immaculate lawn, where two crested cranes strutted and screamed. "I just thought it was a broken-down old yellow strange place." Despite the debris, the house spoke to her. "I just remember walking through the courtyard, and I got this amazing feeling. Déjà vu."

Hans dropped the idea of investing in a casino, and they bought the house for themselves, along with its five thousand acres of land. Former owner Gilbert Colville had grazed cattle on it, and that was about all the volcanic soil was good for. It wouldn't grow anything "unless you put a lot on to improve it," one expert would later tell *The New York Times.* But that something happened to be the Zwagers' stock-in-trade: chemicals.

There was then very little agriculture on the shores of Lake Naivasha. As Hans Zwager wrote in *The Flowering Dutchman,* the story of his flower-farming success, "Round our lake, nothing much was happening agriculturally. There was only one farmer on a small property who was growing vegetables using irrigation. That made us think, *Why not give that a try*?"

Hans sold off his coffee farms around Nairobi and began growing green peppers and other vegetables in Naivasha. "Then some people from Holland paid us a visit," Hans remembered, and the man said the words that would mean everything for the future: "Why don't you grow flowers?"

The man even gave Hans seeds for boric statice, a purple-and-white spray. The statice grew well, and Hans boxed and shipped some blooms off to Holland, from which flowers are sold and shipped around the world. "It was winter in Europe, and the demand was high, so we received what I considered to be reasonable prices," Hans wrote. From statice they branched out to "spray carnations, delphiniums, euphorbia, molecellas, alstromerias, and then, only very slowly, we began to grow roses."

Once they started, roses didn't just grow in Naivasha, they exploded. "In the early days it was said that all you had to do is throw a sheet of plastic over a tree and flowers would grow under it," said one local flower farmer. The lake was the ideal location, for the same reason it was the ideal place for wildlife and naturalists. Thanks to its position on the equator, growers enjoyed twelve months of constant high-intensity sunshine. Plus, since the lake sits at six thousand feet above sea level, it gets cold at night, which gives the flowers' growth a rest. Naivasha even provided geothermal energy from the nearby dormant volcanoes to heat the greenhouses to a constant temperature. It was, in a word, perfect.

Zwager's timing couldn't have been better, since around this same time, the world had developed an insatiable need for flowers. Flowers had been a prized possession of the rich and royal since time immemorial, but by the twentieth century, new technology and airline transportation had created an unimagined market for flowers on a global scale. Suddenly, the fragile blooms could be shipped from anywhere in the world, and they would arrive still fresh; they would last longer and look fuller. "Flowers today may be better traveled than the people who buy them," wrote Amy Stewart in her book *Flower Confidential.* "More people—field workers, supervisors, sales reps, brokers, truckers, auctioneers, wholesalers, buyers, bookkeepers, retailers—have talked about your flowers in more languages than you can probably say 'hello' in."

The rise of supermarket flowers proved even more of a boon for the farmers interested in growing their crop in Naivasha. Worldwide demand rocketed for quality flowers at the lowest possible price, which meant low overhead and cheap labor, which meant more crops from third-world countries.

The Zwagers were the first to cultivate flowers on Lake Naivasha, but by the early 1990s Kenya's largest flower producer was Sulmac, which had a farm on Lake Naivasha as well and claimed in media accounts to be "the largest carnation farm in the world." A stampede of industrial and independent flower growers soon rushed into Naivasha, including Sher Agencies, a Dutch firm whose Naivasha farm was soon producing millions of flowers a year, making it the world's largest flower farm; Homegrown, a massive facility sitting on thousands of acres of land; Flamingo, which would boast about "400,000 stems of perfect roses picked each day . . . in greenhouses that cover over 200 football pitches." With the flower farms came the hothouses to control temperature—endless rows of white plastic-covered units—until whole sections of Naivasha's lakeshore were blanketed with them, to the point where they blocked wildlife patterns, disrupting the ecological balance of the lake and the land around it.

Except, June Zwager emphasized, for the Zwager family, who "demoted" a parcel of their land once used to grow carnations and turned it into what became the massive Oserian Wildlife Sanctuary, to allow the free passage of wildlife—45 different mammals, including two rare imported white rhino, and 300 species of birds—from Hell's Gate National Park almost to the lake. To safeguard the animals from poachers, the preserve is protected by twenty-five rangers on twenty-four-hour lookout. She said they could have covered every inch of open land with hothouses, but they didn't. "Uh-uh. Not the Zwager family," June Zwager said of the preserve. "Because this is not for my glory today, but it's part of something of leaving, as Joan did leave it in her way. Which is why she was a good friend of ours. Because she knew what we also believed. It's not all money, money, money."

Yet, June Zwager admitted, other flower farms did not follow the Zwager family's—and Joan Root's—lead.

By the time Joan took up life as a single woman in Naivasha in the early 1990s, Kenya was ranked sixth in global flower production. Flowers were now doing for Kenya what coffee had done in its colonial era. And with coffee prices stagnating, coffee companies got special permission from the government to pull up coffee plants and replace them with flowers. The government, of course, was for whatever made money. Only eight years after flower production started in Naivasha, flowers became Kenya's fastest-growing industry. In 1990 alone, Kenyan farms had exported over 400 million flowers, and that number was steadily going up at an annual rate of 35 percent.

Both growers and business visitors to the area were astonished and proud. "I had a visit through a friend of mine from the brother of the South African president Thabo Mbeki," said Count Peter Szapary, a young Austrian-born flower-farm owner and the head of a consortium of local flower growers called the Lake Naivasha Growers Group. "He's an economist, and we went to see one of the farms down the road, and he said there is no other region started by a few individuals without money from the World Bank, without money from donors or government or soft loans, based on pure business principles only, that has established a market share in a world market like Naivasha has. This is absolutely unique. So from a commercial private-sector point of view, the flower horticultural industry in Naivasha is probably the biggest success story of Africa."

Between the late 1970s, right before Hans Zwager planted his first flowers, and 1998, Kenya's annual flower exports grew nearly tenfold, according to one study: from 3,265 metric tons to 30,221 metric tons. By 2005 the Kenyan flower industry would employ 100,000 people directly and 2 million more indirectly. It would rise in annual export values from 1 billion Kenyan shillings ($15 million) to 22.8 billion Kenyan shillings ($340 million). Between 60 and 70 percent of Kenya's flowers were coming from Lake Naivasha.

The flower business dominated the community and the landscape, turning a once dry, dusty railroad and lakeside town into a center of commerce, a money machine of massive proportions. It wasn't just flowers but what the flower farms brought—Kenya's most abundant natural resource, cheap labor. In this impoverished country, where the annual per capita income is about $880—one of the lowest in sub-Saharan Africa—the scant hope of work was enough to lure workers to the area in droves.

Here was a migration as wild and savage as the wildebeest migration Joan and Alan had filmed. This time it was massive numbers of people, hundreds of thousands of hungry, desperate, out-of-work men and women. It was an African *Grapes of Wrath,* an exodus of poverty-driven refugees from across Africa, headed to Naivasha. Many of the penniless multitudes imagined that life on a flower farm was easy, just one long Valentine's Day. True, that is the big annual event in Naivasha, when the farms add labor and produce more flowers. The problem is that afterward they scale back radically until February 14 rolls around again. All too soon the new arrivals would discover just how false their hopes had been.

"The new immigrants are mainly from Western Kenya, spit out by the 'push factor' of collapsing local economies—too much competition in the Lake Victoria fishing industry, flooding in Nyando and Budalangi, AIDS. It's a long list," wrote the prominent Kenyan writer and journalist Parselelo Kantai in the October–December 1990 issue of the Kenyan ecology magazine *Iko.* They expected to find work, but most—

especially men—were unlucky. By the mid- to late 1990s, the new immigrants had pushed the population of Naivasha to 350,000—from what had long been 30,000 at the most—only to discover that 65 percent of the workers were women. Handling flowers was a delicate matter, the flower farmers were quoted as saying, adding in a whisper, "Women work harder, have better output."

Parselelo Kantai described the situation in the workers' slums in a 2004 issue of *Iko* magazine:

> At dawn, the lucky ones queue in front of their company buses at the roadside in Karagita and the two other slum villages located a few kilometers from the farms. During the day, new immigrants and old workers recently recovered from farm injuries and sicknesses, planned and unplanned pregnancies, form long, patient lines at the farm gates. Foremen march up and down the line, picking and choosing temps with life-and-death authority. Generally, men are shunned: they don't have the dexterity the industry requires, the patience for long hours at minimum wage. Besides, in the event of unrest, they will always be more difficult to manage than the women, to placate, to threaten into silence.

Wearing uniforms and headdresses, women served on precise and efficient assembly lines inside the white hothouses along the lake. Here, according to media reports, millions of roses—each an exact copy of the next—grew for a preprogrammed length of time, after which they were individually graded for quality. They were cut just before opening to ensure that the flower was at its fullest possible bloom when it reached the buyer. To prevent premature blooms, the laborers hand-wrapped each rose with mesh that prevented the bloom from expanding; then the flowers were exposed to myriad chemical preservatives to ensure maximum freshness. Naivasha flowers provided "exceptional value for money," said one flower grower. "What the flower growers want is more households buying flowers two times a month."

While the laborers turned their attention to the next rows of perpetually growing hothouse-covered fields, the roses began their trip to the markets, where they bloomed as if on command, not bearing a trace of the world from which they came.

In Naivasha, the misery and destruction were impossible to ignore. Even Dodo Cunningham-Reid, a rich European landowner whose own glorious Hippo Point Lodge on the lake hosted visiting Hollywood A-listers, was exasperated by the state of Naivasha and voluble in her criticism: "Naivasha is the perfect microcosm for the larger picture of Kenya: lawlessness, poverty, collapsing infrastructure, corruption—abuse on all levels. The sad story of a displaced society where money talks. If the consumer in Europe knew the misery caused by one rose, they wouldn't buy it."

The laborers have been described as the de facto detritus in the flower farms' wake, living out what the book *Flower Confidential* called the "blood-and-roses story": low pay, mass exploitation, overexposure to chemicals. In 2001 the Kenya Human Rights Commission issued a damning report listing hundreds of abuses. Paid only "starvation wages," the women were forced to meet unreasonable work quotas that pushed them into unpaid overtime. Many companies denied most workers access to unions. Sexual harassment was reportedly common, especially because it's not considered an offense in Kenya. Medical care and expenses—outside of the few Naivasha flower farms with on-site medical facilities—were nonexistent. One media source conservatively estimated that at least two flower workers die from illnesses linked to chemical poisoning each year; another five go down to conditions related to unsafe exposure to pesticides. Furthermore, the housing provided by some flower farms was miserable. The commission quoted workers as saying these accommodations were grossly overcrowded and unhygienic. Some fifty thousand people lived in squalor, with no electricity or sewage facilities, four or more to a room, and from eighteen to twenty "rooms" to a "plot." Frequently, a torn sheet was all that divided family from family, bachelors from married couples, gangsters from kids, according to the report.

The massive influx of people and the unhygienic conditions inevitably led to an increasingly dangerous situation, not just for the migrants but for the lake itself. Denying their own role in polluting or draining the lake, the flower farmers had plenty of problems of their own, including frustration over the government's failure to create sewage systems to dispose of human waste properly. In other words, they contended that the lake was polluted not by flower-farm chemicals and runoff but by human feces.

Without running water or sewage facilities for the burgeoning population, the human waste from Karagita and the surrounding shanties and *shambas* (small itinerant farms) went into "long drops," big holes in the ground. Long drops dotted the landscape, and their contents eventually found their way into the waterways of the basin, which all ran into one central drain, Lake Naivasha.

"The main threat, obviously talked about a lot, is the flower farms poisoning the lake, releasing the agrichemicals used to protect the flowers from pests and disease—which supposedly go straight back into the lake—and destroying the ecosystem of the lake," admitted flower-farm owner Count Peter Szapary. Yet he said independent studies made by scientists in a Swiss laboratory—who took water samples from six or eight different areas in the lake as well as samples from the fish in the lake—showed, surprisingly, that not one agrichemical product in Kenya could be found in the lake water or in the fish. "What they did find was a high concentration of nitrate," the count said, adding, "a chief property in human waste."

Even if the lake was not sullied by the chemicals that the flower farms expelled—and others disputed the claim that it wasn't—it was surely poisoned by the flood of people the flower farms attracted to the area. Nor was pollution the only threat to the lake. When the migrant men discovered there was little chance of a steady job at the farms, they began doing what they knew best: fishing. Lake Naivasha was still full of fish and overrun with game, and the men rushed to it. Soon poaching—the unlicensed, illegal snaring of fish and game—was occurring on such a grand scale that it practically constituted an industry.

Who would take a stand? Not the Kenya Fisheries Department, locally housed in a Quonset hut, which rarely even had gas for its vehicles, much less resources or incentive to fight the lake's frequently armed and dangerous bands of poachers. "Kenya is full of corruption at all levels, so you don't know if officials in the Fisheries Department were part of the poaching or just turning a blind eye," said one observer. And certainly not the government, justifiably proud of the prosperous flower industry, one of the greatest economic booms since Kenya's independence in 1963. A 1991 *New York Times* article summed up the government's devotion to its new favorite crop: "As worldwide coffee prices remain at depressing lows, Brooke Bond, the largest coffee company in Kenya . . . has received special permission from the Government to pull up coffee plants, traditionally considered almost sacred, and replace them with roses."

So as the old industry of Kenya—coffee—was literally pulled up at the roots to make way for the new—flowers—Joan Root, daughter of a coffee farmer, would be perilously caught in the middle, between past and future, coffee and flowers, the wondrous, game-filled land juxtaposed with the harsh realities of cold and unbridled commerce.

The whole situation went against everything Joan Root stood for: In a world of profits, she cared more for others than herself; in a world of mass-market beauty, she remained a genuine product of the environment from which she came. She was furious at what was happening to the land, to the workers, to the lake, but she couldn't bring herself to blame the impoverished workers, and it wasn't long before she began to stand up against the industry. "I think that Joan Root would have personally preferred no horticulture or floriculture around the lake at all," said Naivasha flower-industry business consultant Rod Jones. "But she understood there was an economic benefit from it, which she tolerated in the early years. Joan was outspoken about the impact the flower growers were having on the lake. I heard Joan have a bit of a rant every now and then and claim that pesticides and nutrients from the fertilizer were running into the lake, affecting the makeup of the lake, its toxicity sending it into a downward spiral."

But complaining was like blaming the wind for the dust. Who could fault a flower company for maximizing profits? Or for bringing desperately needed employment to a region where there had previously been little work? Or for growing a rich business where nothing but nature and wildlife had previously held sway? It was just one more only-in-Africa situation, a scenario as insane as a wife leasing her husband to a terminally ill woman until she died. And in the final irony, her precious homeland was now being destroyed by, of all things, roses: the international symbol of love.

Chapter Eight

One of Joan's first acts as a single woman had been to finally get her pilot's license so she could fly *Oscar Charlie,* the beloved single-engine Cessna she received in the divorce. She would take off from her grass runway and fly above it all over the lake, so serene up there, high above the calamities down below.

Over this land of contrasts she would fly—the great and legendary estates juxtaposed with the tin roofs of the teeming slum, the endless stretches of open land surrounding the tight, crowded white hothouses of the flower farms. She would fly toward the mountains, amid the dormant volcanoes dotted with geysers emitting jets of white-hot steam, flying so high she could almost forget the problems that marked her new life on the ground below. Sometimes she would turn from the controls expecting to find Alan, who was so much at home up here, to be sitting beside her, as he so often had, filming the vanishing world. But she was out of his orbit now, at least while Jennie was alive, and for the moment grateful to be so. "I will finally have the time to find my own feet," she wrote to her friend Anthony Smith. "I don't need him to fire on all cylinders. . . . I've *changed.*"

She was in her mid-fifties, her blond hair long gone gray, but she had had the good fortune to have spent her life in the most beautiful place on earth. Like a wildflower, she had always bloomed where she'd been planted, whether it was the harsh lion habitat of Tsavo, a burned-out hut in the middle of gorilla country, or on the banks of a crocodile-infested river in the Congo. Now, with everything ripped away from her, she would live again, bloom again, be Joan again. She would land her plane in Naivasha, and here, with a lifetime of bush lore and learning behind her, she would begin again.

And with the cause she would embrace—the struggle to save her beloved lake—she would finally succeed in breaking free of the role she had played so long for Alan. She would now become a respected, powerful, independent woman, determined not only to chronicle but also to preserve the continent and the animals she loved. She was appalled by what was happening on Lake Naivasha, that something akin to the ecological horror she had witnessed in Central Africa and Tsavo could soon be occurring right in her own backyard.

Joan sat on her wide veranda, noticing the myriad ways in which things were going wrong, studying the enormous blisters of white hothouse sheeting that cloaked her lakeshore. In those hothouses, grow lights were blazing day and night, disrupting the life cycle of insects, which she knew to be the foundation of the ecosystem of Naivasha. The hothouses were also limiting the nocturnal feedings of hippos and other animals on land, while sucking up water for irrigation and, she suspected, spitting back fertilizer and pesticides. Human waste was contaminating the lake, she knew, though she sympathized with the poor in the slums. She understood that the men, emasculated by being denied employment on the flower farms, were left with no other option than to become poachers.

All the poachers needed was a cheap net in order to launch a thriving little business. They typically worked in teams of three, specializing in a method of fishing called *korosho:* The men would cast four circular nets of fine mesh into the water, then pull them up in such a way that they caught everything in their path. Soon the poachers started employing even smaller-meshed nets, snaring not only the smallest fish but also the fish eggs. This alarmed Joan, who saw that the poachers were disrupting the natural growing cycles of marine life and depleting the very source of their existence.

Feeling energized by her victory over the Kenyan Cowboy who tried to steal her land, she wrote in her notebook:

> *Responsibility is a position. An attitude towards events. You can either take responsibility or you can feel victimized by the world. Your choice of whether to play the victim or take responsibility will determine whose power grows—yours or someone else's. If you take the position of victim, you lose power. If you choose responsibility, you have power then, to do something about what's happening—to choose your next step. It's all about attitude.*

"Oh" now turned into "No!" No to the poaching. No to the degradation of the land she loved, now sheathed in miles of plastic hothouses, beyond which lay the slum of Karagita and Moi South Lake Road, choked with never-ending caravans of trucks belching soot and kicking up dust, ferrying flowers to the airport in Nairobi and, from there, to the world.

Joan's frustration soon turned to anger. She wasn't angry at the existence of the flower farms, exactly, but at what they had done to the lake. Flying over her home—marked by two tall eucalyptus trees on the shore—she could see clearly the ragged armies of poachers in the papyrus and deep inside the lake, barebacked, in patched swimming trunks, throwing their crude nets out to seine fish of all sizes. She could also make out poachers on the land, killing wildlife for meat, trapping whatever they could eat or sell. She didn't blame them. She knew they had been pushed into a world where they had to do whatever it took to survive. She knew that more than half of Kenya's population was under the age of eighteen. She knew that the average Kenyan child had never seen an elephant. She knew that living in slums and limited by their chance for an education, most of these men had no future other than the flower farms or illegally fishing the lake. She wanted to help them. But how?

In early 1994 she wrote in her diary, "Too many fishermen fishing and walking across. Lake down. So they are dragging nets on open side of papyrus." A few months later, she wrote, "So many Africans walking on my land to access road, as everything else closed off." The hothouses blocked travel between the lake and the main road, so Joan's property became the only open thoroughfare. The fishermen tramped through her land to access the lake, then fished from her shore. Almost overnight these lawless men had virtually taken over her precious riparian land, poaching fish, snaring animals, and lighting fires to cook what they caught.

Her suspicions about how dangerous all of this was for the lake would soon be validated.

She lived by herself, but she was rarely alone, not with a sizable revolving staff and a stream of constant visitors. Friends, both new and old, found a temporary home with Joan, whose doors were always open and whose time was given freely. Anthony Smith came to live in Joan's house to write a book about the Great Rift Valley. Their friendship had come a long way since the balloon trip with Alan on which she had blended into the background. Not only did Joan give Anthony a place to stay, she served as "my man in Kenya," he would later say, researching what he wanted to write about, planning his itineraries, getting the required contacts and permits, and even accompanying him on his research trips.

Filmmakers also came to her property. BBC wildlife filmmaker Richard Brock came often to dream up or work on projects, relying on Joan's intellect, advice, and hospitality. Family members also dropped by, including a young cousin who stayed for months. Joan wrote about all of these visitors in her diaries, but the one who appeared with most regularity was Dr. David M. Harper, a senior lecturer at the University of Leicester in England, who arrived, by chance, in Naivasha in the 1980s and, again by chance, commenced what would become a twenty-year study of the lake, eventually sponsored by the Earthwatch Institute, the global environmental charity.

When Harper first appeared in the area, Joan began attending every lecture he gave about the lake, which he presented to half-empty meeting rooms at local tourist lodges. She would always sit in a back row in her neat cotton clothing and matching headscarf, listening intently. But as Harper's research went on and his prognosis about the lake's future became darker, Joan pushed through her shyness and introduced herself. "There is *a lot* the flower industry could do to mitigate its impact on the lake and the environment," Harper remembered her telling him.

Harper thought that perhaps by studying the chemistry of the water in boreholes—deep holes dug in the earth through which the lake water rose—they could get a clue about what was happening to the lake water. Everyone on the lake got their water from boreholes, and Joan knew the location of every one of the literally hundreds of boreholes on the lake.

Harper climbed into her old Pajero and off they went. Not only did Joan take Harper to almost every borehole in the area, helping him analyze the water in each, she also introduced him to every owner of every borehole, becoming his emissary on the lake.

As his study of Lake Naivasha grew and intensified, Harper needed a place to measure the changes the lakeshore had experienced over the last hundred years. He needed a baseline, a piece of lakefront property that was the same as it had been a hundred years ago. There was only one place where the flower farms hadn't encroached too close to the lake or landowners hadn't destroyed the natural vegetation. There was one place that was still accessible to animals, said Harper: Joan Root's eighty-eight acres.

So Joan invited him to base his ongoing investigation on her land, and of course, he could stay in her house along with his team. She would gladly volunteer her services. What was good for the lake was good for Joan Root.

Around 1995, Harper gave Joan a prognosis she probably already suspected: If restraints weren't instituted, the lake would diminish and die in fifteen years. By 2006 Harper's verdict was that "The lake has about five years' life left in it in its present state if people don't do something to restore the damage." He knew that Joan saw the lake deteriorating on a daily basis, and she was particularly upset over the refusal of the authorities to prevent its deterioration.

Joan began to study the poachers on the lake—most of them between eighteen and twenty-one, Africans from a dozen tribes, reduced to scavenging. Some were castoffs from the flower farms. Others were on the lake by choice, since pay for a part-time male worker in the flower farms was 85 to 150 Kenyan shillings a day ($1.50 to $2.25) for eight hours' work, whereas a poacher could make twice that much in half the time. Plus, on the lake, you didn't have to endure tough bosses or chemicals or risk being fired. As a poacher, you could work six days a week in the water, beneath the sun.

The story of a young man named Simon was typical: Like his fellow poachers, Simon would fish in the shallows with a tattered net held together by pieces of papyrus stalks tied into the mesh. At thirty-three, he was a "half-caste" member of the Luo and Luhya tribes who lived with his wife and four children in one room in a clay hut in Karagita. "It's not an honorable profession," Simon said in precise British-inflected English, standing in the waist-deep water with the tail of a small fish protruding from his mouth. "I do it because there is no other way to make a living." He worked in the "spray department" of the Homegrown Flower Farm until he was "declared redundant." He had tried a lawful profession—shaving people in the slum for 20 shillings (a quarter) a pop—but couldn't earn enough to feed his family. "My friend told me, 'There is another way to make a living, and all you have to do is buy your own net.'" And just like that, Simon became a poacher, feeding his family with the fish he caught and supporting them with the ones he sold. He had been arrested for poaching four times, and he once spent three months in the Naivasha jail. "It's hell," he said.

Even if poaching was a shameful activity, it nevertheless seemed the only way out. How else could a man bring home food for the wife and children, pay the 800 shillings ($12.58) a month to the landlord for a single room in Karagita, and still have a little jingling "in the pocket"? In Naivasha, a man was judged by what was jingling in his pocket, especially if he needed to bribe a cop when he was caught poaching. If the pocket was empty, the poacher would be hauled down to the Naivasha jail, where fifty or more men and women had to sleep on the cement floor of a group cell. Once a poacher was released, he went straight back to the lake, hungrier and more desperate than ever, now no longer just a fisherman fighting for survival but a criminal with a police record.

Many of the fish poachers turned to game poaching, using circular wire snares they fashioned from the fences on the land. With a couple of mongrel dogs trained to drive game into the snares, they would catch everything from the hare-sized dik-dik to the grand impala, prized for its sweet meat. As the poachers multiplied and the competition for fish and game intensified, the men began carrying weapons—staves (pickax handles) and pangas (one-edged machetes)—to protect themselves from rival poachers. Desperation had created desperadoes who were turning Naivasha and Joan Root's eighty-eight acres of placid lake property into a battleground.

Every morning Joan and her household staff would go on "poacher patrols," not to confront poachers but to release animals caught in the growing number of snares. She was determined that her property would always be a haven where animals had clear passage to the water. "Sometimes I feel I am living on a different planet," she wrote. Her diary chronicled her escalating call to action. "Feeling motivated!" she wrote in early 1995. She wrote of her increasing frustration, intensified by the ineptitude of the police and government agencies in coming up with any solution to what had become an impossible problem. "Long talk with [a neighbor] about the depressing situation here at Naivasha."

Things only got worse, and Joan looked in vain for anyone to come to her rescue. The landowners provided no solutions. Many members of the Lake Naivasha Riparian Association owned flower farms or leased their land to farmers. "There are some members who would probably admit to being primarily concerned with the value of their land and the amount of fresh water available for their economic activities," Lord Enniskillen, chairman of the association, told the magazine *Iko*.

Considering the roaming bands of poachers and rising numbers of criminals, nobody wanted to stand out in increasingly lawless Naivasha.

Indeed, standing out or speaking up was considered a suicidal gesture. Yet it was not in Joan's nature to give up. She drove to her wise friend Ian Parker's little house on the big piece of land in a lush Nairobi suburb where the wildlife expert lived with his wife, Chris. In their living room, beneath the picture that Ian had taken twenty years before of Joan and Alan's hot-air balloon flight over the summit of snowcapped Kilimanjaro, Joan went on a rare rant. She told Ian of the endless poachers wreaking havoc, coupled with the endless Riparian Association meetings where landowners droned on about the compounding problems but never took any action. "It's all talk, talk, talk!" she said. "But nothing ever gets done."

Ian Parker knew Lake Naivasha extremely well. He and his wife had lived in and maintained Joan and Alan's house while they were on safari. He felt he, too, had a stake in the lake's survival.

"You get nowhere by constantly shouting no!" he told Joan. She knew what he meant: Conservation, in most cases, was confined to attempts to stop people from doing something, which was why, especially in hungry, impoverished, complicated Africa, those attempts failed.

"If you want to stop them from doing something wrong, propose something right," Parker said. "If they're going to fish, encourage them to do it legitimately."

It made sense. After all, if she could rehabilitate a skunk, teach a porcupine to shake its quills, and house-train a hippo, why couldn't she reform a poacher and get him to follow the rules? What if she could turn him—and so many like him—into a licensed fisherman governed by the laws of the lake? Then the fish, the wildlife, and the whole ecological balance, would be in much less danger.

Back on the lake, with fish poaching at an apex, with hundreds of human silhouettes casting nets and wreaking havoc, Joan finally took a bold action that would have monumental repercussions. She walked out and talked directly with some of the poachers, asking if there was anything she could do to correct the situation. Their first response was to try to sell her irrigation pipes stolen from her own lakefront property.

Even though the pipes and the poles were the property of the landowners who had installed them, the poachers sawed off sections of pipe and pulled up poles and attempted to sell them back to their rightful owners. They hadn't found any takers until Joan came along. Before that, the poachers had always been met with a scowl or a shotgun.

But Joan didn't care. She knew it was a scam, but to start a dialogue she bought her own pirated equipment back from them. "Paid 1,500 Kenyan shillings [$22.50] for pipe and 1,050 [$15.75] for 51 cedar poles," she wrote in her diary on June 15, 1994. In return, she began talking to the young men about the importance of responsible fishing as opposed to poaching. They explained to her that they had no choice. To become a legal, licensed fisherman required capital; you had to buy a boat, a license, and regulation-size nets, none of which a poacher could afford. The conversation left Joan feeling even more frustrated.

Soon after that, a legal Kenyan fisherman landed on her property; his insight and advice would prove helpful. His name was David Kilo, and his Lake Naivasha Anti-Poaching and Conservation Lobby was actively trying to put an end to poaching on the lake, but with very little success. Kilo met Joan Root when his outboard engine happened to break down right in front of her house. While illegal fishermen had no problem trespassing on Joan's land—or anyone else's, for that matter—Kilo and his two fellow fishermen felt they needed permission. He could see the white woman in the headscarf feeding birds on her veranda, so he whistled and called out to her: "Memsaab! We need help!"

She walked close to the lakeshore as Kilo waded up through the papyrus and asked them who they were.

"We are licensed fishermen," said Kilo, explaining about the problem with the boat and requesting permission to walk to the road through her acreage.

Joan said sure.

The fishermen docked their boat and crossed Joan's yard with their day's catch. The next morning, before they returned to repair their engine, they called the cell number Joan had given them to alert her of their coming. Eager to show her support for legal fishing, Joan struck a deal within hours to buy fish regularly from Kilo for a pelican and a marabou stork she was rehabilitating. In subsequent meetings, she began to talk to him about what she could do to stop the rampant increase of poaching.

She told him about her idea of rehabilitating poachers. "What would this require?" she asked Kilo. First, he said, she would need a boat built by a *fundi* (a licensed builder of fishing vessels), along with ten nets of specified size, as authorized by the Fisheries Department. "Once you have a boat, you are guaranteed to get a license," Kilo told her, adding that the meager fee was 350 Kenyan shillings ($5.24) a year. He complimented Joan on her idea: "It's a great idea, and you certainly won't run into any obstacles," he said.

All she needed now was a poacher.

In February 1997, however, her focus was temporarily distracted from the lake. The last link to her past, her ninety-year-old father, Edmund Thorpe, was dying of pneumonia in a hospital in Amarillo, Texas. Since her mother's death eight years before, Joan had visited her father often and communicated with him regularly, usually about their shared passion for nature and wildlife.

Immediately upon receiving news of her father's hospitalization, Joan flew to America to be by his side, finding him in a semiconscious state. "Joan," he said from the ethers of his hospital bed. "Don't go." The next day he didn't recognize her. The day after that he was dead. The last influential man in Joan Root's life had left her, but a new, even more controversial one was on the horizon.

Back in Naivasha, she always awoke each morning before dawn. No lingering in bed for a Kenya girl, at least not Joan Root, who was usually in bed by seven, to watch a movie, and lights-out by nine or ten. In her Spartan bedroom, she would walk to her little closet, where every item of clothing was neatly stacked or hung according to color and item, and slip on what had become her uniform: the rubber-soled sneakers called "tackys"; cotton shorts, slacks, or skirt; and a short-sleeved shirt of the same color, all topped by a colorful large bandanna worn in the African style, more and more often red, "which made her instantly recognizable," an AIDS counselor at a neighboring flower farm would tell a newspaper reporter. "Usually it is us black Africans that wear scarves like that."

Unlocking herself from her bedroom, which already had bars on the windows, Joan would head immediately to feed the animals; the animals always came first. They were everything to her now, her constant companions and the source of comfort she depended on most. Some felt that Joan's intense allegiance to her land and its animals was because it was all she had left of Alan. "That house kept something of Alan for her," one friend said. "She didn't change *anything*. I think she wanted to but couldn't bear to."

She also obviously loved the land for what it gave her: wildlife, beauty, and the challenge of saving it against incredible odds. "At Naivasha, there is always plenty to keep me occupied," Joan wrote to friends in late 1996. The letter was to inform them of what she considered a monumental change that she had stubbornly resisted for a long time: fencing in her land. By then the lake had been designated a Ramsar site. (The international treaty for the conservation and sustainable utilization of wetlands had been signed in Ramsar, Iran, in 1971.) Every landowner but Joan had already erected fences, as well as shut down the corridors that allowed access to the lake by both wildlife and the public. The lake's original sixteen corridors had been reduced to one, and that one was so narrow and infested with hippos that few people dared to cross it. Instead, the public found easy access through Joan's eighty-eight acres.

"I had become the last unfenced property along South Lake Road, which meant a lack of security," she wrote. "My land was the recipient of human trespassers and Maasai cattle, hyenas and packs of dogs hunting my wildlife. So in mid-1996, I put up a 7-foot-high game fence along the road and the side boundaries in order to better protect my sanctuary. Leopards and pythons still roam along the lake edge, which give a tolerable level of protection."

The fence served a dual purpose: It kept predators—both human and animal—out, and it kept wildlife in. In times of drought, animals made their way from the nearby Kedong Ranch onto Joan's fenced compound, "where they felt safe," she wrote. "As well as the usual waterbuck, gazelle and dik dik, there were zebra, giraffe, eland and impala all around the house. When the rains came in April/May they all returned to the ranch, which gave my land time to recover from so many animals. The only tame animals I keep now are Chekky, the porcupine, who is 20 years old this year, a red-flanked duiker from the Sudan, and three crowned cranes."

Yet the fence couldn't block the encroachment of the increasingly desperate human world that lay just beyond it.

Joan's poacher patrol on the morning of August 16, 1997, brought fresh outrage. *Dogs.* Not domesticated dogs but mongrel poaching dogs, which, trained to herd game into snares or simply kill it, are the poacher's most effective weapon—one the animal conservationists despise. There were three dogs that morning, encircling and terrorizing a waterbuck. Since one woman and two Kikuyu are not reasonable odds in a dogfight, even if that woman is Joan Root, she braced herself for the worst as the dogs moved in on their prey.

Suddenly, there was a flurry of motion from the lakeshore. Fish poachers. Three of them. Wet and dirty, they had bolted through the papyrus, though, as it turned out, not to work the dogs or to ensnare the waterbuck. Amazingly, they were leading not an attack but a rescue mission. Why they did this, Joan would never truly know. The obvious leader of the group was an athletically built Kikuyu dressed in old wet swim trunks and a ratty T-shirt, but blessed with the speed, agility, and natural beauty of the wild. He rushed the snarling dogs and called a friend who came with a gun and shot one of them; the others retreated and dispersed, leaving behind the trembling waterbuck and an extremely impressed Joan Root.

"Hello," said the poacher who had saved the waterbuck. His name, he said, was David Chege.

By the time the next morning rolled around, Geoffrey, Joan's gardener, was knocking on David Chege's door in Karagita. "Mama Joan wants to see you," he said. Chege headed over to Joan's acreage and immediately began giving her what she treasured: information. Did she want to know where the mongrel dogs lived, meet their owner, and ensure that the dogs never came on her land again? Chege could arrange that and did. Did she want to know who had stolen her equipment that had gone missing over the years? Again, Chege could arrange that and did. Did she want to know *everything* about the lake and its poachers, the armies of men who overfished the water and slaughtered game on the land? David Chege could help.

Chege tracked down the thieves who had recently stolen her pump switch and starter. He led police to them, and they caught the thieves red-handed and returned the stolen goods to Joan. He knew who had cut the wires of her fences, who was crossing her land at night to poach fish from her lakefront, who was burning her papyrus and ensnaring her precious animals.

The next question was: Who was this whirling dervish who knew everyone and everything in the corners and eddies of the lake, where few *mzungu* dared to go? He was part of the sorry exodus that had poured into Naivasha, a resident of Karagita with a wife and two children. Originally from Molo, sixty miles away, Chege had seven brothers and a sister. Their father had run off, leaving their mother to work on the flower farms and the kids to scramble. A member of the majority Kikuyu tribe, Chege had remarkable intelligence, financial cunning, and good looks. He had been poaching fish since his teens and, it was widely agreed, had developed into the best, toughest, most determined, and wiliest poacher on Lake Naivasha. Usually clad in wet and weathered swimsuits, Chege and colleagues worked their nets in the most ecologically destructive *korosho* way, and each evening they would divide up their bounty and sell it in the nearby market or in the slum, earning just enough to buy food and perhaps a dram of whiskey.

Chege was in his twenties when his impoverished life as a poacher collided with Joan Root's post-Alan existence. Within a month of meet-

ing her, Chege became Joan's constant stream of information, her strength, and her protection.

The socioeconomic world of the poachers that David Chege began showing Joan Root was as strange and fascinating as the hidden corridors of a termite mound, only this world was literally playing out in Joan's backyard. It was a complex universe that she knew very little about and had no entry into, in spite of having lived on this lake for almost forty years. After giving her information about the men who owned the mongrel dogs, Chege expanded his intelligence. "Chege phoned from Karagita. . . . Chege brought me info. . . . Chege wants names of guys who stole my wheels. . . . Chege came and keen to work with CID [Criminal Intelligence Department of the Naivasha police]."

David Chege didn't merely talk; he acted and accomplished, and in this way, he gained Joan Root's respect. So she began following David Chege, listening to David Chege, allowing her faith in David Chege to grow. How could she or any devoted naturalist not? He was not only the ultimate guide to the ultimate hidden world; he was also the key to helping her save it.

In turn, Joan Root introduced David Chege to an equally fascinating world. He knew who she was, of course. Most of the children of Karagita did. They had watched *Two in the Bush* and the other films of the famous wildlife adventuress and her husband at the Longonot Primary School in the slum. But the world she was now allowing him access to was beyond even the marvels of *Two in the Bush.* It was a seemingly unlimited world of money and the Kenyan's most prized possession, land. Though it existed just across the road from his own, he had never even begun to imagine this land of plenty, and now he was inside of it. Within days of meeting him, Joan Root bought Chege a new mattress for his home in the slum and found him a temporary job with one of the landowners on the lake.

Then Joan made Chege an astounding proposition: She was not only going to pay him for his information, she was going to teach him how to legally fish and *sponsor* his fishing with her own shillings. Within a year, she had gotten him and his colleagues everything they needed. "3/10/99 Went to Fisheries—Got licenses for boat, me, Chege,

Isaac, and Joseph," she wrote in her diary, including his two fellow poachers in her rehabilitation plan.

She also bought them the ten required legal-size fishing nets. Instead of continuing with the destructive *korosho* method, they could now cast their regulation nets in the proper way, ensnaring only fish of legal size. Joan began patiently teaching David Chege and his team the basics of legal fishing: the legal size and quantities of nets allowed, with mesh that would avoid trapping small fish and their eggs; the critical importance of not fishing the ecosensitive lagoons, bays, and papyrus belts that served as spawning grounds for fish; the times that fishing was allowed, the maximum bag counts, and other regulations specified by the Kenya Fisheries Act. Joan also tried to make them understand that following these practices and policies would create a sustainable lake and, according to the Fisheries Department, "provide employment for many of the jobless youths in Naivasha."

She taught them not only how to fish but how to sell the fish they caught. In exchange for everything she had done for them, all they had to do was keep the poachers away from her land. And so a new force was unleashed on Naivasha—Boat #8, a legal fishing vessel, sponsored by a *mzungu*. She had visited the office of the Kenya Wildlife Services (KWS) "to find out how I can have a lakeside guard like Chege that can collaborate with KWS," she wrote, and when the KWS officers said they thought it was a good idea, she sent Chege and his team into the lake with her boat, her equipment, her shillings, and her blessings, to protect and defend her lakefront from the scourge that had surrounded it.

Joan Root wasn't a crusader, her friends insisted, just one woman fighting to protect what she so desperately loved: her own land and, with it, the land in general. Yet one gets a sense that Joan was looking at a larger picture: the mission of her lifetime, bigger and bolder than any film. If she could rehabilitate David Chege, the most notorious poacher on Lake Naivasha, well then, why couldn't she rehabilitate every poacher on the lake? If she could do that, she could save a generation of young Kenyans from lives of crime while simultaneously saving the lake she loved. By protecting the environment she controlled, she might be able to save the environment at large. If she succeeded, all would benefit, black and white, and maybe others would follow their example.

Of all the thousands of destitute poachers Joan could have chosen to rehabilitate, Chege was both the best and the worst candidate. He was the best because he was, as one landowner put it, "a rough diamond"—the consummate poacher, as quick with his wits as he was on his feet. He was the worst, according to many, because he was the ultimate opportunist looking for an easy mark, which many, including the police, say he found in Joan Root.

For the white community of Nairobi and Naivasha, as well as many of the Africans there, Chege had come to personify all the ills of the area. People insisted that not only was he a poacher, but also a conniver, a thief, and more. "He is a survivor," one longtime Naivasha local explained. "He can fit into any situation. You take him up, he can fit there. You drop him down, he can fit there. He is a Kikuyu, a sweet-talker. When someone is a sweet-talker, you cannot know what is inside of them. You don't know his real motives. His first motive, however, is to benefit himself."

"Chege knew all the tricks," said Joan's neighbor Sarah Higgins. He knew when, where, and how the poachers worked. He knew how to snag the nets they hid just below the water's surface, and he knew how to get in the first punch. Soon poachers were on the run, their nets confiscated, their hideouts blown. But despite what Joan assumed were Chege's best efforts, the poaching continued.

Fresh waves of poachers invaded Joan's lakefront through the flower farms and wreaked havoc on the marine life and the landscape. "12 shots [fired] last night. . . . I was hopping mad. . . . Papyrus tramplers, I chased them off. . . . Gave them a talking to. . . . Fish poachers are threatening. Felt exhausted about all this."

The number of poachers just kept growing. They not only killed her fish but also consumed her time. Without realizing it, she had been transformed from the levelheaded person who wanted to reason with the poachers to just another white landowner chasing them away.

Coupled with the problem of the poachers was increasing crime, and here, too, Joan Root took a stand.

"We used to have a security network, so if anybody got broken in to, we could put out an alert," said Annabelle Thom, Joan's tenant and close friend. "We had radios and code numbers."

One night a gang with guns raided a young couple down the road, and they put out an SOS on the security radio. "Joan and one other woman were the only ones who heard the call," Annabelle continued. "Joan jumped in her old cream-colored Pajero and drove up to the house to see how she could help. She was fearless."

The thugs had left by the time Joan arrived. When congratulated on her rescue attempt the next morning, Joan would say only, "Oh, it was nothing."

But on April 7, 1999, she recorded in her diary news of something even darker: "2 a.m. woken by Melissa's voice on radio calling for help. Phoned a few people and the police and drove down to Three Point Ostrich [farm]. Three dead in Duncan Adamson's house. One wounded and another who had hacked his way through kitchen ceiling and fallen outside."

The dead men were thieves who had broken into Adamson's farmhouse, though guards on duty were firing shots into the air. One thief, who had been holding a pickax over Duncan Adamson's head, was shot dead, and the other two were gunned down. "This will make us more aware of how to take security seriously," Joan wrote. However, it didn't stop her from fighting for the lake, and she fully trusted David Chege as her protector.

Chege played an important part in Joan's mission for the lake, but the young Kenyan fascinated Joan on a broader level as well. She became a part of his life, which meant being a part of his drama—his problems distracted her, in a sense, from her own, and they gave another dimension to the mission she was on. "Long talks with Chege," she wrote repeatedly in her diary. Chege was on Joan's property so much that he married Esther, a member of her staff ("I am but a mere housewife," Esther would later tell police in her defense). Esther was his second wife, polygamy being a badge of honor in a country where a man's status is often gauged by how many wives he has. Soon Chege and Esther had children of their own. While his first wife and children lived in the Karagita slum, Chege lived with Esther most of the time in Joan's more comfortable staff camp. Now Chege wasn't merely the leader of Joan's private security team but also a de facto member of her staff, living on her property. She was quickly entangled in his private life. "Last night, Chege caught [another man] in bed with his wife, and he is most upset." Several months later: "Esther told me Chege's wife came to see me and stayed until 4:30," Joan wrote. "Says he gets money from me under false pretenses."

To compound the drama, Joan received a phone call from Karagita that evening. "Chege missing, wife kidnapped child, unborn not his." Then Chege's mother came onto Joan's land to say that Chege's first wife had kidnapped their son from outside of church and was using the child as a bargaining tool against her husband. "She is pregnant and wants Chege to take her back," Joan wrote. "She ran away and took his furniture [six months prior]." The mother even knew the identity of the true father of the unborn child: a low-level politician in the slum. But she advised her son to take both the wife and baby and nip all of these problems in the bud. "I told him to take his mother's advice," Joan wrote.

And how could Chege not be endlessly fascinated by the equally wild scenarios Joan was telling him of Alan Root and their quarter century as the world's greatest wildlife filmmakers? Even more enthralling was her post-Alan life on Naivasha, Chege would later say, and how she desperately needed, missed, and longed for her former husband. "She would say that if her husband was there, she could not have problems on her farm," Chege said. She talked about how people harassed and tried to take advantage of her because she was a woman on her own, without a husband, standing up in a world of men. "She would say, 'If Alan was here, people could not play with me,'" Chege remembered. "Mostly, she spoke of her husband. Because so many people were harassing her because she didn't have a husband." If Alan had been there, Joan assured Chege, no one would have dared erect electrical poles on her property without her permission; no one would have dared cut down her cypress trees or encroached upon—and destroyed—her property. It became a litany. "If Alan was here, he was going to take care of her," Chege remembered. "She would say, heartbroken, 'If Alan was here.'"

But Alan wasn't there—only a dirt-poor Kikuyu poacher from the Karagita slum.

Chapter Nine

During this same period, in early 2000, Alan Root was at Jennie's side as she died. It had been eighteen years since they had piqued each other's interest at the wedding at Naivasha, fourteen years since her diagnosis of leukemia, ten years since Alan and Joan's divorce. "Don't you want to die in the Africa that you love?" Alan had asked Jennie in their home in Nairobi during the final stages of her cancer, but she had insisted that she wanted to go back home to London. By then Alan had postponed much of his filmmaking activity for her. "I've done my bit for posterity, if that doesn't sound too grand," he told a reporter. "I'm not burning to get on to the next job anymore, and a lot of that is being married to Jennie. I have found at last that there is something more important than work." So he flew with her to the London Clinic, where he stood by her through her last days, until the ordeal ended on January 11, 2000. "Sue Allan phoned, and also Ian Parker, to tell me Jennie died early this morning," Joan wrote.

"Jennie died." Such a succinct diary entry for this monumental event. If anyone had dared to wonder whether Joan had moved on from Alan, or even forgotten him, in her new life on the lake, the answer was revealed one afternoon a few days later. As she sat with David Chege on her veranda, going over the problems he was encountering in their project to stop poaching on the lakefront, the conversation was disrupted by the sound of a helicopter. Joan smiled. "*Bwana yangu sasa atarudi,*" she said to Chege, Swahili for "My husband is coming home!" She added, in English, "Because his second wife has just died." Sure enough, the helicopter came closer and closer until the sound of its rotors was so close that they thought they could hear it landing. Suddenly, the sound began to dissipate and then slowly, finally, disappeared, leaving Joan silent on the veranda with the poacher. After a moment she simply excused herself and walked into her house.

He hadn't come back. So where, then, was Alan? Was he ever coming back to her? In truth, things had grown even more complicated for Alan. He had stuck by Jennie's side through all those years until there was nothing left but her skin, bones, and constant excruciating pain; even his lightest touch was torture to her. This still-vital man who had spent his life in the wildest, most exciting places on earth was now surrounded by the stench of disease and death. No longer free to fly across the Serengeti or over Mount Kilimanjaro, he was confined to a succession of doctors' waiting rooms and cancer wards, intermittently hearing from mutual friends that Joan was still hoping that he would eventually return to her, even after eighteen years of separation. "In some awful sort of way, she was waiting for me," Alan remembered. "I did actually have an outburst once and said to her, 'You've got to make your own life!' "

In the last months before Jennie's death, he met a young woman named Fran Michelmore at a dinner hosted by Cynthia Moss, who had spent her life studying the elephants of Amboseli. Jennie was spending some of her last days in the thatched guest cottage of a friend on a beautiful stretch near what used to be the Great Kikuyu Forest (the very land where Karen Blixen had fought the fire that destroyed her coffee crop in *Out of Africa*). Fran was smart, beautiful, and vibrant, and she and Alan had a great deal to talk about: She had a zoological background and was a cartographer, biographer, artist, and violinist.

4/1/00. Adrian told me that Alan had told him he had a lady, Fran Michelmore, & he would bring her "out of the closet" soon. . . . I saw him with her at an art exhibition on 26 Nov., so he started chatting her up before Jennie died. I felt shattered with many confused emotions. . . . I went to see [friends] in duka *[a shop], & told them both. Drove back to Naivasha in a daze & tossed & turned all night, but on Sunday was adjusted. In a way a relief, because I know where I stand.*

Eight days later, Joan received more unexpected news: Alan had not simply fallen in love with another woman. That woman was expecting a child. "4/9/00. Long call with Adrian about Alan's & Fran's situation. Not so amusing for him as conceived before J died. . . ."

On a piece of notepaper, she wrote to Alan expressing her feelings, but she never sent the letter:

A., a great awkwardness about contacting you, and so I put it hastily on the back burner. But the months go by and this is getting ridiculous. You must realize that you and Fran having a baby is a great emotional thing for me, though I am extremely happy for you. I was especially touched by you naming your little boy Myles Nicholas. I guess the Myles is for North and Turner [Alan's early friend Myles North, a bird expert, helped inspire Alan's love of the lily-trotter; Myles Turner, another friend, had been the chief park warden of the Serengeti National Park], which is so wonderful. What say did Fran have in this?

Still, Joan sent along some gifts for the new baby, as painful as that must have been. Not long afterward, she received this letter from Alan:

Dearest Joan,

I guess—Nairobi being what it is—that you have heard that I am getting married next week. I find it hard to talk to you about it—or anything else for that matter. We always did find it hard to communicate, except when we were whispering to each other in the bush. . . . Anyway, I just wanted to let you know myself—even if I have left it very late.

I never really understood why our partnership went off the rails—or at least my half did. For so many years you were the wind beneath my wings and helped me to fly so high . . . and then I flew off—ungrateful sod—but I guess we'll never understand what makes us tick. I know I paid a heavy price for my move, but through all the pain I learned so much about life and myself. Now I only know that, although I am scared of dying while [Myles] is still young and needs me, I have never been as happy or fulfilled as I am now with little Myles.

Thank you so much for Old Myles' stool and the records. . . . It was a very loving gesture . . . and thank you for everything else. I know it's bloody late, but I can't move on without finally saying thank you for your love and support back then when we were so young, for all the fun we had, all the hard work, and the great things we achieved together. You will always have a special place in my heart. I'm sorry I seem so unable to show it.

I hope you are happy in your life. You are such a great lady. Please don't let this upset you.

Lots of love, Alan.

Did her faith in Alan, the only man she ever loved, finally fly away now that she must have seen he was never coming back to her? Did the blood rush to her head in embarrassment when she thought of the recent day when, walking with an old friend in England, she had asked, with Jennie's demise imminent, "Do you think I have a chance?" It was laughable now, humiliating, even. One thing is for sure: Eventually, she did cry. Annabelle Thom said Joan came running to her cottage one day, carrying the letter from Alan, and cried when she let her read it.

Then, as she always did, she became stronger, more resolute. She soon packed up everything that remained of Alan in her house in Naivasha and shipped it all off to the home he now shared with his new wife outside Nairobi.

Here are 5 boxes of your early books. . . . Also a few mementos, such as your finger [the one lost to the puff adder, preserved in

> formaldehyde], a picture you painted in New Guinea, and a wax mold of a Galápagos tortoise foot. We had planned to get it cast in bronze but were always so busy in the years following. . . . Have you room to take over the pile of 16 mm films that I still store in the big cupboard in your old editing room? There are many 1-hours and early half-hours from Australia and South America. . . . I'll type out a list.

Safeguarding the lake had given Joan a new purpose and a cause to fight for. She was producing and directing her own wildlife story, not a nature film for television or classrooms but a real-life drama that could make a vital difference in Africa. A chief character in this drama, the man she had empowered and entrusted to bring the changes the lake so desperately needed, was, of course, David Chege. "Madam Root had taken Chege as an adopted child," mused the fisherman David Kilo, "so you couldn't say anything bad against Chege that Madam Root would accept."

If she did see him as an adopted child, as David Kilo suggested, then it was up to her to protect, defend, and support him in whatever ways he needed toward their mutual goal of saving the lake and, in the process, saving David Chege himself. She needed to believe he was good, and indeed, Chege was a brilliant sweet-talker who could tell her what she wanted to hear. David Chege was not perfect, Joan knew from everything her staff and neighbors told her. But he was a natural-born leader and an extremely effective force. She and Lake Naivasha *needed* him. Everyone agreed that something had to be done *immediately* or the lake would soon be dead, "a desert," as she once told Chege, benefiting nobody. By this point the number of poachers had reached crisis level; they were hungrier and more desperate than ever. Some of them were also armed and dangerous.

By late 2000 the poaching had increased to such an extent that Lake Naivasha was running out of fish. Over the years, the number of legally registered boats had increased fourfold, and the poachers had become too numerous to count. Everyone agreed that if something wasn't done immediately, the fishery would collapse. Urgent meetings were called to bring government agencies together with the legal fishermen in an attempt to find a solution. Eventually, it was decided that the lake needed a rest so the fish stocks could rejuvenate. A six-month ban on fishing was established, to begin February 10, 2001.

The Lake Naivasha Riparian Association helped find some of the licensed fishermen jobs on the flower farms and paid an educational stipend for their children, as well as some living expenses, while the ban was in effect. Joan, ever concerned about the welfare of others, was at the forefront of these efforts—and payments.

However, the lawmakers neglected one critical question: What good is a fishing ban if poachers ignore it or even flaunt it? The number of poachers didn't drop during the ban—it increased, frustrating both the lawmakers and the legal fishermen who wound up being punished by the situation. "In front of me, boats fishing korosho and poachers on foot. Infuriating!" Joan wrote.

On February 6, 2001, right before the ban went into effect, Joan noted in her diary that her friend Barry Gaymer, the longtime local and honorary Kenya Wildlife Services game warden, had met with the powerful national director of the Kenya Department of Fisheries, Nancy Gitonga, presumably to tell her about Joan's plan to clean up the lake with a private security force. In her diary, Joan described Nancy Gitonga as "an amazing woman . . . busy changing the laws at the coast and Kisumu." Gitonga was enthusiastic, telling Gaymer to "go ahead" with the "plan to clean up the lake" and stop the poaching on Lake Naivasha.

Part of Joan's plan involved pairing Chege's tougher patrols with a softer approach of her own: She actually tried paying poachers—some of whom were off-duty flower-farm employees, others simply unemployed—not to poach. By approaching them on a personal level, Joan Root was now standing up and standing out, and therefore entering dangerous territory.

As the ban and the rise in poaching continued, Joan's security force expanded and a few more men were added to Chege and his team of two. Soon there were two small groups of security personnel: one to patrol one corner of the lake and another to patrol another section or, as Joan wrote, "to do pincer action." This pincer action was a bit like *korosho,* pulling in a circular net and capturing everything in its path. Now Joan's ragtag team of refugees was metaphorically pulling the net around poachers, capturing supplies, boats, and the trespassers themselves.

The poacher problem wasn't confined to the water. Soon they were coming at her land from all sides. Joan wrote of constantly having to change her guards (they were letting in poachers for bribes), losing respect for neighbors who did nothing ("No courage"), of chasing poachers on foot, screaming at them to leave, and of how everything she did had no effect. "Felt anxious about everything," she wrote. "Trust people and get stabbed in the back." The peace she loved so much on the lake was beyond shattered; the only solace she had was in her animals and in the rare moments of solitude at night, when she would watch a movie on the VCR in her bedroom, always noting the film and a short review of it in her diary. "TV. Watched *Titanic.* An amazing movie," she wrote one night. As a friend would later point out, "She felt like the *Titanic* was sinking before her eyes, and she was trying to save it."

As days went by, it became increasingly clear that the ban was not working. On March 8, 2001, an emergency meeting of the stakeholders of the lake was called. Joan made phone calls urging everyone to be there. Local landowners, flower farmers, businessmen, legal fishermen, and a deputy from the national Fisheries Department in Nairobi all crammed into a room at the Kenya Wildlife Services Training Institute in Naivasha town, with everyone talking at once to suggest ideas of how to rid the lake of poachers, until finally someone—or everyone—realized that what Joan was already doing on her land could be a successful route to safeguard the entire lake.

"A thief to catch a thief," one person said. "A former poacher makes the very best gamekeeper," said another. The only answer was to meet force with force. "You can't blame [the poachers]," one Riparian would later say. "These guys have nothing. Not only them, but the next thousand behind them." However, he added, "If you don't challenge them, they'll take every fish and every animal."

Since poachers know the secrets of other poachers, the reasoning went, why not select an even larger group of the most effective poachers on the lake; give them boats, licenses, and instructions on proper fishing rules and regulations; and have *them* protect the lake?

"A vigilante group?" someone asked.

It wouldn't be called that, it was agreed. Since the group would be working for the restoration of the lake with the full compliance and support of the police, Kenya's wildlife and fisheries agencies, the flower farmers, the landowners, the legal fishermen, and the merchants, it needed a more dignified name.

"Why don't we call it the Task Force?" someone proposed. Thirty men—half of them poachers and half of them legal fishermen—would constitute the group, including as foreman the best rehabilitated poacher-turned-legal-fisherman of all, David Chege.

What Joan had been doing as a private citizen would now be a communitywide effort: The landowners and stakeholders of the lake would contribute their time and money, and the government entities—the local Kenya Fisheries Department and the police—would handle the law-enforcement aspect. "It was entirely Joan's initiative, her idea, and it coincided entirely with the Riparian Association's management plan," said Lord Enniskillen. And with the Task Force, Joan Root became "a champion for the livelihoods of impoverished fishermen," he said. "How? By promoting fishing as a sustainable activity rather than allowing the illegal element to just clear out the lake."

Word spread instantly through Karagita of the promise of work, from the butcheries to the bodegas that sold everything from meat to sex to cell phones, from the South Lake Club to the Millennium bar, and all the other ramshackle storefronts that lined Moi South Lake Road. One hundred Kenyan shillings ($1.50) per man per day. Not in the flower farms but out on the lake! Legal work! Thirty strong and able fishermen needed for a Task Force. "Many people, very many," Chege recalled of the men who were eager to join the Task Force. Only thirty would be selected. Competition got even tougher when the budget was cut and the number was reduced to fifteen.

The men selected—including some of Chege's brothers—were instructed to gather in an unmarked building in Karagita. Each received a white cap to wear as a uniform, and Chege gave them their marching orders: to ambush and apprehend poachers, confiscate their nets, and instruct them to immediately stop fishing.

According to one original plan, a landowner was to fly over the lake in his plane to spot poachers and catch them in the act. He would call Chege on the cell phone Joan had given him and tell him where the poachers were working. The Task Force, having ridden a *matatu* (bus) to the lake from Karagita, would rush to the scene, hide in the papyrus, and then bolt out in ambush. As time went on, Task Force members said, Chege included his own twist: Out on the lake, he would instruct his men to lie down on the bottom of the boat so all the poachers could see was a single man at the helm. Once they were in striking distance, Chege would scream, "*Toka!*" (Swahili for "Get out!"), and the Task Force would leap from the boat like a storm cloud from hell. "We'd beat them, whip them, screaming abuse," recalled one member of the team. Not inclined to argue or debate, the Task Force simply attacked. If you were on the lake with a net during the fishing ban, you were guilty. Upon apprehending the poachers, the Task Force would confiscate the nets, then take them to the Kenya Fisheries Department Naivasha headquarters and the poachers to the police station. Joan didn't condone the violence, but she couldn't help admiring the results: The balance of power on the lake had shifted from poachers running roughshod, and the rule of law was finally being enforced.

That was the way it was supposed to work. But things rarely work as planned in Kenya, and there was one important detail they failed to consider: Poachers worked at night. Who would transport the nets and men in the middle of the night? Joan was the treasurer of the Riparian Association and the treasurer of the Task Force; she wasn't supposed to be the coordinator. However, she soon fell into a routine that cost her not only more money but also massive amounts of time.

She kept her cell phone and charger beside her bed. It began ringing night after night, with incessant calls from Chege. "Mama Joan, come quick, ten poachers and thirty nets confiscated at Hippo Point. Mama

Joan, rush over immediately! Eighteen poachers and forty-five nets confiscated at Fisherman's Camp. Mama Joan, come now! The Task Force is beaten, bloody, stranded, hungry, broke . . ." And Joan, as always, would not merely come, she would handle everything.

Whenever her phone rang—two, three, or four A.M.—she would leap from her bed, slip on her clothing and her red headscarf, jump into her Pajero, and race to whatever corner of the lake her "chaps," as she called them, had conducted an operation in. Upon arriving, her doors would fly open, and the men—both the poachers and the Task Force—would pile inside. The poachers would be ferried to the police, and the Task Force frequently to Joan's staff camp for sustenance and, of course, when the donations didn't pour in from landowners, Joan began to underwrite the entire enterprise. "Each man was paid forty-five hundred Kenyan shillings a month, all by Joan," said Barry Gaymer. Every month Joan would put each man's pay in separate envelopes that she would give to David Chege, entrusting him to pass out the payments to the men.

It was a loose-knit operation, desperately in need of funding, organization, and everything else. "They do nothing without my leadership," Joan wrote in her diary.

At the outset, Chege and his men found themselves apprehending members of the very entity that was supposed to be assisting the Task Force in stopping poaching on the lake: officials from the local branch of the Kenya Fisheries Department. At the height of the fishing ban in 2001, Chege watched Fisheries officials push out from the shore in the government agency's boat. With them was a group of Japanese businessmen who, dropping anchor in a picturesque corner of the lake, cast their lines and began fishing. Further detective work by Chege proved that the guests were paying the Fisheries officials 10,000 Kenyan shillings ($150) for the trip, ludicrously calling it "research." "Will discuss how to trap," Joan wrote in her diary.

By the next day, she and Chege had a plan in place. Joan sat by her telephone most of the day, receiving progress reports from the team. As soon as the Fisheries boat returned to the shoreline with their catch, the Task Force, in a brazen show of power and reverse authority, pounced, apprehending both the fishermen and the Fisheries Department representatives. Detaining the men until the vehicle arrived, Chege and his team discovered that one of the Africans who had taken the businessmen on the illegal fishing trip was married to an official in the Kenya Fisheries Department; they even had a letter from the official authorizing them to fish "for research purposes."

The Task Force was unimpressed. The entire group was hauled off to jail, where they spent the night on the squalid concrete floor with the riffraff in the group holding cell. The next day Joan contacted the head Fisheries office in Nairobi; the officer who arranged for the illegal fishing expedition was transferred and some members of the staff lost their jobs.

It was a stunning victory, and Joan relished it. The Task Force was taken to the Bell Inn to celebrate over icy cold Tusker beers. With the bust of the Fisheries Department officials, a line had been drawn in the sand. From then on it was Joan and the Task Force against pretty much everybody else.

3/22/01. Chege phoned. Sounds frightened under threat from Fisheries people who lost their jobs.

A few days after that diary entry, a group of fifteen men lay in wait for the Task Force as they made their way back to Karagita after a day's work. Though they went after Chege and his men with fists, sticks, and cudgels, the Task Force fought back, not only overpowering the thugs but hauling them off to jail, where a political leader tried to bribe Chege to forget the whole thing and let the men go, Joan wrote.

The lines between law and order were bleeding into each other. Who were the lawmakers and who were the lawbreakers? In Naivasha, no one knew for sure.

—

> Everybody in Naivasha has an angle, and for every allegation there are counter-allegations motivated not so much by truth or the lack of it, but by interests; it is not so much what is said as it is about what is emphasized.
>
> —*Iko* magazine, 2004

Interests and angles. Hidden agendas. Forces at work behind the scenes. If Joan Root thought the microscopic world of a termite mound was complex, she must have been endlessly fascinated by the machinations going on around her lake.

Was Joan aware of violence the Task Force employed? Maybe not at first, people insisted. She did not go on patrol with them. Yet she saw the results—the apprehended and frequently bloodied men whom she was called upon to ferry to the police. As time went on, she must have understood the fear instilled by the mere sight of the Task Force. In general, the members of the Riparian Association didn't seem overly bothered by the Task Force's controversial methods—after all, meeting violence with violence was a necessity in turn-of-the-twenty-first-century Kenya. "Desperate measures for desperate times," more than one Lake Naivasha landowner said.

Yet like a mother with an errant son, Joan tried to rein in the increasingly outlaw actions of the young Kikuyu entrusted to lead the Task Force. "David Chege wanted us to beat up those poachers we arrested," said Absolom Mulela Letta, the Task Force's oldest member, whose hands and feet were thick with white calluses from decades of fishing. This was against Joan's wishes: "She would tell us, 'When you are doing this job, don't beat anybody up, because you are all brothers staying together.'"

Still, she knew they had to make a show of strength. To further demonstrate her commitment to stopping poaching on Lake Naivasha during the fishing ban, Joan and some of the other landowners, Fisheries representatives, and legal fishermen borrowed a public-relations move from her earlier fight against the elephant poachers: They piled all of the confiscated nets—"worth millions" of shillings, said David

Chege—and lit them in a massive bonfire seen from all corners of the lake. "They wanted me to talk," Joan said of the bold event. She didn't have to. Her actions spoke louder than she ever could.

With the bonfire, every poacher on the lake soon knew that Mama Joan was the key player in stopping them from earning a living and feeding their families. It may have been easy to forget that she was fighting for the overall future and survival of the lake, giving money to those in need, paying for their children's education, doing whatever she could to help support all sides of the Lake Naivasha tragedy—frequently even the poachers.

But the poachers' anger over the Task Force, and the *mzungu* woman who ran it, couldn't help but grow, especially when it became clear that the Task Force had become criminals again. There had long been rumors, which Joan ignored, that Chege and his men had never stopped fishing themselves. To make it worse, Chege and his team were not just poaching but also, many said, charging the poachers a "protection fee"—bribes that had to be paid by poachers if they wanted to fish illegally on the lake.

Chege was equally duplicitous when it came to his own men, according to Task Force member Absolom Letta. Apparently intoxicated by the power he held over the Task Force, Chege began withholding their wages unless they met him in the bars of Karagita, Letta said, where they would be paid only after they bought beer for him and his growing circle of friends. "It was a must to buy the beer," the Task Force member added.

No one on the Task Force dared to cross their boss, "because Chege became so powerful that he could dismiss anybody," remembered David Kilo. Dismissal was a dreaded fate. "The ones who fell out with Chege, who disagreed with Chege, ended up going back to fishing and were tortured by the illegal fishermen because they were traitors." Meanwhile, David Chege was becoming accustomed to the finer things in Kenyan life: his wet swimsuit and ratty T-shirt replaced by *mtumba* apparel (the Swahili word for secondhand clothes sent from around the world into Africa and sold to retailers by the bale); his poacher friends replaced by members of the local government and police; his thirst slaked by cold Tusker beer in the company of both the authorities and the fast women of the Karagita slum, who flocked to Chege now that he had something jingling in his pocket. No longer was he forced to forage for the poacher's meager diet of fish, beans, and greens. Now he enjoyed Kenyans' most prized dish, *nyama choma*—the choicest cuts of goat and game meat, roasted to perfection and dripping with fat and natural juices.

Chege's new lifestyle was made possible by Joan, and some say he jealously guarded their relationship, allowing no other Task Force member to have direct contact with her. "He was saying, 'I am the son of Mama!' and that one day he would be given part of her farm," Absolom Letta said. "He then borrowed money from Mama and bought a piece of land."

Chege could hardly be expected to stay in his old quarters in Karagita, he insisted to Joan. He was a marked man there, residing among the very poachers he was preventing from making a living. Besides, Joan was already dishing out money to others in need. To note just one of many instances she recorded: "Three ex-fishermen came, pleading they have been ejected from their houses, with families sleeping outside plus landlord locking their effects inside." She gave them the equivalent of two hundred dollars in shillings. So how could she turn down Chege when he came to her a few days later asking for her help to buy a piece of land of his own?

That was just the beginning of Chege's never-ending cycle of need: Joan paid for his children's education; she hired lawyers to defend him when he was charged with what she was convinced were bogus criminal charges ranging from simple assault to rape, designed to destroy the Task Force and allow poaching to return to the lake (with the help of the lawyer, he was exonerated of each and every charge); she paid his hospital bills for all the times he was attacked and beaten; she bought him vehicles so he could do his job, beginning with a bicycle and escalating to a motorcycle.

He had been blessed gloriously by fate and Joan Root. Practically overnight, he was the undisputed leader of fifteen men and, better yet, enjoyed the complaisance of the police and other authorities.

"Chege's sweet talk can move mountains and make you give him your own child," said one of the men who spoke of him one day in the slum. "He can easily convince you. Within a very short time, he used the name of Joan Root to get to know big names in this country. He had the power to convince the director of Fisheries, the Kenya Wildlife Services, even the police."

"He became a king," said his friend.

"He was the King Solomon of Karagita!" added the first man.

"He used to say that it was God who helped him and that he would not suffer again," Absolom Letta said.

David Kilo tried to alert Joan that her star ex-poacher and members of his team had reverted to their former roles. He even brought it up at the Lake Naivasha stakeholders' meeting—the gatherings of concerned citizens, licensed fishermen, and others living and working around the lake. But Joan didn't want to hear it. She was still too shy to engage in public conversation, especially debate, and furthermore, she still believed in Chege.

Joan's diaries in the spring and summer of 2001 were filled with Task Force operations, often involving substantial cash outlays.

> *5/1/01. Chege came to collect Task Force wages, and I was persuaded to give Chege another 2,000 Kenyan Shillings [$29.90] to look after his mother, Absalom 3,000 Kenyan Shillings [$44.84] for school fees & Isaac 3,800 [$56.80] for school fees.*

Through the multiple arrests, the infinite charges, the increasing evasiveness and evidence of lies, all of which she recorded in her diary, Joan steadfastly continued to defend Chege. How could this have happened? How could a woman who had always been so intimately attuned to the world around her that she could tell the presence of a snake by the sound of a worried birdsong, could read the emotions of a brooding lion a split second before it attacked, not be able to see the duplicity of David Chege? How could a fish poacher from the Karagita slum have conned Joan Root?

The most likely answer is that he didn't, at least not in the beginning. Joan seemed to know what he was up to but tolerated it when she weighed the alternatives. As early as 1999, Joan was getting "tipped off," as she wrote, that Chege and her supposedly rehabilitated fishermen were poaching again in the shallows and casting nets in the papyrus in front of her land.

Yet as the situation around the lake intensified—with the Fisheries Department collapsing, some members of the law-enforcement agencies clearly corrupt, the legal fishermen pursuing their own frequently questionable agenda, and crime becoming an almost everyday occurrence—Joan Root's dependence on David Chege grew.

To his credit, he was not just a charmer; he was an amazingly hard worker. And it was clear that, for reasons justified or not, people were out to get him. It was also evident to Joan that he had done a great deal to clean up the lake. Her diary was filled with the triumphs: poachers apprehended and arrested, illegal nets—wheelbarrows full of them!—pulled up and destroyed, fish stocks rising, the papyrus belt thick and green again.

In these very rare moments of triumph—and even rarer moments of tranquillity—when Joan walked through her favorite spot in her garden, she was reminded of a happier, peaceful, and more triumphant period of her life. Whenever she had screened her and Alan's old films for the staff in the mud hut that served as a TV room, the scene that always brought down the house was the image of Joan sitting on her enormous lawn with her sewing machine, repairing the damage to a torn, ripped, and waterlogged balloon, its orange fabric billowing hundreds of yards around her, practically covering the endless expanse of their acreage.

Joan could do anything she set her mind to. But the battle of Lake Naivasha was different; she knew she couldn't do it without Chege. For the greater good of the lake, she tolerated his indiscretions, which showed up first in talk by others: Chege duplicitous, Chege squandering the money she'd given him as payment for supplies or transportation, Chege straying from not only his first wife but his second. If pressed, Joan could dismiss it all as the smears of those whose livelihoods Chege had interrupted or whose corruption he had exposed.

"She so wanted to trust him," remembers a friend who had once asked her: "Do you really think that the twenty thousand shillings you gave to Chege yesterday is really all for the Task Force?"

"Of course not," Joan replied. "But he's working really hard."

She could even tolerate the escalating charges on the cell phone she had given Chege. Because how else could he relay news of operations in progress and poachers apprehended? Even when his phone charges went to 20,000 shillings a month ($274) and she checked the bill—discovering "Most calls are work related, too many to women"—she tolerated it. Because she knew if she dug too deep, the Task Force would fall apart and the lake along with it.

Chege stepped up his efforts with the Task Force, busting poachers, confiscating their nets, and burning their boats. The poachers became increasingly hostile and violent, as did the Task Force. By now the fifteen young men were practically living in Joan's staff camp—especially Chege, even after buying his own plot. Joan's property had become the Task Force's base of operations. ("Chege & Task Force slept in TV room, ready to leave at 3 a.m," she wrote.) The pressure took a toll on her. "Feeling close to a mental breakdown," she wrote in her diary on May 21, 2001. "So exhausted. After dark Chege came to give me LOTS OF SERIOUS INFO."

> *12/13/01. Had a toss and turn night about what I should be doing, but feel overwhelmed. . . . Feeling cross with Chege because he seems to be evasive, not bringing all the books [for Task Force payments and advances]. Came at dark and brought books and asked for one month's wages (6,000 Kenyan Shillings [$89.69]).*

As late as 2004, Joan continued to defend her supposedly rehabilitated poacher, as did others. Although most everyone in Naivasha was against him, he got support from a member of one of the highest government offices in Nairobi:

3rd June, 2004—Ministry of Livestock and Fisheries Development, Fisheries Department.

LETTER OF APPRECIATION

Dear Mr. Chege,

Your role and contribution towards sustainable fisheries utilization, management and conservation of the Lake Naivasha fishery has not skipped the attention of the Fisheries Department. We are aware that you are the team leader of the community vigilante group, which has been actively involved in policing the lake in partnership with the Government and other stakeholders.

This office acknowledges your personal effort despite sometimes working under very challenging situations. Your dedication to the lake patrols to flush out illegal fishers has greatly contributed to bringing order in the fishery of Lake Naivasha.

I take this opportunity to thank you and other members of your team, most sincerely for your continued support. You are always welcome to share any information or ideas that you may feel would enhance surveillance and management of fisheries in Lake Naivasha with us.

Your services are highly valued and appreciated. Please keep up the good work.

Yours Sincerely,

Nancy K. Gitonga, Director of Fisheries

Even Nancy Gitonga was praising Chege and his good work on the lake. What else could be said about the carping of the corrupt, envious, and lawless legions that cursed, charged, punched, and arrested him? He always denied everything, pointing out that the accusations came from people he had angered, jailed, or prevented from poaching.

All of Naivasha was corrupt and against him, Chege claimed; he and Joan Root were the rare honest souls on the lake, which was why her faith in him was merited and justified. It was a pretty amazing defense, but coming from Chege—a Kenyan who could come off as kind, peaceful, and well mannered—it somehow seemed plausible. "Four times I was arrested," he said, insisting that it was all blowback from the lawless lake he had brought under control.

Aside from the question of Chege's guilt or innocence, the lake was in better shape with the Task Force than without it. Since the fishing ban had gone into effect on February 10, 2001, poaching had been "more or less contained," according to a report from the Kenya Fisheries Department entitled "The Lake Naivasha Task Force." It was essentially a request for contributions to the cost of running the force, whose expenses to date—1,318,963 shillings (approximately $20,000)—had been paid almost exclusively by Joan Root.

"Since the start of operations the Task Force has arrested 121 men, confiscated 23 boats, 218 nets and 7 fishing rods and lures," read the report. "The ban on fishing has had many positive consequences. The lake edge vegetation is recovering and wildlife and birds are seen in abundance. . . . Research shows that the fish are now having a chance to increase in numbers and size."

The lake was finally allowed to take a breath and a break: the papyrus belt rejuvenating and the animals returning to nest and feed within it; the fish eggs escaping the nets and allowed to grow; the fish maturing; the birds feeding; and the vast cycle of life that depended on all of it was beginning to be restored. Poaching was reduced, but the job was only halfway done. Even though rebirth was at the core of Joan's existence, both as a woman and as a naturalist, she knew there could be no victory in allowing the lake to rejuvenate at the expense of the people who depended on it for survival.

Many of those driven to live illegally off the lake with their undersize nets now stepped out of the water and lined up at Joan Root's door. Alan Root had once famously said that, upon his death, he wanted his corpse left on an African savanna to be consumed by the wild that had given him so much in his lifetime. Joan was giving herself, body and soul, to Kenya. "Isaac came to request loan to buy donkey to cart water," began a typical diary entry. "Gave him a lecture about having seven children, but loaned him 7,000 Shillings [$96]."

Shillings. The word runs through her diaries like a litany—shillings to the unending stream of needy people, many of them poachers, shillings to do right by the Task Force, shillings to the members of her staff . . . "When I went with her through her papers, every single member of her staff had loans that they could never, ever consider paying back," said Adrian Luckhurst.

It was all Joan could do to stem the tide rising all around her on both sides of the lake, the Task Force and the poachers, but it was more than one person could do or conceive of doing, and soon the dam that she had built in hopes of sustaining and preserving the lake amid the pressures of modern-day Kenya would burst.

Christmas was coming to Naivasha, but it would provide no respite from the intensifying conflict into which Joan had inserted herself.

> *12/20/01. At night something frightened Pongo [a goat Joan was rehabilitating]. She raced around and bucked. Waterbuck also did alarm calls.*
>
> *12/28/01. 3 a.m. Chege rang and woke me from a deep sleep. His wife had come and created a disturbance and broken up his room.*
>
> *12/31/01: Moses and Kamau told me a woman had overheard poachers talking that they would kill Chege tonight. I got Chege on mobile . . . to tell him direct and he said a letter had been left at his house saying the same. . . . Chege came to spend the night here [in Joan's staff camp].*

As the conflict at the lake intensified, it was hard to keep perspective. Joan tried to get away, visiting her many old and new friends in Nairobi and beyond, including a trip to Antarctica with a Nairobi-based British businessman with whom she had become friends.

"He was virtually the opposite of Joan," Adrian Luckhurst remembered. "A very successful businessman, but he wasn't into wildlife and conservation. So off they went on this trip. The boat stopped someplace to have maintenance done on it, and Joan's companion started wedging away about the safety of the boat. Joan had serious guts. She wanted to go down there, and that's where she was going. So she turned to this gentleman and said, 'If you don't want to go to Antarctica with me, why don't you get on a plane and go home?' Here's this big chap, and Joan is saying, 'If you can't cut it, *leave.*'" He did leave, and Joan continued on, sailing from South Africa to South America, alone on the faltering ship, which got stuck in sea ice along the way.

Lake Naivasha was a portion of her life, one friend insisted, but it wasn't her entire life. Yet as time went by, the real-life drama of the lake, with its great victories and stunning defeats, its espionage and shadows, its crimes, deceits, crosscurrents, and whirlpools, began to suck Joan into its vortex.

"There was a dinner and a lecture one night at the Muthaiga Club," remembered Esmond Bradley Martin, the Save-the-Rhino crusader from Karen. "It was an extremely interesting lecture by a man who brought pictures of the lions being poisoned and speared in Nairobi National Park. To lighten up things, I asked Joan how she was spending her time. And she started talking about the illegal fish poaching, and how the authorities were doing nothing to stop it, and all that she was doing to curb the poaching." He shook his head. "I'd known Joan for thirty-five years, and I had never seen her so worked up about anything."

Chapter Ten

With the reduction, if not eradication, of poaching on the lake, some of the massive numbers of unemployed men turned to an even more dangerous enterprise. "I've sat here and watched everything coming into Naivasha," one old-timer said in his house near the lake. "In America you have your gold rushes and oil booms. When people went into the mines, others came in to live off of the miners—prostitutes, shop owners, bar owners, thieves. If fifty people came to work in the mines, there must've been another three hundred to live off of them—people selling things, people stealing things. It's the same thing here, only here the gold rush is flowers."

Naivasha had always held a certain degree of frontier danger, even in Joan's early days as a single woman after Alan left. Her diary includes mention of suspicious calls and other worrying mysteries: "3/10/91: Woken up by phone call. Wrong #. Woman threatened, 'Keep an eye. Keep an eye.' . . ." She had to leave her phone off the hook until the calls stopped. In the decade since those calls, things had gotten progressively worse. By 2004 Joan's diary had gone from being a chronicle of adventure to being a chronicle of crime. In her office, surrounded by the detritus of her and Alan's film career, or in her living room, surrounded by shelves of books about Africa, she wrote of the horrors that were becoming almost routine.

Around this time, a friend of Joan's wrote a five-page single-spaced letter to the CEO of the Kenya Association of Tour Operators, detailing the felonies committed in the area over a two-year period. "Below is a brief history of violence, murder, intimidation, robbery, carjackings, farm invasions and arson that I have assembled since 2003," the letter began, then went on to detail each horrific case, ending with a mention of an unsigned leaflet written in Swahili and English that had been sent to the area's flower farmers. The leaflet read:

> TIME BOMB ABOUT TO EXPLODE!!!!!!!!!!!!!! The various tribes have noted with concern that you, the so-called investors, have been sidelining other tribes and ganging up with the Mount Kenya cannibals [the Kikuyu] to have their kinsmen dominate employment at the farms. You are actually not investors but infestors since you have infested our land with Kikuyus. WARNING: WE ARE VIGILANT. THIS PRACTICE MUST STOP WITH IMMEDIATE EFFECT.

"This is not Happy Valley—it's a valley of fear," one resident told a reporter from *The Scotsman,* the national newspaper of Scotland. The sensational quote, which became a headline, infuriated many locals whose love of Naivasha outweighed their fear of it. Even when the seemingly impenetrable Djinn Palace was hit—"fourteen guys with guns," said June Zwager—the family calmed the staff members whose quarters had been invaded, felt blessed that the thugs hadn't gotten into the main house, beefed up the security, and moved forward.

Naivasha was plagued not only by a crime wave but also by constant conflict among Kenya's forty-some tribes, including the ongoing threat of the Maasai to take back by force the lands they claimed white Kenyans had stolen from them at the start of the previous century. This boiling anger would erupt in tribal warfare, with Kenyans brutally killing one another in the streets, following the disputed 2007 presidential election.

By 2004 Joan's friends in Nairobi were all giving her the same clear message: *Get out now. Dissolve the damned Task Force and leave the lake before it swallows you.* According to Alan, Joan was very well off financially, from her share of the Roots' film proceeds and her inheritance after the death of her parents. She could have gone anywhere, done anything.

"Get out of it," Alan remembered everyone telling her. Yet he knew it was just like Joan to see the whole thing through, to do things properly and to take care of the details. "I wouldn't have expected anything else of her when she was involved," he remembered. "If she was doing a job, knowing she was doing it well, she wouldn't have been happy handing it over to someone else, even if the consequences were frightening. She would have said, 'Well, they don't spend as much time as I do on it or won't care as much.'"

Everyone also knew that you couldn't tell Joan Root what to do. Fiercely independent, she found it difficult to retreat or, especially, concede defeat. No one tried harder to persuade Joan to leave than Adrian Luckhurst. He often played polo in Naivasha and would frequently call on Joan at home. "Joan, please, listen," he told her on numerous occasions. "You're vulnerable. You're isolated, and you're involved in a fairly delicate thing here. With all due respect, Joan, I really don't want to drag you out of the gutter or find you somewhere you shouldn't be. You've got to think about this very carefully."

Her reply was always the same: "I just want to do the right thing for the lake."

When she refused to ease up on her fight for the lake, Luckhurst advised her to rid herself at least of the role that he felt marked her for trouble: chief financier of the enterprise. "Keep the Task Force if you want, but have somebody else be perceived as its controller—not you, not Mrs. Root," he told her. "Right now you are perceived as the sole orchestrator and manager of a Task Force that is doing something very good for the lake, but you are seen as the driving force behind it and the financier behind it. So obviously, people know you have the money."

She couldn't argue with that, having dished out more money than she could count.

"In addition," Luckhurst said, "the Task Force will perceive you as their employer. Now, what's going to happen to you five years down the road when you say to everybody, 'Right, I'm too old now. We're shutting down the Task Force. Bye-bye. Everybody go home'? They're going to turn around and say, 'Well, Mrs. Root, you've employed us for five years. We need to be paid off.'"

According to the Kenya Employment Act, anyone employed for ninety days straight is classified as a permanent employee, entitling him or her to such benefits as paid vacation and severance. The Task Force had been running for three years, and since Joan had been paying their wages, she could be considered the employer of fifteen full-time workers.

"You can work as hard as you like for this, but at the end of the day, somebody is going to stab you in the back or kick you up the backside and tell you, 'Get lost. We don't need you here anymore,'" Luckhurst continued. "You will have burned up all this fantastic positive energy, but at the end of the day, they will shaft you for it."

She knew he was right. In addition to alienating herself from the Fisheries Department when her Task Force had busted its members for illegal fishing, she had alienated herself from parts of Naivasha's white community. "She was getting resistance from flower farmers," Luckhurst said. "She wasn't included in the social circles as much as she used to be. She was perceived as stirring up this whole scenario of the ecology of the lake, but also now she was getting into agriculture [the flower farms]. And so the farmers were beginning to pull away and distance themselves. That hurt her a lot."

Finally, Joan relented. "Okay, let's try it," she said of Luckhurst's suggestion to funnel her money to the Task Force through the Riparian Association. Luckhurst called Lord Enniskillen, the head of the association, and told him the plan. From then on Joan would write a check for a donation each month to the LNRA, and the Riparians would use it to pay the Task Force's wages.

"[The payment] supposedly had nothing to do with Joan anymore," Luckhurst said. "But the Task Force still perceived that it was Joan who was the driving force behind it. Whenever they wanted anything, it was always Joan. Chege would still deal only with Joan."

Despite the Riparian Association ruse, everyone in Naivasha knew that Mama Joan was still the power behind the Task Force, and most saw her as a source of good, even amid the evil that the Task Force came to represent: *Mama Joan rehabilitates poachers and turns them into kings. Mama Joan has an endless stream of shillings. Mama Joan has a heart bigger than Kenya. Mama Joan lives alone on a big piece of land on Moi South Lake Road with very little security. Mama Joan always wears a bright red headscarf, which makes her easy to identify and just as easy to befriend.*

Her last extended journey was to Egypt, a weeklong tourist trip with friends in 2004. She marveled over the Egyptian Museum in Cairo, with Tutankhamen's gold coffin and artifacts and the Sphinx and Pyramids of Giza and the Luxor Museum. Then into the Valley of the Kings with their colossi. And yet even here, among the treasures of the world, she thought mostly of the lake, of home. She rushed through the trip, taking a deep breath of relief only when she arrived back in Kenya and was able to note in her diary, "All well at home. No tragedies."

The peace didn't last long. By the spring of 2004, Joan wrote, the rains came, torrential, washing everything into the lake, rising with new intrigue, new injustices, new outrages. She wrote of boats being stolen from jetties, of a "traditional healer" selling lion fat.

When Joan went out from her beloved home—usually to make the hour-and-a-half drive to Nairobi—she would often take some of her wounded animals with her: a dik-dik, a python, an owlet, a baby duiker that had to be fed every three hours. Sometimes she would also take David Chege.

By the fall of 2004, Chege was under fire for charges not only of corruption, extortion, and rape. He was also a main suspect in a brutal assault. It happened on a normal raid, involving ten poachers, nets, and a stolen pump on March 24, 2004. Chege and his team were on the lake; Joan was monitoring everything from her house. The Task Force chased after a poacher in the shallows of the lake, and when the man was apprehended, he suffered a broken leg. Some claimed that Chege was responsible for it; Chege insisted that the attack had been made by a member of the anti–stock theft unit, which policed Naivasha for cattle rustlers. Either way, unbeknownst to Joan, the man couldn't afford medical care and returned to his village, where he died shortly afterward.

At Joan's urging, Chege went to the Kenya Human Rights Commission to file a report about what he claimed was the bogus assault case against him involving the poacher who died. Even the new Naivasha director of Fisheries was convinced that the man's broken leg had been caused when he fell, not when anyone struck him. The Task Force members wrote letters saying as much to the police. For her part, Joan once again called Nancy Gitonga "to talk about the future of the Task Force and how to prevent Chege from being framed."

The police were looking for Chege to question him about the poacher on a day in November 2004 when he and Joan drove to Nairobi. Joan went to the bank to get the payroll for her workers, did some shopping, and on the way home stopped to meet with a former mayor of Naivasha to discuss the assault case against Chege. Chege later said he had kept telling Joan to hurry, because it wasn't safe to drive the Nairobi-Nakuru Highway at night. But Joan insisted on completing her errands.

It was dark by the time they got back to Joan's land. As soon as they drove through the gate, they saw two men run and hide. Joan cut her lights and inched forward. Once they arrived at the carport, Chege went to the servants' camp to get assistance in unloading the SUV, and Mary, the housekeeper, came out to help Joan. Suddenly, six men appeared, at least one of them with a gun. They pushed the two women into the Pajero, and one of the assailants got in behind the wheel. The other five crowded inside, and they squealed off into the darkness.

The men made ugly threats as they drove over rutted roads and into the bush, with the Pajero bouncing crazily. They demanded the money they were sure Joan had on her, saying they would kill her if she didn't cooperate. Joan refused to give up even a shilling. They parked in a moonlit field on a very large ranch miles from the main road, snatched away Joan's purse, and rifled through it. They found some shillings but somehow seemed to know there was more, much more. Joan's purse had various hidden compartments in which she had hidden her cash, and when she wouldn't answer to the whereabouts of the whole amount, they began beating her. "Where's the rest?" they yelled with every blow, until finally, bruised and bleeding but still showing no sign of fear, she gave it to them. They jumped in her car and sped away, leaving Joan and Mary in the dark of night.

When they got back home the next morning, Joan calmly entered an account of the event:

> *11/25/04. Carjacked. Well after dark we met Fariz [former Naivasha mayor] at Caltex station to ask him about [Chege's] case. Near my gate, two men quickly hid. Chege was suspicious. I drove down the drive with lights off. Chege left to go to camp. Soon I was surrounded by 6 men wanting to rob. Mary and me carjacked.*

She went through the motions of an investigation—took the police to the scene of the crime, gave statements, offered a reward, and attended a police lineup that included two of her former employees but not the men who had robbed and beaten her. As usual, it all came to naught. Many of her friends insisted that Chege had staged the whole thing—why else would he disappear at the moment the thieves arrived, and how else would the thugs have known exactly how much money she had in the purse?—but Joan refused to believe them.

In the end, it wasn't Joan who elected to end the Task Force; it was the official bureaucracy. A new head of the Naivasha branch of the Fisheries Department cut off all government support. Having had enough of financing and organizing everything on her own, Joan sought help from the Lake Naivasha Growers Group, but they weren't inclined to get involved. Neither were the members of the Riparian Association, except for continuing to funnel Joan's money to the men.

Joan began by reducing the number of men in the Task Force. Whereas the formation of the vigilante group had been something of a community effort, its dissolution fell completely on Joan. She had to tell the group of supposedly rehabilitated poachers that their jobs were gone. They would have to return to the lives they had led before they got the white caps and the stable income—despite the fact that they had alienated themselves from their Karagita neighbors by busting so many of them for poaching.

In a Riparian Association meeting, she said she was unable to continue looking after the entire lake by herself. Her friend and fellow Riparian Dee Raymer suggested that perhaps she confine herself and her Task Force to a single area and that other members of the association help out with the rest. She looked around the room. Where was the support of the other landowners who lived around the lake? Where was the time, money, and sacrifice of the Riparians? "The Lake Naivasha Riparian Association could have been much more participatory," Raymer said. "But no, it fell on Joan. But Joan as the person in charge of this program made herself a target."

Security was becoming an even more pressing concern. A solution arrived in the person of John Sutton, who came to Naivasha in May 2005. Joan had known him since he was a child living on Karen Blixen's estate in Karen, a part of which had been turned into the Karen Blixen Coffee Garden, which Sutton's father owned and operated.

Sutton was soft-spoken but tough, a former police reservist. He was recruited by the Lake Naivasha Growers Group and other concerned citizens to head up the Naivasha Community Project, a private security force set up to protect the ever more threatened white residents around the lake.

Sutton asked Joan if he could run his security operation out of her property, where his cousin was already renting a cottage. Ever accommodating, Joan said yes, and the Naivasha Community Project moved into the rooms that had originally been Alan Root's film-editing quarters. What had once been a haven for filmmaking in paradise became a command post for security in a war zone, with Joan once again providing oversight and impeccable organizational skills.

By then Joan was as determined to disband the Task Force as she had been to create it. Now her diaries reflected her realization that what she had started as a force for good had backfired. "Gave Chege 10,000 Kenyan shillings to look for five bicycles for Task Force . . . Task Force came without their new bikes, expecting me to pay for first service. Long talk with John [Sutton] about Task Force etc. Advises to completely close down and get rid of Chege and all . . . of them. At night, stayed awake worrying what to do about Chege . . . John adamant Chege must go. . . . Talked to Chege and told him we should withdraw from lake issues. Suggested I phone for him to join [elephant expert Daphne] Sheldrick anti-poaching teams in Tsavo." Before he went for the interview, however, "Chege phoned saying he thinks no future in Naivasha for him . . . Asked if I could finance him to start something. Pointed out that he already had a plot [of land], house and motorbike etc."

He was hired for the job Joan had found for him in Tsavo National Park. She laid off the others, paid their outstanding wages, helped some of them start new businesses, even bought back some of the bicycles she had given them—anything to smooth their transition back to Karagita.

But nothing concerning the Task Force could ever be smooth. Predictably, an officer from the Kenya Department of Labor soon contacted Joan, hectoring her "about days off" for the fifteen men she had "employed." She wrote in her diary, "Finally, agreed I would pay extra for holidays and fifteen days per year and leave pay for six months." The Task Force wanted more, and her diaries were soon filled with their endless demands, as well as her own despair—sleepless nights, staff betrayals, neighbors getting robbed and shot, money missing from her kitchen cupboard.

By then three white Kenyans had been shot dead within a matter of months, each murder more violent than the last. "9/24/04. Martin

Palmer shot," Joan wrote. He was a good friend, a British-born farmer and horse breeder, who had been murdered by eight thugs dressed as policemen and driving a hijacked cargo truck. After killing Palmer, the men tied up his girlfriend and forced her to lie beside the dead body. Joan also knew Lloyd Schraven, the Dutch flower farmer killed near his front gate during a robbery attempt. He had just returned from the bank in Naivasha town with the payroll for his workers. And Joan knew John Goldson, the sixty-nine-year-old owner of Naivasha's exclusive Crater Lake Lodge who was gunned down when he stepped outside the confines of his hotel to check on a watchman who had been attacked by a gang.

"Drove to Crater Lake for remembrance of John," Joan wrote. "Someone told me what happened that night. John left the lodge, after saying good night to kitchen staff, climbed the stairs and met the gangsters in the car park."

She wrote of these horrific events in a cool, almost detached manner, though she must have noticed that the murders shared a common theme: The victims had been targeted. Armed robberies averaged eighteen a month in the Naivasha area, and people felt under siege. There was talk of drawing up lists of blood types, since hospitals were far away, and transfusions were invariably needed in the wake of shootings. A website was created so that motorists could log in and arrange to travel in convoys on the increasingly dangerous Nairobi-Nakuru Highway. The night after John Goldson's memorial, Joan noted in her diary that a dozen fish poachers had entered her gate and cut across her land to the lake. "Now, no Task Force," she added. The poachers multiplied, in fact, cutting the wires of her newly installed fence, burning papyrus, snaring animals, seining baby fish—as if her attempts to rescue the lake had never occurred. She suspected that former members of the Task Force might even be plotting against her.

No more Task Force, no more Chege, no more three A.M. reconnaissance calls. She had turned another page in her life, and with it came renewal and new confidence that things would heal, as they always did in nature.

"9.26.05. Intruders into house."

Her burglar alarm had gone off at three A.M. "Very deep sleep," Joan wrote in the diary. Thinking it was a false alarm, she fumbled with the keypad to turn off the siren. Then she heard a voice outside her bedroom window: "Mama, *fungua malango.*" Mama, open the door. "First, I was sleepily puzzled," she wrote. "Then he said again, 'Mama, *fungua malango.*' "

John Sutton, in his security quarters, had heard the alarm and had also heard the night watchman screaming, "*Munyama ame kuliwa!*" The animals have been eaten! Sutton took that to mean that a leopard had gotten into Joan's compound of orphaned and injured animals, which was behind her bedroom, and eaten a bushbuck or a gazelle. But as the watchman's voice came closer and clearer, Sutton realized he was saying, "Mama has been taken! Down toward the lake!"

Was it a ploy to separate the two of them? Sutton didn't pause to consider it. Instead, he grabbed his pistol, ran outside, and fired two shots into the air. He was thinking, Oh my God, this is it. He was running toward the lake, his cell phone in one hand, his pistol in the other, when Joan called him to say she was in the camp. When the experienced bush girl had heard the whispered threat, she had known exactly what to do: She let herself out the side door and ran silently into the servants' camp, where she called out to John. As he headed back toward her, he heard gunfire. Was it warning shots from white landowners on neighboring estates, he wondered, or shots fired by the intruders? It turned out to be both.

Joan and Sutton returned to her bedroom, "where we saw the huge 20 kg [44-pound] rock they had thrown at my door," she later wrote. The intruders had gotten into her living room. "Opened two drawers, pulled antenna wire from my radio and stole mobile [phone]." They saw the broken dining room window through which the thugs had thrown a rock. Within a half hour, Joan wrote, the police arrived, but they soon left, since nobody was injured and not much had been stolen.

It was just another night on Lake Naivasha. "I made tea for John," she wrote, and then she and Sutton retired to their respective beds "and tried to sleep for a short time before dawn."

The next morning Sutton insisted that Joan reinforce her security. The thin bars on her bedroom windows were an open invitation for robbery or worse. She needed steel doors, he told her, like the ones so many people around the lake had installed.

"Security doors and window grilles for bedroom," she wrote in her diary in late 2005, noting that she had visited friends to see what they had done to secure their homes. One of the houses was an Italian-style villa overlooking the lake; it belonged to Tony Seth-Smith, the former big-game hunter and his wife, Sarah. Seth-Smith was in his seventies but robust and determined to guard his property and his family at any cost, as was his wife, a slight, pale woman who wore her hair in a bun.

"Someone had a go at shooting me on the road six months ago," Tony Seth-Smith would later say. He explained that he had been driving by Joan's land when two Africans tried to carjack him. They ran off when he pointed his revolver in their faces. "The flower-farm laborers get hijacked on payday," he continued, "when they are given their wages. The baddies, posing as flower-farm workers, get on the buses with the workers and rob them."

Seth-Smith showed Joan their security system in hopes that she would install a similar one. "Joan was quite calm," he said. "She was a Kenya girl who didn't panic. You would think she must have been frightened, as an older woman on her own. But she had spent her life in the bush, dealing with Africa and the unexpecteds that Africa can throw at you."

There were bars and gates and security fences around the exterior of the Seth-Smiths' home. In addition, there were steel doors and gates at each passageway inside the house, from the front door to the living room. Standing at the landing leading to the master bedroom, Seth-Smith reached up and pulled down a louvered door with a deafening crash. "It's like a jeweler's door," he said. "It's meant to stop an AK-47. Then you close this wrought-iron grilled door."

Behind the louvered door was another door, with thick wrought-iron grillework, in case burglars somehow managed to open the louvered door. Next, Seth-Smith walked into his bedroom. "The dogs sleep in here, too," he said. "So someone would have to go through all of that, making all kinds of noise, which the dogs should hear. But if they did step into the bedroom—not impossible, if they are determined enough—I have this."

He opened a drawer beside his bed that held a sizable revolver. "I would shoot if I had to, if the life of my family was in danger," he said. He was licensed to have the guns, he explained, "because I am an honorary Kenya Wildlife Services game warden."

Joan didn't have a license, so she didn't have a gun. Seth-Smith asked her what security precautions she had in place in case of an "unexpected" in the middle of the night.

"I have flares," she replied. Her plan was to fire them through the window if there was trouble.

Probably sensing how ineffectual her flare idea might be, Joan relented, just as she had relented on installing a fence around her property. She reluctantly installed heavy sliding metal doors on two sides of her bedroom and reinforced the steel bars on her bedroom windows. The doors were painted orange-red. With that, she became what she had always dreaded the thought of: a living creature confined to a cage.

In the fall of 2005 David Chege returned to Lake Naivasha from Tsavo National Park, having been fired from the job that Joan had gotten him. Joan's diaries show her increasing suspicion of him, his motives, and his evolution from poacher to licensed fisherman back to poacher or even worse, an alarm expressed in many diary entries: "Talk with Chege—so much intrigue and deviousness," she had written earlier in the year, followed by a report that "Chege has a gun."

Soon even the authorities were reluctant to come to her compound;

one even "came with a bodyguard!" she marveled. Reports multiplied about the "*wakora*" (thugs) she had employed in the Task Force, most notably its leader. "Long talk with John Sutton," she wrote. "Very astute about how Chege has been manipulating me. Dangerous for him and me. Advised me to count my money." She fired a guard she had employed for six months. "Full of lies and is a relative of Chege." On November 13, she wrote: "Chege and Esther back in Karagita," adding that a well-placed source informed her "that Chege was behind my Sept. 26th intruders and last November carjacking" and was now pressing the labor office in his complaint against her for overtime. At this point her diary items about David Chege—and presumably his place in her life—stop.

"Chege went from the leader of the Task Force to the bottom of the ladder in Tsavo," said one landowner. "He came back to Naivasha with nothing to do. He had been walking around like a tin god, and then he was nothing." After Joan cut off her support, Chege was reduced to driving a motor-scooter taxi through the dirt streets of Karagita. "Chege was a *madaraka ndogo,* a little man with a little power, but he thinks he's a king," added one Kenyan. "It's not a lot of money you're giving someone like Chege, but it's a lot of power. And when you yank them out of the gravy train, *boom*!"

By the fall of 2005, Joan was regularly awakened by her askari's panic button alerting her to invasions at the front gate. "4 A.M. Siren. The buzzer in my room is so loud I get bombarded by noise and can't think straight to communicate with John [Sutton] on the mobile or walkie-talkie. Hard to get to sleep again. My heart was pounding."

The alarms were real: poachers, thieves, and frequently both. "I counted 18 poachers," she wrote. The next time it was twenty, then thirty, then too many to count. She also began receiving threatening text messages on her cell phone, so disturbing and violent that later none of her friends—or even the police—wanted to quote them. It would be reported that some Task Force members had threatened that if she didn't continue to pay them, "the poachers would get her." Worst of all in her mind was the effect the escalating crime was having on the most important residents of her land: "Animals running," she wrote—which she knew to be nature's signal that something was amiss. Then someone cut the brakes to her car, which was luckily detected by a mechanic before she drove. "She made very little of it," said her friend Annabelle Thom.

Less concerned about her own safety than the fight she was determined to win, Joan made up her mind to make one last attempt to save the lake in a way that had worked for her in the past—by means of a film. Richard Brock, who was a senior producer in the BBC natural-history unit when she and Alan were making films for the BBC, regularly came to stay on her property, and the result was a series of educational films about the devastation of the lake and ways to prevent it. Brock filmed ongoing anti-poaching efforts, and David Harper, whose scientific study had predicted the lake's demise, provided a running commentary. One of the resulting films, entitled *Lake on the Edge,* was shown at a meeting chaired by Lord Andrew Enniskillen. "Only 25–30 people turned up," Joan wrote. "Absolutely shocking. Feel sorry for Andrew, who has done so much."

The film was a noble attempt, but it did not succeed in inspiring much action. The battle for Lake Naivasha seemed to be over.

Joan's friends continued to urge her to leave the lake, but she continued to refuse. "Where to go?" she wrote in her diary.

Behind the bars and steel walls of her bedroom, with the head of the community's new private security force living only a few yards away and new guards on duty, Joan could finally feel secure. "12/22/05. 8:30 P.M. My siren went off. John Sutton went with shotgun. Pleased to see all my chaps out and armed with pangas, rungus [clubs], etc." She spent this Christmas alone, "in a total conversational vacuum," she wrote. Two days later, on December 27, 2005, she wrote in her diary: "Area been quiet from crime this Christmas. Police and Naivasha Community Project have caught thugs at Karasani that terrorize Karagita."

The New Year brought new challenges. "Dear Frank and Peggy," she wrote two American friends on January 4, 2006. "I am well and healthy, but feeling rather exhausted from dealing with the challenges of living in Kenya nowadays. I feel like I live on a different planet to the U.S.A. A planet where corrupt governance and the burgeoning human populations are increasing poverty, crime and destruction of the forests, savannas and wetlands of this lovely country. My property at Lake Naivasha continues to be a haven of peace for birds and animals, despite the surrounding pressures."

She ended the letter on an upbeat note. "Tourism has picked up recently after a few years of U.S. advisories against travel to Kenya, which kept the tourists away. . . . Whatever the reason, the influx of tourists is helping the economy, and if they continue to come to the beaches and the wildlife parks it may help the conservation of the wildlife. This year I finally got myself a computer and am slowly joining the computer age! So my e-mail address is above. Much love to you all, Joan."

The Task Force was gone, poaching and crime were on the rise, and yet she had hope, although it was coupled with frustration. As her friend Jean Hartley pointed out, "Things weren't going well, but she wasn't one to give up."

Joan was weeks away from her seventieth birthday, and she had come too far to stop now.

Chapter Eleven

In late 2005 a young resident of Karagita under questioning revealed to the Naivasha police that his cousin led a group of thugs "planning to attack that old Mama" on Moi South Lake Road, whom he identified as Memsaab Joan Root. It was a gang of eight men, he told the police, "and all have pistols and four AK-47." Why they were out to kill Joan Root, the snitch didn't reveal, but he said the attack was scheduled for the night of December 31. He had taken an oath with his cousin's gang and was supposed to accompany them to Joan Root's land.

The attack was postponed because the attackers worried that security would be too tight around the holidays. The police asked the informer to play along with his cousin's gang to find more information about the proposed attack. But when a new date, January 12, was set, the police asked the snitch to postpone the attack so they could be better prepared. The gang apparently didn't go along with the request.

The night of January 12 was clear and moonlit. That day had brought twin attacks: In the morning poachers had ensnared and slaughtered a waterbuck near Joan's house, and in the afternoon a leopard had killed a gazelle and dragged it across her acreage. The trail of blood went cold near the lake, so despite a lengthy search, the leopard was still at large. Joan finished her dinner at six P.M. An hour later she said good night to Samuel, her cook of fourteen years, and then locked herself inside the steel walls of her bedroom. Her two new Somali night watchmen reported for duty. Her eight-member staff watched TV on the set Joan had given them, and she most likely watched a movie. By ten P.M. Joan, her staff, and her animals were all sound asleep.

At one-thirty A.M. the guards saw two men sneaking into the compound from Moi South Lake Road. One carried an AK-47 semiautomatic rifle, the other a panga. The guard who spotted the intruders later said that they were wearing hoods over their faces. He set off the alarm, but John Sutton was on a security assignment in Tanzania, and the guards, due to Kenya's strict gun laws, were unarmed. Instead of charging the intruders, they ran and hid. One of them later said he heard the thugs discussing whether they should shoot the watchman who had sounded the alarm, but they thought better of it. "Let's do the work," he heard them say.

They walked around the house, skirting the electrified fence that now guarded part of Joan's property, and walked through the unelectrified gate that led to Joan's bedroom. They crept through the grassy animal orphanage, home to several giant tortoises with cracked and broken shells in various states of recuperation. Coming to Joan's back bedroom door, they shot off the outside lock with the AK-47, but the inner steel doors stopped them from going any farther. Awakened by the alarm and startled by the gunfire, Joan heard the same frightening words she had heard three months before: "Mama, *fungua malango*." Mama, open the door.

She managed to reach John Sutton on her cell phone. "John, they're back," she said in a whisper. She heard the steel bars rattling as the intruders frantically tried to enter the bedroom.

"Okay, Joan, turn off your light," Sutton said. On the phone, he could hear the alarm siren and the men's voices getting louder, and he realized that Joan's first move in such a dangerous situation would have been to switch on a light so she could operate the keypad that controlled the security alarm.

"Switch off the light," Sutton told her again. "Get on the floor and get into the bathroom and stay put. I'm going to call my people to come right away."

As soon as Sutton had called his security team and the Naivasha police, his phone rang again. Joan's voice, usually so quiet and calm, was frantic and trembling. "John, John," she said. The men's voices were louder, and he could hear them shouting repeatedly, "Mama, *fungua malango!*" He heard them ordering Joan to open the door, adding in Swahili, "Or we will fill you with so many bullets you will look like a sieve." Then Sutton heard the gunshots, so many that at first he thought the thugs were banging on the steel doors.

"John, help, John, help!" Joan implored, and then the phone went dead.

She had been shot in the thigh, and she dragged herself across her bedroom floor, trying to stanch the bleeding with bedsheets, leaving a trail of blood. When there was no longer any sound coming from inside the house, the gunmen, believing the woman was dead, started to leave. But then a spark lit up the darkness in the bedroom.

Whether it was a flashlight or the light from her cell phone, no one would ever know, but the police would later say that the light told the men that their victim was still alive and their work was unfinished. With a barrage of fresh gunfire, they completed the task. By the time the police and private security team arrived, the killers were gone, the servants were crying, and the blind bushbuck in the pen beside the bedroom was in a state of panic. Joan Root, struck by at least five bullets, was dead.

"She died while on the forefront of fighting illegal poachers . . . in and around Lake Naivasha, but may have made enemies that conspired against her," read the police report on Joan's death. Her friend Delta Willis put it better: She died because "she turned on a light."

She always knew that he would come back to her. Someday, some way, she would have him back, on their land, beside their lake, on the safari that would last forever. And finally, after all those years, Alan did come back. Climbing into his helicopter as soon as he got the news by phone from a friend in the early-morning hours of January 13, 2006, he rose out of the cacophony of Nairobi and into the majestic Great Rift Valley, flying, at long last, home to Lake Naivasha and to her. People later recalled that they had heard the helicopter crossing the mountains, flying over the dormant volcanoes and the farms, and coming in for a landing on Joan's landing strip beside the lake.

By the time Alan arrived, neighbors had already gathered outside Joan's bedroom, which had become a crime scene. "It was chaos," said one of the first neighbors to arrive shortly after two A.M. Some people were gaping through the lace curtains on her bedroom windows, which had been blackened by gunfire, while others tried to get through the bars and steel doors to see if there was any life left in the body that lay sprawled in a pool of blood on the bathroom floor.

The police were soon there, too, gathering evidence, of which there was very little. Alan and Barry Gaymer crawled under Joan's bed and retrieved a few of the spent casings from bullets that had riddled the walls and broken the windows. But it was too late. The killers were long gone.

There was one hope for justice, though not the informer who had originally gone to the police. His statement had been recorded, but it doesn't seem that anyone followed up on it. Instead, the investigation fell into the domain of a dog. "The bloodhound," someone suggested, and urgent calls were placed to the Mugie Ranch, which quickly flew in Chief Inspector Baucis, the most highly trained bloodhound in Kenya. Joan had welcomed him onto her land for training drills months before. At eight-thirty A.M. the dog arrived by private plane and was led to the animal orphanage outside Joan's bedroom, where his nose was directed to one of the footprints the killers had left behind.

The dog took off running, trailed by two handlers, across Joan's lawn, down Moi South Lake Road, through the streets filled with people, then turned right and ran straight into the calamitous heart of Karagita, where he bolted down the rutted dirt streets and stopped in front of a shanty and put his paws up on the door. It was the cramped quarters of two families, headed by a welder and a teacher, both of whom worked in the slum. Police contended that these men were the assassins. They believed they had been organized by David Chege, along with a "hocker," a buyer and seller of odds and ends in Karagita.

Chege was apprehended through the promise of work. He was pushing the out-of-gas motorcycle Joan had given him, now his taxi, through Karagita when his cell phone, also given to him by Joan, rang. It was one of the landowners on the lake, asking him to come over for some part-time work. When Chege arrived, the police were waiting. He was arrested and jailed, along with the three other suspects, at Naivasha Maximum Security Prison on the charge of attempted robbery with violence, an offense that carries the death penalty by public hanging.

The other murder victims who had been gunned down around Lake Naivasha were relatively unknown; this was the murder of a wildlife filmmaking star. Too much in love with the lake to leave it, and too stubborn to surrender, she had made a last stand on her land. What she left behind would tell the story of what she had tried to accomplish. The media attention was an international onslaught. Overnight, shy, quiet, unassuming Joan Root was thrust from the shadows and into the spotlight—as was her story about her mission to save the dying lake.

PASSION FOR CONSERVATION OF KENYA'S BEAUTY MAY HAVE COST . . . FILMMAKER HER LIFE headlined a story in England's *Guardian*.

FRIENDS FEAR THAT THE KILLING OF A RENOWNED FILM-MAKER MAY BE CONNECTED TO HER CONSERVATION WORK IN KENYA was the headline in *The Times* of London.

The *Standard*, a daily newspaper in Nairobi, featured a six-column spread, complete with a photograph of a black Kenyan placing a bouquet of flowers—one of a dozen that people had left for her—at Joan's gate. "Root's death is a major blow not only to her family . . . but the larger Naivasha community and Kenya," reporters wrote in the *Standard*. "Many will remember her for her endless efforts to save the ailing Lake Naivasha that has been under attack from various quarters. Until her death at 69, she was an outspoken campaigner against poaching and illegal fishing on the lake, a section of whose shore is named after her." The newspaper quoted an employee who said, "she was no longer just my employer but more like a relative," and a Naivasha business leader who said, "Joan's death is a great loss to . . . all those who champion the beauty and conservation of Africa's wildlife."

Among those left behind on Joan's land was Richard Waweru, a twenty-four-year-old black Kenyan Joan had employed, housed, and paid 4,500 shillings a month to monitor a nesting box of white-headed barbets, according to Lady Sarah Edwards in a moving tribute to Joan published by a nature journal. "He told me how she would walk him around her property in the evenings and show him leopard spoor, how to handle a python and a myriad other things. She lent him books on natural history and ornithology. He wept when we met soon after her death."

"Naivasha is *Chinatown*," said a Nairobi journalist, referring to the Academy Award–winning movie in which violence and conspiracy plague a once-sleepy town, and which climaxes with a twisted and shocking murder. "It's a fucking pressure cooker," added someone very close to Joan.

In late February 2006, when I went to Naivasha to attend Joan's memorial and write the *Vanity Fair* story about her life and death, I saw what they meant. Arriving in Naivasha is like landing in one of the area's famous hothouses, where everything, good and evil, is in one compressed and crowded place.

I was driven to Naivasha by Adrian Luckhurst and his smart blond American wife, Vickie. From the glory of the Great Rift Valley, we drove in broad daylight down the Nairobi-Nakuru Highway, where few dare to drive after dark, and through Naivasha town—the market town where the legal fishermen sell their catch on the main street. From there, the road twists, pitches, and turns onto the terribly rutted Moi South Lake Road, choked with eighteen-wheel trucks ferrying roses to the world and kicking up such a cloud of fine white dust that it's hard to see through. When the dust cleared, I could see the people, the destitute, hungry, and out-of-work people, many with their hands out, along both sides of the road.

"When people talk about places in Africa and Asia where people live on less than a dollar a day, you're looking at them now," Adrian Luckhurst said from behind the wheel. We passed Karagita, with its shanty bars, clay huts, mud streets, and desperation, broken by throngs of uniformed schoolchildren who shouted a chorus of "How are you! How are you!" the second they saw a paleface.

Turning right onto Joan Root's land was like arriving at an oasis in a land of barren desperation. It had been less than a month since her murder. When I arrived, the blood had been cleaned from her bedroom and bathroom floors, but bullet holes still riddled the walls. An amazing menagerie of wild animals pranced across her lawn; her clothing hung in her bathroom; and her staff was still in deep mourning. Everything was almost as Joan had left it, along with the lingering mystery of who killed her.

Hoping for answers to that, I went to the Naivasha police station, where Chief Simon Kiragu, a compact, friendly African in a crisp khaki uniform, flashed an exuberant smile in his bright blue office near the Karagita slum, assuring me that he had solved the murder of Joan Root primarily on the testimony of a dog. "A bloodhound! Super!" he said. After all, Chief Inspector Baucis was the best tracker dog in Kenya, and he exhibited neither hesitation nor doubt from the second he sniffed the killer's footprint until the time he put his paws up upon the Karagita door of two of the accused.

Chief Kiragu pulled out a thick report that listed five possible motives for the murder:

1) Ex-workers involved.
2) The deceased had acrimonious partings with some of her ex-employees. Some of them were bitter with her and there is a possibility that some of the disgruntled, sacked employees could have conspired to eliminate her.
3) Revenge deal gone sour.
4) Normal robbery.
5) Organized crime against state tourism. The deceased was an influential personality in wildlife matters worldwide and maybe a group of people who intend to tarnish the good name of the gov-

> ernment and tourism sector in order to cause donors to suspend aid to projects in this country that may have organized this murder to discredit the government and show that Kenya is an insecure country.

As for the connection of David Chege, Chief Kiragu was emphatic and harsh. "This group of four, they're very close to each other," he said, showing me Chege's statement, written in his own handwriting, which slanted down the page. "Although he was trusted, he was a crook," said the chief, listing a litany of Chege's deceptions that included "masterminding" both Joan's carjacking and her murder.

"A crook," the chief continued, elaborating on how Chege sold the boats he and the Task Force had confiscated, how he got money from Joan for operations that he never mounted, and how he extorted money from the poachers for allowing them to continue fishing illegally.

Chief Kiragu continued, "She protected and defended Chege. There was a time an investigation was being conducted on allegations that Chege could be having guns or associating with people with firearms. Root herself was saying, 'It cannot be true.' She told the criminal investigating officer in charge, 'Chege is a very good person. There is no way he could be involved with those kind of people.'

"Although Root had trusted him, he was not a very good worker. He was tricky, dishonest, but Root discovered a bit late."

Here the police chief said he had found the motive for the killing: shillings, pure and simple. "Basically, when we look at it, this was an attempted robbery," he said. "Based on circumstantial evidence leading us to him as a mastermind or the person who could arrange the whole thing. . . . You know, he is from inside. He knows the compound, in and out. The people who went there, they did not approach from the front. They approached from the rear, meaning they knew the setup of the house."

The word had gone through Karagita that Joan kept four million shillings ($59,000) in the safe in her home. When the safe was opened later, it was found to contain only 16,000 shillings ($237). A life for $237?

The chief nodded. People had been killed in Naivasha for a lot less.

—

When I told Joan Root's friends about the police conviction that her killing was the result of a normal robbery, they all said emphatically that the theory was, well, bullshit. "It was a known fact that Joan never kept a lot of money in the house," said Adrian Luckhurst, who pointed out that the murder had been committed in the middle of the month, not at the end, when Joan's workers got paid. "It was a vendetta based on a combination of a number of things, one being her conservation work around the lake and the efforts she made to preserve the lake. She crossed a lot of people, and so if you suddenly take a livelihood away and you're perceived to be the person behind it? Without a doubt, it was a contract killing."

Who paid for it?

"That is the mystery," Luckhurst said.

"Joan was hated by the people who were sponsoring the breaking of laws which related to the lake's ecosystem," said another neighbor. "I've had about eight of my friends murdered in the last few years, and no one has come to trial," Alan Root told me. "They're such bloody bastards," said a doyenne of Kenya's wildlife community, referring to Joan's killers and their ilk. "All these war zones! Somalia, Burundi, Tanzania, and Uganda—they've brought in so many guns. You can get an AK-47 for nothing." She was disappointed by the reaction to her friend's murder. "I felt we should have organized a demonstration, seen the minister of the interior or even the president," she said. "We should have used Joan's murder to say enough is enough!" Lord Enniskillen added. "The tragedy is that she died trying to alleviate the very poverty which creates the insecurity."

Others lamented Joan's death by saying "if only": If only she had stood back instead of standing out; if only she had taken a more conventional route to the problems instead of facing them head-on; if only she hadn't been so stubborn, single-minded, strong . . .

"The actual cause of the murder of Joan was, I think, her mission and absolute total absorption of protecting the wildlife she loved," said one white Kenyan in his magnificent home beside the lake, as music played and champagne was poured. He was all for protecting animals and the environment, he said. *But.* "How Joan did it was a dangerous way. You know, employing poachers and this and that. I'm not making any judgments. I don't want to be quoted out of context in this respect. She was doing what she was passionate about, and had been passionate about, all her life. But she approached it, and she wanted to deal with it, at her doorstep, in her way."

"She fought for what she knew was right," interrupted one of the women in the room.

"She should have joined Andrew Enniskillen on the Lake Naivasha Management Implementation Committee, which I was on," the gentleman continued. "Because Andrew was creating a structure in which one could work and deal with these problems. As an individual, you always have risks."

Committees and structures and meetings, meetings, meetings . . . Three years after her death, it's been mostly talk and little action, except by the poachers, who have returned to Lake Naivasha in a huge, unbridled wave. While crime in white Naivasha has been controlled to some extent by the private security force led by John Sutton in Joan's guest quarters, crime in black Naivasha has grown to the point that the Nairobi *Standard* newspaper would feature this September 22, 2008, headline: NAIVASHA, KENYA'S CAPITAL OF SHOCK AND HORROR STORIES. The story recounted a wave of murder, rape, cannibalism, incest, and "the weirdest happenings," including a witch doctor who kept pictures of "prominent people in Naivasha town," presumably to curse them. "Shocked residents flocked to the house to check if their pictures were there."

"The only person who can save us is God before we all perish like in Sodom and Gomorrah," added one Naivasha resident.

What will happen to the thing Joan cared about most—her land? Her friends hope that the Swiss trustees Joan put in charge of the property will follow her wishes to maintain it as an admission-free and unfettered wildlife preserve and not sell it for millions to a flower farmer or let it sit idle. At this writing, it is sitting empty and idle, except for the community security force.

One of the last films Alan and Joan Root produced together was entitled *The Legend of the Lightning Bird.* As always, she and Alan spent a year together in the bush, persistently filming the hammerkop—known as the lightning bird and regarded as the king of Africa's birds—in its inexplicable annual ritual: building a massive and flamboyant nest, a stack of scavenged vegetation as big as a bathtub, complete with a thick thatched roof crowned by feathers, animal hooves, and sometimes even wildebeest tails, only to have the magnificent structure decimated by time and predators. By the film's end, the intricately constructed nest is abandoned, then invaded by a relentless procession of opportunists—pythons, hyenas, owls, rats, genets, and baboons—seeking either a free meal or a comfortable nest in which to bed down for the night. Yet no matter the futility of building their magnificent nests, the lightning birds begin their excruciating nest building all over again, season after season, year after year.

"Why do the hammerkops build these ridiculous nests, and why do they fly hundreds of miles and carry enormous loads to build structures that are far too large to make any sense in terms of survival value?" asks the voice-over of the Roots' film. "And why do they so often move on without even using them? Scientists say there must be some benefit gained from all of that outpouring of energy. But they cannot say just what. Others say that the lightning bird's nest is a flamboyant gesture, a defiant challenge that overturns all our laws and theories about natural selection. . . ."

"Africa is the continent of legends," the narrator states earlier. With her death, Joan Root becomes one more of them, a legendary life forever caught between the continent's great extremes of beauty and brutality. Why did this woman, fighting to save the land and people she loved, have to die—and as with the lightning bird involuntarily leaving its nest behind for other species to inhabit and feed upon, who will continue the work that Joan dedicated so much of her life to in vain?

This question had no answers on March 4, 2006, when I sat among a hundred mourners, including many of the world's leading wildlife experts, at Joan's memorial service on her property by the lake. The mourners came by plane, car, and foot, black and white, rich and poor, to celebrate what the memorial program called "this sweet and gentle woman." They came to celebrate who she was and what she had done. She was but one person, a breed as endangered as the species she filmed and fought for: the elephants that once thundered across Tsavo; the flock of pink flamingos that flew free from their shackles on Lake Magadi; the endangered fish and fowl given a temporary reprieve on Lake Naivasha. Yet for those who loved her, she was one more devastating domino to fall, and behind Joan Root, who knew what would come next?

The cover of the memorial program featured a watercolor painting of Joan's garden with her two crowned cranes in the foreground and Lake Naivasha in the distance—the exact scene where her memorial was held, with a hundred chairs set up around a small podium.

"Not far from where we're gathered now, Joan Root was murdered in cold blood," a priest said at the opening of the service. "It's hard to get our heads around it," he continued, trying to grasp why her life was "brutally and shamefully cut short. Although bullets could cut her down, no brutal killer could kill what she did and what she stood for."

The program listed three people who would deliver eulogies: Joan and Alan's longtime friend Ian Parker, who had filmed the epic footage of them flying over Kilimanjaro in the hot-air balloon; Dee Raymer, Joan's friend in various conservation societies; and David Coulson, who hailed Joan's bravery and hard work as his assistant on his rock-art expeditions in the Sahara and Chad, only to return to his seat to find a threatening text message on his cell phone seemingly referring to something he'd just said in his speech, as if Joan's killers might be listening in on her memorial. This did not dampen the celebration, however. All of the speakers spoke eloquently and lovingly of their fallen friend and colleague.

Then Alan Root, sixty-eight, with his beard gone gray but still strong and limber, stepped out of the audience and walked up to the podium. At the same instant, as if Joan were standing there to call them, two crowned cranes swooped in and began strutting and dancing before the audience.

"I do not appear on the program, for the simple reason that I was not sure I was able to speak today," Alan said. "I'm still not sure I can, but I shall try. And if I didn't try, I know Joan would call me a wimp." He thanked everyone for coming, then spoke of Joan and their early life together—of how they had found this gorgeous Naivasha landscape back in the 1960s, "on our way up to the Congo," of Joan's bravery and her unflinching courage in the face of all manner of danger, of the debilitating myasthenia that she had managed to conquer, and of how she had saved him on countless occasions, including the time she caught him as he was falling out of the basket of the balloon when they were high over Kilimanjaro.

"Many of you know what a wonderful helper Joan was to me," he said. "But she was much more than that. She was really the producer of all the films we did together. Joan was my right arm. She made it all possible. And if we flew high and far together in those years, it was because of her."

He broke down and cried. When he regained his composure, he said in summation, "Modest, loving, funny, committed, courageous—that was my Joan."

Only she wasn't Alan Root's alone anymore. Her mourners were now global, and the story of the endangered lake that a woman loved so much she died trying to save it had become international news. Joan Root was no longer in anyone's shadow, and she hadn't been for a very long time.

I looked through the crowd of mourners to where, weeks before, Alan had buried Joan's ashes beneath a mound of earth and planted a small fig tree above her. There she would remain forever, looking over Lake Naivasha.

POSTSCRIPT

On August 10, 2007, the four men charged with attempted robbery with violence went before a judge in the rudimentary Naivasha courthouse. The defendants, including David Chege, looked glum, having spent almost two years in jail awaiting trial. Thirteen witnesses were called for the prosecution. The defense called no witnesses, preferring to stand by their own sworn statements.

The spectators consisted mainly of the defendants' families. Not a single white Kenyan attended the trial. There was no jury. A lone judge would decide their fate. He sat above the proceedings, and when he began to speak in a deep voice with a strong English accent, it was clear that he had already made up his mind.

No one had seen the accused at the scene, he pointed out. The guards had hidden, and the killers had been wearing masks. There was no evidence to link the accused to the crime. The only thing that linked anyone at all was the ludicrous accusation of a dog, he said, adding that it had been a civilian dog with untrained handlers, and with no police present. Even the charge was defective. "The deceased was shot dead . . . ," he said. "There was really no reason for preferring the charge of attempted robbery with violence. They should have preferred the charge of murder." Then he banged his gavel and ordered that the four men be set free.

Three months after he was released, David Chege was back on the run. "He is a ghost these days," people said. Chege was in jail on the charge of attempted robbery with violence in connection with Joan Root's death when I first went to Naivasha to write the magazine story about Joan Root. When I returned to do more research, he had been acquitted and released. I began looking for him the moment I returned, to no avail. He didn't answer his cell phone; he was never at the places where he was known to stay in Karagita. He was underground, I was told. Some people even insisted he was dead.

I enlisted some Karagita insiders to help me find him. Despite its burgeoning flower industry, Naivasha is still a very small town. We began putting out the word in the slum and the shanty bars that a *mzungu* writer from America was eager to see David Chege. Then we drove through the mud streets of Karagita to the mud-and-wattle houses of his mother and his first wife. Again, no luck. After two weeks of trying, my Kenyan cell phone rang. "It's Chege," announced the voice on the other end. He did not want to meet in Naivasha, he said. Things had become too dangerous for him to be seen in public; he insisted that he had been receiving threatening phone calls. However, he said he would be happy to meet me in Nairobi. I suggested the bar of the Nairobi Safari Club hotel, the urban outpost of the famous club near Mount Kenya, founded by the American actor William Holden.

David Chege was waiting for me when I arrived in the bar. A strong, young, handsome Kikuyu straight out of central casting, he wore bright blue pants, mismatched with a well-worn plaid double-breasted blazer, a polo shirt, and a baseball cap emblazoned with the name David Beckham. Chege's face was smooth and his skin was the color of dark chocolate. He slumped in his chair, eyeing me warily, unsmiling, suspicious.

He was accompanied by a beautiful young African woman in a blue-jean skirt and jacket. She was the sister of Chege's second wife, Esther, who had worked for Joan. She acted as if she were his media representative. It was clear they wanted to check me out before he said anything.

Chege spoke in Swahili to an interpreter I had brought along. His first question: Was I writing the screenplay of the movie being made about the life and murder of Joan Root, which he and everyone else in Kenya had been hearing about?

"No," I said. "A professional Hollywood screenwriter is writing the script for the movie."

He turned to the woman at his side. She nodded. Then he nodded. I had passed some sort of test. When beers arrived, he poured his delicately into his glass, staring into the bubbles, and began painting a radically different picture of himself, the polar opposite of the story that everyone had told me about him.

"There were people who tried to spoil my good name," he said. Just the fact that he was there, drinking the beers in the bar that day, instead of in the jail where he had spent the last two years, was proof of one thing: David Chege was indeed a survivor.

He had brought along a folder filled with papers, police reports and photographs, all of which, he said, exonerated him, just as the judge had done, in the killing of Joan Root. He loved Joan Root so much, he said, he called her "Mama" and told me, "She was a wonderful lady, a merciful lady." He talked about how much she had done for him and for Naivasha, and he said that when he'd heard the news of her murder, he'd gone into mourning. "I even did not eat for two days." To each and every one of the endless allegations against him, which I listed one by one, he said either "no," "never," or "not even for one single day!"

Like Joan, I wanted to believe him. When I asked him point-blank, "Are you a thug?" he answered without hesitation, "Not even a single day have I been involved with any criminal act." His record was clean, he insisted. As to who might have killed her, he said, "I tried to investigate it myself, but it defeated me." Was he telling the truth or was it just an extremely convincing performance?

"We are monitoring him," the police told me of David Chege.

I was thinking about all of this a few days later while sitting on the wide lawn of a restaurant, a pastoral setting traversed by monkeys and filled with birds whose species were recorded in a log at the entrance under the heading BIRDS SEEN TODAY! On the day of my visit, the list included: giant kingfisher, African fish eagle, hadada ibis, superb starling, little egret, cormorant, yellow-billed stork.

But as with many of the beautiful places I visited in the course of my research, there was an undercurrent of intrigue. I was at the club for tea with a Kenyan law-enforcement officer. After tea, he told me that he thought some payback was due for the time he had spent with me. "You make money on your stories, right?" he asked.

The talk of money by an officer of the law made the blood rush to my head. The conversation had shifted drastically, from an interview into what seemed to be a shakedown. I stammered a bit and said I appreciated his help.

"If you make money for stories, I should make money, too," he said. "You should give me two thousand dollars for the stories I have just told to you."

I shut my notebook with a loud slap. The interview was over, and I hoped that something sinister wasn't about to begin.

"Do you have a car?" he asked. His jovial disposition of a few minutes earlier had been replaced by a steely-eyed glare.

"Yes, do you need a ride somewhere?" I asked.

"No. I have a car. But I have no petrol."

I asked how much he needed for gas.

"Five hundred bob," he said, meaning five hundred Kenyan shillings. It amounted to $7.45—not much of a shakedown. I passed it to him in a handshake gesture and hurried away.

It's safe to say that the police investigation, if there ever really was one, has gone cold. To this day, the murder of Joan Root remains a mystery, and its perpetrators are still at large.

"Whoever killed her threw that gun into a long drop," a woman told me at Joan's memorial service.

"A shit hole in Karagita," added her husband.

And there it mixed with the wastes of the slum and the runoff from the flower farms and then flowed, like everything in Naivasha, into the lake.

AFTERWORD

Not long after I left Kenya, where I was researching this book, the country exploded. Sparked by what people saw as a rigged presidential election, voter outrage turned to carnage, and protest turned to tribal warfare, as mobs from Kenya's more than forty different tribes began killing opposing tribesmen and women in January 2008. The weapons included everything from sharpened sticks and stones to bows and arrows and guns. More than a thousand people were left dead; hundreds of thousands were wounded, displaced, and on the run. Women were raped. Slums, churches, stores, and villages were torched, their inhabitants, including children, burned alive. The government ordered a media blackout as the economy collapsed; tourists were evacuated and riot police marched through Nairobi, the capital, firing guns and tear gas to disperse rioters and kill looters.

Some of the worst violence happened in and around Naivasha, but after it subsided, people there returned to asking, *Who killed Joan Root?*

More than four years after her murder, as many questions as answers remain. But less than two years after her death, a new wrinkle arrived in the deepening mystery. It all began when a British safari operator named Brian Freeman and his Kikuyu wife, Esther, rented a house on twenty-two acres near Joan's land.

The Freemans had only recently moved onto the property by the midnight Joan was murdered; from their compound, they could hear the gunshots coming from Joan's property.

"We were afraid to go out and see what was happening," Esther Freeman told me later. "Very early the next morning, the landowner came over to the main house, where I was. She told me, 'That evil woman is dead! She's *dead!*' And she was dancing when she got into the house. As if she was relieved in some way." Until that incident, she added, the owner had been kind and accommodating, "a polite good woman. So to me I thought, 'This Joan Root must be an evil woman, because [the owner] is so good.'" Brian Freeman had the same early impression. "She was quite religious," he said. "When I moved in, I felt sorry for her, that she was quite isolated and maybe people were taking advantage of her."

There had been something of a feud between the Freemans' landlady (to whom both Freemans refer by her first name, and whom I'll call O.) and Joan Root, mostly over land boundaries. I had heard about it during my stay in Naivasha, and Joan had written about it in her diaries:

> *7.16.04: [O.] accused me of bringing the [police] Chief to investigate her tree cutting. . . . She accused me of threatening her on a phone call, + I told her I warned her, not threatened. Felt shaken up but may have saved the bushes. . . . Got to Eugene's at 1:30 for lunch + told him about [O.]'s unbalanced behaviour. . . . 8.17.04: A.M. I drove down to pumps + looked at [O.]'s front land with all the cut stumps + the line she plans to fence. Feel very distressed. . . . 8.9.05: John sent Alex + Waweru. They saw about 11 poachers in the water. [O.] told them she was very worried about security because I harboured group of bad men.*

John Sutton, who heads the Naivasha private security force based on Joan's land, had told me that his team had been called to Brian Freeman's house to investigate evidence of black magic—witchcraft. "[Freeman] found a sheep's head on the doorstep. . . . Obviously there was blood and there were signs of witchcraft," Sutton said.

"The police traced the sheep and other parts of the animal to the staff quarters" of the property, and to the neighbor's main houseman.

It was the beginning of some very strange happenings in and around the Freemans' compound, which Brian Freeman referred to as "bad juju": he soon found an earthen pot "full of blood and gunk" placed in the middle of his driveway, dogs poisoned, dead chickens hung on his fence, "a bit of black magic at the gate"—all of which began, he said, after he told his landlady he would be interested in buying the land where he had been living. (Joan had also found evidence of witchcraft on her property.) "She wanted me out," Freeman said. "But being very British, I was not going to be forced from my castle." That's when the problems began. Aside from the black magic, Freeman said his landlady turned his water off, followed by "an escalation of harassment to get us out of the property."

Shortly after noon on March 30, 2007, Freeman returned to his compound to find it empty, which caught him by surprise, as his staff was supposed to be preparing for an upcoming safari. Unbeknown to Freeman, his employees had been rounded up and locked in a storage container. A group of thugs were lying in wait for him, one of whom aimed a rifle at him and misfired. "Then they set upon me," he said, "cutting my head with a panga, clubbing me, and I fell to the ground. I knew that I was exposed and I would die."

He managed to crawl under his Land Rover and fight them off, as the men kicked at him and sliced the air around him with their pangas while trying to pull him out. When they couldn't pry him from beneath the vehicle, they began shooting at him—"five shots, the last of which blew my arm to smithereens."

The similarities between the attack on Freeman and Joan's murder were strikingly apparent, down to the weapon: an AK-47. Unlike Joan, Brian Freeman survived to tell the tale, and to follow, to the best of his ability, the somewhat murky trajectory of the police investigation thereafter. According to Freeman, an informant told police after the attack that the men were contract killers, hired by the landlady and her houseman for 16,950 shillings (about $220) to kill both Freeman and his wife, Esther. For two days before the attack on the Freemans, the informant reported, the would-be killers stayed and were fed in the landlady's compound. A police investigator with whom I corresponded later relayed a slightly different story, apparently the one given to police by some of the men rounded up after the events of March 30, 2007: "Two suspects . . . told police that prior to attack they were hosted at [the landowner's] residence and told by [the landowner's houseman] that they stood to make a lot of money if they robbed Freeman." Shortly after the attack on Brian Freeman, the landowner, along with her houseman, was arrested and charged with conspiracy to commit a felony. The landowner recorded a statement for police, according to the police investigator, "explaining [that] the suspects spent [time] at her place [and that] she understood . . . that the suspects were to assist [in having the Freemans] evicted from her house." However, the landowner later changed her version of events, vigorously denying any connection with the attack on Brian Freeman, much less the murder of Joan Root. Acquitted of all charges, she left Naivasha after her release from custody. "Unfortunately, people can't be prosecuted on their own evidence in Kenya," said Freeman.

As of this writing, the mystery of the murder of Joan Root remains unsolved. As for the state of Lake Naivasha: the droughts of 2009–2010 pushed water levels to historic new lows, stranding papyrus and poachers, who find increasingly fewer fish to ensnare. To Joan, however, the biggest travesty might have been the state of her land itself. She had intended the property to become a nature preserve, a place for education and an enduring example of the wonders of the wild. But it presently remains barren, with only the guest house inhabited by the private security force headquartered there, which guards the lake against those who trespass against it. Lying eternally beneath the ground of this haunted but still extraordinarily beautiful place, the woman I have written about in *Wildflower* is unable to do anything about the declining state of her beloved homeland. But her story remains a beacon of activism and, it is to be hoped, a lesson in the importance of preserving the wild places on earth.

ACKNOWLEDGMENTS

I am fortunate to have Susan Mercandetti as my editor at Random House. Her endless encouragement, boundless enthusiasm, and editorial expertise, as well as her fantastic team—including Millicent Bennett, Abby Plesser, Ben Steinberg, and Steve Messina—pulled me through. Thank you, Susan, for all that you did to make this book a reality.

The story of Joan Root was first published in the August 2006 issue of *Vanity Fair* magazine. For that, I want to thank Wayne Lawson for championing the story, first as editor on the magazine piece and later on this book; *Vanity Fair*'s great editor Graydon Carter for sending me to Kenya and publishing the resulting story; and Matthew Pressman for his invaluable and constant help both on the magazine story and on this book.

Thank you to the brilliant John Ruddy, who was my invaluable editorial assistant on this project.

In New York, endless thanks to the acclaimed author and travel and wildlife writer Delta Willis, my early ally on this project, whose help opened many doors.

Thank you to Guillaume Bonn for your great company in Kenya and your incredible photographs, and Annabelle Thom for your insightful remembrances of Joan.

Before I left for Kenya, where I had never been before, my first call was to Pamela Lassers, director of media relations for the international tour operator Abercrombie & Kent, which started in Nairobi. Pamela immediately connected me with Marett Taylor, who grew up in Kenya and is now director of sales and marketing for Abercrombie & Kent Europe. Marett's guidance and connections in Kenya made me immediately feel at home.

In Nairobi and Naivasha, I found a community of gracious and friendly people who opened their doors and their hearts to me about their friend Joan Root. These include, first and foremost, Alan and Fran Root and Adrian and Vickie Luckhurst, who spent innumerable hours with me. I am also eternally grateful to Jean Hartley, who runs Viewfinders, a company that outfits and facilitates wildlife documentary filmmakers in Kenya. Jean read the manuscript before publication and offered her factual corrections and wise advice. Thanks also to Oria and Iain Douglas-Hamilton, Ian and Chris Parker, Sarah Higgins, Lord Andrew Enniskillen and Lady Sarah Edwards, Barry and Linda Gaymer, Felix Munyao, Count Peter Szapary, June Zwager, Peter and Teresa Zwager, Parselelo Kantai, Francis Erskine, Reuben Chege, Richard Waweru, Mark Kariuku, Claus Mortensen, Dr. Richard Leakey, Jeremy Block, Dodo Cunningham-Reid, Robert Hammond, Rod Kundu, David Kilo, Aidan Hartley, John Vaughn, Dieter Rottcher, Norbert Rottcher, Mike Eldon, William Murai, John and Elli D'Olier, Bosire Bogonko, John Sutton, Valerie Sutton, Tom Cholmondeley, Sally Dudmesh, Esmond Bradley Martin, Chief Simon Kiragu, Rod Jones, Tony and Susie Church, Tony and Sarah Seth-Smith, Dr. David Coulsen, Dee Raymer, Sue Allan, Natasha Illum Berg, Kuki Gallman, Errol Trzebinski, the wonderful staff of the Nairobi Serena Hotel, and the women who make up the team at Balloon Safaris, who so capably assisted me in copying thousands of pages of Joan Root's letters and diaries.

In England, I found a friend in Anthony Smith, who flew over Africa with Alan and Joan in his balloon and became one of their closest friends. Thank you to Alan's former assistant Giles Camplin, whose memories were so vivid and exciting. William Hutton gave of his time and provided his impeccable notes and memory from Guernsey. Thanks also to Jonathan Kenworthy, John and Meta Wells-Thorpe, Senga Thorpe, Des and Jen Bartlett, Richard Brock, Aubrey Buxton, Barry Paine, James Fox, Mike Hay, Jeffrey Boswall, Alison Aitkin, Cindy Buxton, and Stuart Wheeler.

In South Africa, I would like to thank Otto Poulsen, Lindy Lawrie, Dr. Holly Dublin, Jacky Walker, and Mary Stanley-Shepherd (and all of the dancers in Mary's Mob).

In the United States, many thanks to Jeff Rich; John Heminway; Beth Conlin; Martin Bell; David Magee; Rosanna Sguera; Shannon Marven and the staff at Dupree/Miller & Associates literary agency; Tom Colligan, who doggedly fact-checked every line; and Liz Suman, who found key sources.

Last but far from least, thanks to my wonderful family: the amazing Evelyn Abroms Kraus and Melvin Kraus; the late, great Berney Seal; Eddie and Melissa Seal; B. J. and Alana Seal; and all of the many members of the extended Seal, Abroms, Kraus, and Blocker clans.

NOTES

PREFACE

ix Joan Root letters, May/June 1996.

INTRODUCTION

xi "Conservationist Killed": World Briefs, *New York Times,* January 17, 2006.

xiii *Vanity Fair:* Mark Seal, "A Flowering Evil," *Vanity Fair,* August 2006.

xiii "I hear you are looking for me" and "Dear Mark": Alan Root email to author.

xiv *"Doctor Dolittle* times one thousand": Author interview with John Heminway.

xiv Description of memorial and flower farms: Seal, "A Flowering Evil."

xiv about a hundred dollars a hit: Author interview with Thomas Cholmondeley.

xv "Everyone here knows what I mean": Ian Parker, eulogy at Joan Root's memorial.

xvi When five soldiers: Author interviews with Ian Parker.

xvi "I've crashed two of these": Author interviews with Alan Root.

xvii Working Title Films optioned the movie rights: BBC News, May 21, 2007.

xvii Another stroke of luck: Author interview with Anthony Smith.

CHAPTER ONE

3 Kenya history: Robert Edgerton, *Mau Mau—An African Crucible* (New York: Free Press, 1989).

3 "The British people came to Kenya": Author interview with Otto Poulsen.

4 ended with a bloodbath: Caroline Elkins, *Imperial Reckoning* (New York: Henry Holt, 2004).

4 Kenya history: David Anderson, *Histories of the Hanged* (New York: Norton, 2005).

4 Joan Root later told a friend: Author interview with Otto Poulsen.

5 "When the British arrived": Edmund Thorpe letter.

5 Kenyatta quotes: John Frederick Walker, *A Certain Curve of Horn* (New York: Atlantic Monthly Press, 2002).

6 Edmund Thorpe biography: Edmund Thorpe's résumé; obituary in *The New Mexican,* March 4, 1997; and Jim Thomas, "Former Safari Boss Recalls Kenya Days."

6 a derelict 240-acre estate: Edmund Thorpe letter.

6 He planted thirty-nine thousand: Author interview with Elizabeth Conlin, Edmund Thorpe's sister-in-law.

7 a mile of coffee beans: Thomas, "Former Safari Boss."

7 a hundred workers: "Adventurers and Explorers, Jean and Edmund Thorpe," *The Santa Fean,* January/February 1981.

7 "I could swim": Ibid.

7 *Tarzan* films: Ibid.

7 "A friend had left me Mabel": Ibid.

7 In a country where little child-rearing: Author interview with Alan Root.

8 Edmund had become a professional hunter: Kenya Thru the Lens brochure, 1945–1965; Edmund owned safari business: Thorpe résumé.

8 Few people in the white community: Joan Root interview with Mike Eldon.

8 worked as a secretary for Shell Oil: Author interview with Mary Stanley-Shepherd.

9 roof rack . . . chickens: Alan Root, eulogy at Joan Root's memorial.

9 Driving east across: 1968 Kenya Thru the Lens brochure.

9 The Ngorongoro Crater: www.ngorongoro-crater-africa.org.

9 "These Americans are a very pleasant bunch": Joan Root letter to mother, January 27, 1960.

10 set foot in Kenya at age ten: Alan Root's résumé.

10 rare combination of wit: Author interview with Ian Parker.

10 As John Heminway would write: John Heminway, *No Man's Land* (New York: Warner Books, 1989).

10 son of a Cockney meatpacker: Ibid.

10 The Roots lived on the Athi Plain: Ibid.

10 Alan Root bio: Alan Root's résumé; Heminway, *No Man's Land;* author interview with Alan Root.

11 Armand and Michaela Denis: Michaela Denis obituary by Caroline Boucher, *The Guardian* (London).

12 "What the hell are you doing": Author interview with Alan Root.

12 Bernhard Grzimek: Obituary, Associated Press, May 26, 1987.

12 knee-deep in the Ngorongoro mud: Author interview with Alan Root.

12 "Hi, I'm Alan Root": Ibid.

12 invited the young man to . . . dinner: Ibid.

13 He suggested that she take the day off: Ibid.

13 a pound of butter: Ibid.

14 still hadn't said one damn word: Delta Willis, "The Other Roots," *People*, July 6, 1981.

14 engaged to be married: Author interview with Jean Hartley.

14 "Goosey-Goss": Author interview with Ian Parker.

14 Ted Goss: Obituary, *The Independent* (London), July 25, 2002.

15 heard a cry coming out of a well: "Special Food Came Too Late for Bundu," clipping, newspaper not identified.

15 Feeding a baby elephant was next to impossible: Author interview with Alan Root.

15 invented the formula: www.sheldrickwildlifetrust.org.

16 slept with the animal . . . she would be *right back:* Author interview with Senga Thorpe, Joan Root's aunt.

16 one of her friends had gotten engaged: Author interview with Alan Root.

16 neither . . . had ever known true romantic love: Ibid.

16 She would later claim that she loved Alan: Author interview with Annabelle Thom.

17 How do you get on TV?: "Her Wildlife Is Tame," magazine article.

CHAPTER TWO

18 one goal: to become the greatest wildlife filmmaker: Author interview with Alan Root.

18 The wedding took place: Author interview with Sue Allan, and "A City Wedding After All," clipping, newspaper not identified.

19 "we're either still on our honeymoon": Delta Willis, "The Other Roots (Alan and Joan) Document Africa's Wildlife," *People,* July 6, 1981.

19 "a safari that would last": Joan Root interview with Mike Eldon.

19 elephant dung: Author interview with Alan Root.

19 Alan had telegrammed: Joan Root letter to mother, February 27, 1961.

20 set up camp on the Athi River: Joan Root letter to mother, March 22, 1961.

20 The tent he had brought: Author interview with Alan Root.

20 scorpion: Ibid. and Colin Willock, *The World of Survival* (London: Andre Deutsch, 1978).

20 She took two aspirins: Alan Root, eulogy at Joan Root's memorial.

20 At four-thirty A.M.: Joan Root letter to mother, March 22, 1961.

21 male lions had killed and consumed: J. H. Patterson, *Man-Eaters of Tsavo* (New York: St. Martin's Press, 1986).

21 Neither Joan nor I: Alan Root email to author.
22 "We're off to Karamoja": Author interview with Alan Root.
22 "Dear Mum": Joan Root letters to mother.
22 Alan has gone out: Joan Root letters to mother.
23 all of which Alan was apt to do: Author interview with Anthony Smith.
24 "Romance?": Alan Root email to author.
24 The couple could not live on love alone: Author interview with Alan Root.
24 One day they awoke: *Box Me a Bongo* (movie), 1998.
25 "never been in love ever before": Edmund Thorpe letter.
25 Jean Bowie Nathan Shor: Obituary, *New Mexican,* December 31, 1998.
26 a great colonial lady: Author interview with Alan Root.
26 "No one thinks [ill] of you, Mum": Joan Root letter to mother, July 1962.
26 "Don't let that old": Joan Root letter to mother, undated.
26 "I have a wonderful husband": Joan Root letter to mother, August 24, 1963.
26 expedition across East Africa: Alan Root résumé.
26 balloon expedition: Author interview with Anthony Smith; Anthony Smith, *Throw Out Two Hands* (London: Allen & Unwin, 1963).
27 President [Idi] Amin saw: *The Guardian* (London).
27 "We were having *terrible* trouble": Author interview with Anthony Smith.
28 "She was the spear carrier": Author interview with Dee Raymer.
29 beneficiaries of his will: Alan Root letter to Anthony Smith.
29 After three intimate months: Author interview with Anthony Smith.
29 Details of hornbill: Joan Root letters to mother, July 13 and December 28, 1962.
30 Buxton biography: Author interview with Aubrey Buxton; Willock, *The World of Survival;* www.wildfilmhistory.org (interview with Buxton); author interview with Alan Root.
31 Alan and Joan were camping: Author interview with Alan Root.
32 Joan let out a shout: Ibid.

32 One of their first assignments: Joan Root letters to mother, June 20 and 29, 1962.

32 "Half a century ago": *A Tear for Karamoja* (movie), 1980.

33 eight or nine stages: Joan Root letter to mother, June 29, 1962.

33 "I would have *a child!*": Joan Root letter to mother, July 13, 1962.

33 Lake Magadi details: Author interview with Alan Root; *National Geographic,* December 1962; "Saving the Flamingo," *Sunday Nation,* September 23, 1963; Joan Root letters to mother, October 4 and 11, 1962.

35 Requests for Alan's film footage: Joan Root letters to mother, October 4, 1962, and August 24, 1963.

36 "You know, it never rains": Joan Root letter to mother, December 28, 1962.

CHAPTER THREE

38 "have a coffee": Author interview with Alan Root.

38 Naivasha was a place of extremes: Author interviews with Jean Hartley and Ian Parker; "Relatives Lured into Mungiki Traps and Bodies Left to the Dogs in Naivasha," *Daily Nation* (Nairobi), October 20, 2008.

39 Even President Theodore Roosevelt: Theodore Roosevelt, *African Game Trails* (Birmingham, Ala.: Palladium Press, 1991).

39 Finding house in Naivasha: Author interview with Alan Root; Alan Root, eulogy at Joan Root's memorial; Joan Root letters to mother.

39 "take a stiff gin and tonic": *The Irish Times,* April 4, 2005.

40 "the most beautiful home site": Mark Seal, "A Flowering Evil," *Vanity Fair,* August 2006.

40 Kilimandege: Author interview with John Sutton.

40 belonged to the McRae family: Author interview with Robin Anderson.

40 Description of property: Author interview with Alan Root; Alan Root, eulogy at Joan Root's memorial.

41 Description of Virunga Mountains: Joan Root letter to mother,

October 1, 1963; author interview with Alan Root; Alan Root, eulogy at Joan Root's memorial.

41 Carl Akeley: George Schaller, *The Mountain Gorillas* (Chicago: University of Chicago Press, 2000).

41 Smith collapsed: Author interview with Anthony Smith.

42 They smelled the gorillas before they heard them: Schaller: *The Mountain Gorillas.*

43 We had to get very close for pictures: Alan Root, newspaper interview.

43 Over several weeks: Author interview with Alan Root; Alan Root, eulogy at Joan Root's memorial; Joan Root letter to mother.

44 he came up with a fist: Author interview with Giles Camplin; Colin Willock, *The World of Survival* (London: Andre Deutsch, 1978).

44 Anthony Smith later wrote: Joan Root obituary by Anthony Smith, *The Guardian* (London).

44 the house on Lake Naivasha: Joan Root letter to mother, December 1963.

44 tragedy struck: Alan Root, eulogy at Joan Root's memorial.

45 Additionally, it can alter: Monique M. Ryan, M.D., "Myasthenia Gravis and Premature Ovarian Failure," *Muscle & Nerve* 30, no. 2 (2004):231–33.

45 "You don't know how sick she is!": Author interview with Jacky Walker.

45 Still weak and shaking: Alan Root, eulogy at Joan Root's memorial.

46 *Whoop! Whoop!:* Author interview with Giles Camplin.

46 They sometimes had trouble communicating with words: Alan Root letter to Joan Root.

46 The Roots' property: Author's visit.

47 George and Joy Adamson: Joy Adamson, *Born Free* (New York: Bantam Books, 1966).

47 They could not have picked a better place: Author's visit.

47 Description of house: Ibid.

48 ever-growing menagerie: Delta Willis, "The Other Roots," *People,* July 6, 1981, and other media.

48 red-billed oxpeckers: Author interview with Anthony Smith.

48 Joan's caracal: Author interview with Giles Camplin.

48 "We are presently staying at Alan's house": Giles Camplin letter to Anthony Smith, April 2, 1968.

49 "Alan damaged his knee": Joan Root letter to mother, January 12, 1983.

49 Details on Kiari's family: Joan Root diary; author interview with Anthony Smith.

49 Gichuhi, throttling Kiari: Joan Root letter to mother.

49 These were petty crimes; but perpetrators: Joan Root letter to mother, January 12, 1983.

50 Some nights Alan and Joan would stretch a sheet: Author interviews with various staff.

50 "A lot of the time, Joan was sort of an intensive-care nurse": Alan Root, eulogy at Joan Root's memorial.

52 Details of Fossey killing: Dr. Richard Leakey in media reports; Farley Mowat, *Woman in the Mists* (New York: Grand Central Publishing, 1988).

52 Joy Adamson killing: *New York Times,* August 29, 1981; "Kenyan Convicted in Death of Joy Adamson," *The Guardian* (London), February 8, 2004; "Joy Shot Me in the Leg So I Gunned Her Down," *The Guardian* (London), February 8, 2004.

52 George Adamson killing: *New York Times,* August 22, 1989.

53 Details of puff adder bite: George Plimpton, "The Man Who Was Eaten Alive," *The New Yorker,* August 23, 1999; Joan Root letter to mother.

53 We'll have to amputate at the elbow: Unsigned letter, December 5, 1968.

54 Details of Anglia offices and Alan as star: Willock, *The World of Survival;* author interview with Anthony Smith.

54 His handsome profile gazed: Author interview with Anthony Smith.

54 "He loved it when Anglia TV would send": Ibid.

54 "I mean, there were a couple of": Author interview with Alan Root.

55 "leapt skyward, struck a bird": Delta Willis on www.deltawillis.com.

CHAPTER FOUR

56 Details on Galápagos: Colin Willock, *World of Survival* (London: Andre Deutsch, 1978); Aubrey Buxton, "The Enchanted Isles," *TV Times* (London), November 30, 1967.

56 The untouched beauty: Joan Root letters to mother, April 28 and May 16, 1966.

57 "with plenty of time on hand": Buxton, "The Enchanted Isles."

57 "Film all the wildlife you can!": Willock, *World of Survival.*

57 "It was quite exciting": Joan Root letters to mother, April 28, May 30, and August 23, 1966.

58 shot twenty-three thousand feet of film: Willock, *World of Survival.*

58 "You're an excellent cameraman": Author interview with Alan Root.

58 offering twice the two thousand pounds: Joan Root letter to mother, May 30, 1966.

59 "We have always been very frank": Joan Root letter to mother, October 23, 1967.

59 "It will help get our names out": Joan Root letter to mother, October 23, 1967.

59 "it *is* our film": Joan Root letter to mother, October 23, 1967.

59 the coral fish: Joan Root letter to mother, January 3, 1968.

60 Details on Buxton's wife and shopping for clothes: Joan Root letter to mother, January 3, 1968.

60 "My job is to show what was there": Author interview with Alan Root.

60 Details of meeting queen, premiere and party afterward: Joan Root letter to mother, January 3, 1968.

61 I don't know the names of any of the titled: Joan Root letter to mother, January 19, 1968.

62 The next morning: Joan Root letter to mother, January 19, 1968.

62 Details of programs and bongos: Author interview with Alan Root.

63 Alan left on Tuesday morning: Joan Root letter to mother, August 28, 1969.

63 Details of Alan Root activities: Alan Root résumé.

64 Details of Mzima Springs: Joan Root letter to mother; author interview with Alan Root; Joan and Alan Root, "Mzima, Kenya's Spring of Life," *National Geographic,* September 1971; *Two in the Bush* (movie).

64 Details of *Baobab: Portrait of a Tree:* Willock, *World of Survival; Two in the Bush;* author interview with Alan Root; Mary Riddell, "The Man Who Has Given His Life to Love and Africa," *The Times* (London), July 17, 1996; Joan Root letter to mother, July 17, 1996.

65 We had plenty to film: Joan Root letter to mother, August 24, 1971.

66 Details of balloon flight over migration: Joan Root letter to mother, August 25, 1986.

66 "Okay, Alan, get ready": *Two in the Bush.*

67 Joan was in Durban: Anthony Smith letter to Joan Root, July 1973; Anthony Smith letter to Dr. Eleanor Mears, June 13, 1973.

67 She wanted children: Author interview with Alan Root.

67 Joan returned to Naivasha: Alan Root letter to Anthony Smith, May 30, 1973.

67 "I got the feeling that she felt": Author interview with Alan Root.

68 "She was a Kenya girl": Author interview with Oria Douglas-Hamilton.

68 "I really am a mess these days": Alan Root letter to Anthony Smith, January 5, 1973.

69 Details of Kilimanjaro flight: Alan Root letter to Anthony Smith, March 19, 1979; Joan Root letter to mother, March 16, 1974.

71 "You don't need to be so frightened!": Alan Root, eulogy at Joan Root's memorial.

74 Details of Jacqueline Onassis flights: Joan Root letter to mother, August 20, 1974; author interview with Alan Root.

75 Alan liked to fly home . . . through Hell's Gate: Author interview with Mike Hay; George Plimpton, "The Man Who Was Eaten Alive," *The New Yorker,* August 23, 1999.

76 "He also shares with his fellow filmmakers": Brian Jackman interview with Alan Root, publication not identified.

76 Their balloon flights soon paid an additional dividend: Joan Root letters to mother, January 1976, and May 1, 1980.

76 Details of Mzima hippo attack: Joan Root letters to mother; Alan Root letters to friends; Plimpton, "The Man Who Was Eaten Alive."

78 Details of termite film: *Two in the Bush; Mysterious Castles of Clay* (movie), 1978.

80 *Castles of Clay* is artistically as majestic: John Heminway, *No Man's Land* (New York: Warner Books, 1989).

80 "The Roots may be the last of their breed": Delta Willis, "The Other Roots," *People,* July 6, 1981.

81 "compilation film": Joan Root letters to mother, October 4, 1979, and July 23, 1981.

81 Details of spitting cobra sequence: Joan Root letter to mother May 1, 1980; author interview with Alan Root; *Two in the Bush.*

82 Details of publicity tour: Joan Root letters to mother, June 14 and July 23, 1981.

86 They were a team: Author interview with John Heminway.

87 a friend gave Joan: Joan Root diary.

CHAPTER FIVE

89 "It was a typical Kenyan wedding": Author interviews with Ian Parker and Dieter and Norbert Rottcher.

89 "Isn't he fantastic!": Author interview with Ian Parker.

89 Details of Jennie Hammond: Author interviews with Bob Hammond and Ian Parker.

90 "I just remember being pretty drunk": Author interview with Alan Root.

90 "Your dinner is in the oven": Author interview with Bob Hammond.

90 "I don't know if she actually came with the suitcases": Author interview with Vickie Luckhurst.

90 help find Jennie a house: Author interview with Alan Root.

91 Details of volcano: Joan Root letter to mother, August 25, 1986; author interview with Alan Root.

92 No one will ever beat this: Author interview with Delta Willis.

92 "I had to have this test": Author interview with Alan Root.

92 He felt "trapped": Ibid.

93 "She was willing to make that deal": Author interview with Vickie Luckhurst.

93 Details of scene and dialogue in Wheeler Opera House: Joan Root diary.

95 "It hurts me that I cannot be involved": Joan Root letter to Anthony Smith, July 12, 1987.

95 "I also feel I may have noticed Mushamuka": Joan Root letter to Anthony Smith, July 12, 1987.

96 Alan said it was "killing Jennie": Joan Root diary, July 10, 1987.

97 "Cannot be at the Serengeti": Joan Root letter to Anthony Smith.

97 "She stopped him from making his films": Author interview with unnamed friend of Alan and Joan's.

100 Details of divorce: Joan Root diary.

101 "I can picture her in my mind's eye": Errol Trzebinski email to author (from her diary about Joan Root's neighbor, Doria Block).

101 "I'm selfish and arrogant": Jennie Hammond letter to Joan Root, undated.

102 Divorce settlement: Author interview with Alan Root.

102 Details and dialogue of Jennie Hammond's confronting Joan Root: Joan Root letter to Anthony Smith, March 21, 1991.

CHAPTER SIX

103 Details on Joan Root post-divorce: Author interviews with Adrian Luckhurst, Vickie Luckhurst, and Jean Hartley.

105 Details of elephant counts: Author interview with Iain Douglas-Hamilton; Joan Root letter to Anthony Smith, April 4, 1988; Richard Leakey, *Wildlife Wars* (New York: St. Martin's Press, 2001); *New York Times,* July 19, 1989.

108 "She was not one to stand up in public": Author interview with Sarah Higgins.

109 "She was such a good person" and other rock-art expedition details: Author interview with David Coulsen.

109 "In the Sahara evenings": David Coulsen, eulogy at Joan Root's memorial.

110 Now she would do everything: Joan Root obituary, *The Standard* (Nairobi), January 23, 2006.

110 "I didn't have a lot of time for her": Author interview with Dee Raymer.

111 Adrian Luckhurst to nominate her: Joan Root diary.

111 one negative vote is all it takes: Author interview with Esmond Bradley Martin.

111 "She suffered from a lack of recognition": Author interview with Annabelle Thom.

111 Details of David Attenborough introduction and Alan Root reply: Joan Root letters.

112 "Stayed home all day": Joan Root diary, October 17, 1994.

112 Details of animals seen: Joan Root diary, October 20, 1994.

113 "Some people just see a few animals": Joan Root interview with Mike Eldon, 1992.

113 "She contained herself so much": Author interview with Vicky Stone.

113 "She was so protective": Author interview with Annabelle Thom.

113 Woe to the predators, details of releasing python: Sarah Edwards, "A Tribute to Joan Root."

114 Sometimes she stopped in to see Sarah Higgins: Author interview with Sarah Higgins and visit to her home.

114 Details of Delta Willis trip: Author interview with Delta Willis, and www.deltawillis.com.

114 Throughout these years: Joan Root diary.

114 Details of Edmund Thorpe: Edmund Thorpe résumé.

115 Details of trip with Otto Poulsen: Author interview with Otto Poulsen.

115 Details of Treetops: Paul Zimmerman, "Treetops Hotel: Not a Bit Posh but It Attracts a Posh Clientele," *New York Times,* September 15, 1968.

116 "My dearest Otto": Joan Root letter to Otto Poulsen, undated.

116 Details of fight over riparian land: Author interview with Bill Hutton; letters and documents; Joan Root letters and diary; "Lake Naivasha, Experiences and Lessons Learned Brief," Lake Basin Management Initiative, 2005.

118 Whitney heiress from New York: *Sunday Telegraph* (London), November 3, 2003.

CHAPTER SEVEN

120 Details of Lake Naivasha: Alan Cowell, "Kenya Lake Outlives Comedy of Ecological Horrors," *New York Times,* March 18, 1982.

121 Naivasha's flower industry: Hans Zwager, *The Flowering Dutchman* (Oxford, UK; Victoria, Canada: Trafford Publishing, 2005).

122 In 1953 she met Hans: Ibid.

122 "You've got the bitch": Charles Hayes, *Oserian: Palace of Peace* (Nairobi: Rima Publications, 1997), p. 211.

123 "He imported all sorts of things": Author interview with June Zwager.

123 Details on chemicals: http://www.pesticideinfo.org/Detail_ChemReg.jsp?Rec_Id=PC33671.

123 Hans dropped the idea: Author interview with June Zwager.

124 "unless you put a lot on to improve it": Jane Perlez, "Dutch Flowers? In Name Only. Ask the Kenyans," *New York Times,* February 2, 1991.

124 The man even gave Hans: Zwager, *The Flowering Dutchman.*

124 Details about Naivasha flower farms: Perlez, "Dutch Flowers?"; Steve Bloomfield, "Where Have All the Flowers Gone: Thorns Among the Roses," *The Independent* (London), October 3, 2006; Flamingo flower farm website, www.flamingoholdings.com.

126 In 1990 alone, Kenyan farms had exported: Perlez, "Dutch Flowers?"

126 going up at an annual rate of 35 percent: http://www.dfid.gov.uk/news/files/speeches/trade/naivashaqa.asp.

126 "I had a visit": Author interview with Count Peter Szapary.

127 Kenya's annual flower exports grew nearly tenfold: Chris Collinson, "The Business Cost of Ethical Supply Chain Management: The Kenya Flower Industry Case Study," Natural Resources Institute, May 2001.

127 employ 100,000 people: U.K. Department for International Development, "Questions and Answers About Flower Production at Lake Naivasha," http://www.dfid.gov.uk/news/files/speeches/trade/naivashaqa.asp.

127 annual per capital income is about $880: World Bank report, 1990.

128 the laborers hand-wrapped each rose: Kenya Human Rights Commission.

128 "exceptional value": Author interview with Rod Jones.

129 "Naivasha is the perfect microcosm": Author interview with Dodo Cunningham-Reid.

129 Details on flower-farm workers: Kenya Human Rights Commission; "Kenya: Beauty and Agony," *Africa News,* March 18, 2002.

129 Some fifty thousand people lived in squalor: *Business Daily Africa.*

129 Frequently, a torn sheet: Kenya Human Rights Commission.

130 "The main threat": Author interview with Count Peter Szapary.

131 "Kenya is full of corruption": Author interview.

131 "I think that Joan Root": Author interview with Rod Jones.

CHAPTER EIGHT

133 "I will finally have the time to find my own feet": Joan Root letter to Anthony Smith, July 12, 1987.

134 Soon the poachers started employing: Author interview with David Harper.

135 Responsibility is a position: Joan Root notebook.

135 more than half of Kenya's population: Kari Lydersen, "Chicago Considers Banning Mistreated Elephants," *The New Standard,* March 6, 2006: UNHCR.com, 2004.

136 "Too many fishermen": Joan Root diary, February 18, 1994.

136 "So many Africans": Joan Root diary, June 12, 1994.

136 write a book about the Great Rift Valley: Joan Root letter to mother.

136 "my man in Kenya": Author interview with Anthony Smith.

137 "The lake has about five years' life left": Author interview with David Harper.

138 The story of a young man named Simon: Author interview with Simon.

138 800 shillings: Kenya Human Rights Commission.

139 the men began carrying weapons: Author interview with Tom Cholmondeley.

139 "Sometimes I feel I am living on a different planet": Joan Root letter to Frank and Peggy, December 2005.

139 "Feeling motivated!": Joan Root diary, March 13, 1995.

139 "There are some members who would probably admit": Lord Enniskillen to *Iko* magazine.

140 "It's all talk, talk, talk!": Ian Parker, eulogy at Joan Root's memorial.

140 "If you want to stop them": Author interview with Ian Parker.

140 Their first response: Author interview with Sarah Higgins.

141 Details of David Kilo meeting Joan Root: Author interview with David Kilo.

142 Details of the death of Edmund Thorpe: Joan Root diary, February 28 and March 1–2, 1997.

143 "which made her instantly recognizable": Devika Bhat, "A Colonial Paradise Lost to Violence in Not-So-Happy Valley," *The Times* (London), January 14, 2006.

143 "That house kept something of Alan for her": Author interview with Annabelle Thom.

144 three dogs that morning: Author interview with David Chege.

145 giving her what she treasured: Joan Root diary, August 20, 1997.

145 Chege tracked down the thieves: Joan Root diary, April 29, 1998.

145 Details on David Chege: Author interview with David Chege.

146 Diary items on Chege: Joan Root diary, February 17, August 26, September 1, and September 4, 1997.

146 He knew who she was: Author interview with David Chege.

146 Within days of meeting him: Joan Root diary, September 6, 1997.

146 going to teach him how to legally fish: Author interview with David Chege.

147 She also bought them: Author interview with David Kilo.

147 "provide employment for many of the jobless youths": Rod Kundu email to author.

147 "how I can have a lakeside guard like Chege": Joan Root diary, August 28, 1997.

148 "a rough diamond": Author interview with Sarah Higgins.

148 Chege details: Various sources, including author interview with Naivasha police chief Simon Kiragu.

148 "Chege knew all the tricks": Author interview with Sarah Higgins.

148 Fresh waves of poachers: Joan Root diary, June 5, 6, 10, and 11, and August 21, 1999.

149 "We used to have a security network": Author interview with Annabelle Thom.

149 Details of Duncan Adamson incident: Joan Root diary, April 8, 1999.

150 "Last night, Chege": Joan Root diary, July 4, 1999.

150 Then Chege's mother came: Joan Root diary, March 3 and 4, 2001.

150 Details of Joan talking of Alan: Author interview with David Chege.

CHAPTER NINE

152 "Don't you want to die in the Africa that you love?": Author interview with Alan Root.

152 Alan had postponed much of his filmmaking: Author interview with unnamed friend of Alan and Joan's.

152 "I've done my bit for posterity": *The Times* (London), July 17, 1996.

152 "Sue Allan phoned": Joan Root diary, January 11, 2000.

152 As she sat with David Chege: Author interview with David Chege.

153 "In some awful sort of way, she was waiting for me": Author interview with Alan Root.

153 Details of Fran Michelmore: Author interview with Sue Allan.

153 Details of dinner: Author interviews with Dieter Rottcher and Alan Root.

154 Alan's early friend Myles North: Alan Root articles about Myles North, www.serengeti.org/turner.html.

155 walking with an old friend in England: Author interview.

155 Eventually, she did cry: Author interview with Annabelle Thom.

155 Here are 5 boxes: Joan Root letter to Alan Root, November 14, 2002.

156 "Madam Root had taken Chege as an adopted child": Author interview with David Kilo.

156 the lake would soon be dead, "a desert": Author interview with David Chege.

156 By late 2000: Robert Brecht, "Lake Naivasha: Experience and Lessons Learned Brief," Lake Basin Management Initiative, 2005.

157 The Lake Naivasha Riparian Association helped: Author interview with Lord Enniskillen.

157 "go ahead": Joan Root diary, February 6, 2001.

158 Details of *korosho:* Author interview with David Chege.

158 "Felt anxious about everything": Joan Root diary, March 12, 2000.

158 "She felt like the *Titanic* was sinking": Dodo Cunningham-Reid, *New York Times,* January 22, 2006.

158 Details of emergency meeting: Joan Root diary, March 8, 2001; author interview with David Kilo.

158 "You can't blame [the poachers]": Author interview with Barry Gaymer; Mark Seal, "A Flowering Evil," *Vanity Fair,* August 2006.

159 Details of Task Force: Author interviews with David Kilo and David Chege.

160 According to one original plan: Author interview with Absolom Mulela Letta.

160 *"Toka!":* Author interview with Reuben Chege.

160 "We'd beat them, whip them, screaming abuse": Author interview with Barry Gaymer; Seal, "A Flowering Evil."

160 Details of Task Force: Author interviews with Reuben Chege, David Kilo, and Absolom Mulela Letta.

160 incessant calls: Author interviews with Sarah Higgins and Annabelle Thom; Joan Root diary.

161 Details of Kenya Fisheries Department operation and arrest: Joan Root diary, March 13, 15, 16, and 19, 2001.

162 A few days after that diary entry: Joan Root diary, March 25, 2001.

162 a political leader tried to bribe: Joan Root diary, March 28, 2001.

163 the fear instilled: Author interview with Reuben Chege.

163 "Desperate measures for desperate times": Author interview with Tom Cholmondeley; Seal, "A Flowering Evil."

163 "David Chege wanted us to": Author interview with Absolom Mulela Letta.

163 Details of bonfire: Author interviews with Sarah Higgins and David Chege.

164 "protection fee": Sources including author's interview with David Kilo.

164 Details of Chege as boss: Author interviews with Absolom Mulela Letta and David Kilo.

165 something jingling in his pocket: Author interview with Simon, a poacher on Lake Naivasha.

165 Chege could hardly be expected to stay: Joan Root diary.

165 "Three ex-fishermen came": Joan Root diary, June 30, 2001.

165 hired lawyers: Author interview with Naivasha police chief Simon Kiragu.

165 exonerated of each and every charge: Author interview with David Chege; "We didn't really have any crime record (on Chege)," per author's interview with Naivasha police chief Simon Kiragu.

166 "Chege's sweet talk": Author interview with anonymous source.

166 "He became a king": Author interview with anonymous source #2.

167 "tipped off": Joan Root diary, July 6, 1999.

167 the scene that always brought down the house: *Balloon Safari.*

168 Chege cheating: Author interview with Absolom Mulela Letta.

168 "She so wanted to trust him": Author interview with Annabelle Thom.

168 "Chege & Task Force": Joan Root diary, May 18 and 21, 2001.

169 he and Joan Root were: Author interview with David Chege.

170 Details of Task Force victories: The Lake Naivasha Task Force report, January 9, 2002.

170 Alan Root had once famously said: John Heminway, *No Man's Land* (New York: Warner Books, 1989).

171 "When I went with her through her papers": Author interview with Adrian Luckhurst.

172 "He was virtually the opposite of Joan": Ibid.

172 Lake Naivasha was a portion of her life: Author interview with Dee Raymer.

172 "There was a dinner and a lecture": Author interview with Esmond Bradley Martin.

CHAPTER TEN

173 "I've sat here": Author interview with John Vaughn.

173 In her office: Author's visit.

174 Around this time, a friend of Joan's: Author interview with Tony Church.

174 "This is not Happy Valley": Rob Crilly, "Pioneering Film-maker and African Conservationist Murdered," *The Scotsman,* January 13, 2006.

174 Kenya's forty-some tribes: "Government, Maasai Clash over Land in Kenya," *VOA News,* August 30, 2004; Joan Root diary and letters.

175 According to Alan: Author interview with Alan Root.

175 "Get out of it": Ibid.

175 No one tried harder to persuade Joan to leave than Adrian Luckhurst: Author interview with Adrian Luckhurst.

177 Her last extended journey: Joan Root diary, February 28 and March 8, 2004.

177 She wrote of boats being stolen: Joan Root diary, June 20 and July 28, 2004.

177 Details of poacher with broken leg and aftermath: Joan Root diary, March 25, April 13, April 27, July 8, and November 24, 2004; author interviews with Absolom Mulela Letta and David Kilo.

178 Details of carjacking: Joan Root diary, November 25 and 26, 2004; author interviews with John Sutton and Adrian Luckhurst.

179 In the end, it wasn't Joan: Author interview with John Sutton; Joan Root diary.

180 In a Riparian Association meeting: Author interview with Dee Raymer.

180 A solution arrived: Author interview with John Sutton.

180 the Naivasha Community Project moved into the rooms: Author's visit.

181 "Talked to Chege": Joan Root diary, June 15, 2005.

181 "Finally, agreed I would pay": Joan Root diary, June 24, 2005.

181 money missing from her kitchen cupboard: Ibid.

181 Details of murders: Joan Root diary, July 28, 2005; "UK Safari Boss Shot Dead," BBC News, July 27, 2005.

182 "Drove to Crater Lake": Joan Root diary, August 4, 2005.

182 The victims had been targeted: Author interview with Parselelo Kantai.

182 Armed robberies averaged eighteen a month: Author interview with John Sutton.

182 talk of drawing up lists of blood types . . . A website was created: "Dark Days Put Paid to Happy Valley's Idyll," *London Telegraph,* April 27, 2005.

182 "Now, no Task Force": Joan Root diary, August 4 and 5, 2005.

183 Details of break-in: Joan Root diary; author interview with John Sutton.

184 "Security doors": Joan Root diary, October 13, 2005.

184 Details of security at Tony and Sarah Seth-Smith's home: Author interview and visit.

185 She reluctantly installed: Author's visit.

185 In the fall of 2005: Joan Root diary, October 1, 2005.

186 "Chege went from": Author interview with Barry Gaymer; Mark Seal, "A Flowering Evil," *Vanity Fair,* August 2006.

186 "Chege was a": Author interview with Parselelo Kantai; Seal, "A Flowering Evil."

186 By the fall of 2005: Joan Root diary, October 21, 2005.

187 Then someone cut the brakes: Author interview with Annabelle Thom.

187 "Only 25–30 people turned up": Joan Root diary, December 9, 2005.

187 "Where to go?": Joan Root diary, April 18, 2000.

188 "Things weren't going well": Author interview with Jean Hartley.

CHAPTER ELEVEN

189 Details of police informant: Informant's statement to police.

189 Details of night of January 12: Author interview with Joan Root's staff.

189 An hour later she said good night to Samuel: Samuel Cheriot's statement to police.

190 At one-thirty A.M. the guards saw: Statement of guards to police.

190 "Let's do the work": Richard Coniff, "Death in Happy Valley," *Smithsonian* magazine, February 2007.

190 They walked around the house: Author interview with John Sutton; author's visit.

190 shot off the outside lock: Author interview with Naivasha police.

190 She managed to reach John Sutton: Author interview with John Sutton.

190 Details of murder: Police reports; author interviews with police and John Sutton.

191 "She died while on the forefront": Police report.

191 Her friend Delta Willis put it better: www.deltawillis.com.

192 Climbing into his helicopter: Author interview with Alan Root.

192 People later recalled: Author interview with Tony Church.

192 Details of crime scene: Author interviews with neighbors.

192 Details on bloodhound: Author interviews with Naivasha police chief Simon Kiragu and Claus Mortensen.

193 Details of Chege arrest: Author interview with Naivasha police chief Simon Kiragu.

193 *Guardian* and *Times* headlines: Both January 14, 2006.

193 Nairobi *Standard:* Articles by Anthony Gitonga and Karanja Njoroge, January 23, 2006.

194 Richard Waweru: Author interview with Richard Waweru.

194 Details of Naivasha and Joan Root's land: In addition to police reports and comments, author visited area; author interview with Naivasha police chief Simon Kiragu.

197 "It was a known fact": Author interview with Adrian Luckhurst.

197 "Joan was hated": Author interview with neighbor.

197 "The actual cause of the murder of Joan was": Author interview.

198 What will happen: Author interviews with Adrian Luckhurst and John Sutton.

199 Details of *The Legend of the Lightning Bird* come from the film.

199 Details of memorial: Author's visit.

POSTSCRIPT

202 Details of trial: Visit by Kenyan journalist Bosire Bogonko.

203 Details of Chege and other meetings: Author's visit.

PHOTO: © GUILLAUME BONN

MARK SEAL has been a journalist for more than thirty years. Currently a contributing editor at *Vanity Fair,* he has written for many major magazines and served as a collaborator on almost twenty nonfiction books. Although he has written thousands of stories, Seal says none has struck a chord with readers more than the story of the incredible life and brutal death of Joan Root, which he originally reported in the August 2006 issue of *Vanity Fair.* He lives in Aspen, Colorado.